TRA

Shake
the
Slee
S

To Shake the Sleeping Self

A QUEST FOR A LIFE
WITH NO REGRET

JEDIDIAH JENKINS

RIDER

1

Rider, an imprint of Ebury Publishing,
20 Vauxhall Bridge Road,
London SW1V 2SA

Rider is part of the Penguin Random House group of companies
whose addresses can be found at global.penguinrandomhouse.com

Penguin
Random House
UK

First published in Great Britain by Rider in 2021
Published in the United States by Convergent Books, an imprint of Random House,
a division of Penguin Random House LLC, New York.
www.penguin.co.uk

A CIP catalogue record for this book is available from the British Library

ISBN 9781846047046

Printed and bound in Great Britain by Clays Ltd, Elcograf S.p.A.

The authorised representative in the EEA is Penguin Random House Ireland,
Morrison Chambers, 32 Nassau Street, Dublin D02 YH68.

Penguin Random House is committed to a sustainable future for
our business, our readers and our planet. This book is made from
Forest Stewardship Council® certified paper.

MIX
Paper from
responsible sources
FSC® C018179

Grateful acknowledgment is made to Daniel Ladinsky for permission
to reprint "The Sun Never Says" from *The Gift: Poems by Hafiz, the
Great Sufi Master* translated by Daniel Ladinsky (New York: Penguin
Compass, 1999), copyright © 1999 by Daniel Ladinsky. Used by
permission of the translator. All rights reserved.

For my mom,

who is as giving as spring, as fun as summer,
as sacrificial as fall, and as strong as winter. As
good to me as seasons are to earth.

For my dad,

who taught me to drive down every dirt road,
and who loves me the way sunlight loves us all.

For Phillip Crosby,

who showed me how to let go of my house
when the flood comes, and to build on higher
ground.

Contents

Author's Note   *ix*

THE ITCH   *1*

Part One **WEST COAST**

Chapter 1 **THE PLAN**   *13*

Chapter 2 **IT BEGINS**   *22*

Chapter 3 **THE COAST IS CLEAR**—*Northern California*   *34*

Chapter 4 **THE TEMPTATION OF HOME**—
Southern California   *55*

Part Two **MEXICO**

Chapter 5 **CROSSING INTO BAJA**   *65*

Chapter 6 **SOME BACKGROUND AS I LOSE MY MIND**—
Baja and My Childhood   *91*

Chapter 7 **CARTELS AND COCONUTS**   *106*

Chapter 8 **THE CATHEDRAL SITS ON THE TEMPLE** —
Mexico City   *121*

Part Three **CENTRAL AMERICA**

Chapter 9 **WHAT HAPPENS IF I GO HOME?**—
Oaxaca and Christmas   *137*

Chapter 10 **HARRY DEVERT**—*Panama*   *161*

Chapter 11 **A NEW CONTINENT**—*Crossing to Cartagena*   *165*

Part Four **SOUTH AMERICA** *for the Most Part*

Chapter 12 **COCAINE AND CUTE LITTLE MUSHROOMS—**
    Cartagena and Medellín   175

Chapter 13 **GOD ON THE TRAIL**—*Medellín to Salento*   188

Chapter 14 **SEX HOTELS AND HERE COMES MOM—**
    Cali to Quito   200

Chapter 15 **THE COLDEST NIGHT**—*Quito to Cusco*   216

Chapter 16 **EMPIRE FALLS TO EMPIRE**—*Machu Picchu*   232

Chapter 17 **NEW BLOOD INTO BOLIVIA—**
    Bolivia and Argentina   253

Chapter 18 **ALL BY MY ARGENTINA**—*Solo Down Argentina* 259

Part Five **PATAGONIA**

Chapter 19 **ENTERING THE HOLY LAND—**
    Mendoza to Bariloche   275

Chapter 20 **ALONE IN GOD'S MOST OBVIOUS WORK—**
    The Carretera Austral   290

Chapter 21 **MOM AND THE MOUNTAIN**—*Torres del Paine* 299

Afterword to the Paperback Edition   317
Acknowledgments   319
A Reader's Guide   327
Excerpt from Like Streams to the Ocean   333

Author's Note

The story in this book is based on my memory, which is imperfect. Terrible sometimes. There are parts that I have oversimplified or omitted for clarity. Life is damn complex and a lot happened. Also, I changed some names. Read this the way you would receive a long story told over dinner.

THE ITCH

> *The youth gets together his materials to build a*
> *bridge to the moon, or perchance a palace or*
> *temple on the earth, and at length the middle-aged*
> *man concludes to build a wood-shed with them.*
>
> —HENRY DAVID THOREAU

have learned this for certain: if discontent is your disease, travel is medicine. It resensitizes. It opens you up to see outside the patterns you follow. Because new places require new learning. It forces your childlike self back into action. When you are a kid, everything is new. You don't know what's under each rock, or up the creek. So, you look. You notice because you need to. The world is new. This, I believe, is why time moves so slowly as a child—why school days creep by and summer breaks stretch on. Your brain is paying attention to every second. It must as it learns the patterns of living. Every second has value.

But as you get older, and the patterns become more obvious, time speeds up. Especially once you find your groove in the working world. The layout of your days becomes predictable, a routine, and once your brain reliably knows what's next, it reclines and closes its eyes. Time pours through your hands like sand.

This equation has a crummy side effect: while our child brains are absorbing the ways of the world ... mislabeled patterns of survival get swept in as we grow. Bad examples. Wrong thinking. Mistaken assumptions. They get caught in the flow of time through adolescence and carried into adulthood, buried beneath everything else. You watch your dad fly into a rage while driving, and your little brain logs it away. You overhear your mom talking about hell, and something rearranges in your head. A building block placed so deep and quickly covered. We show up as adults, confused by our own thinking, and with time running out.

But travel has a way of shaking the brain awake. When I'm in a new place, I don't know what's next, even if I've read all the guidebooks and followed the instructions of my friends. I can't know a smell until I've smelled it. I can't know the feeling of a New York street until I've walked it. I can't feel the hot exhaust of the bus by reading about it. I can't understand the humility of walking beneath those giant buildings. I can't smell the food stands and the cologne and the spilled coffee. Not until I go and know it in its wholeness. But once I do, that awakened brain I had as a kid, with wide eyes and hands touching everything, comes right back. This brain absorbs the new world with gusto. And on top of that, it observes itself. It watches the self and parses out old reasons and motives. The observation is wide. Healing is mixed in.

This kind of attention is natural to a child. To an adult, it must be chosen. The trick is: knowing when we are in fact adults, and when attention is asleep.

My name is Jedidiah Jenkins. It's a singsongy name I know, *Jedidiah* is Hebrew and means "loved by God," or "friend of God." My mom was dead-set on giving me a biblical name. I mean, damn. She went straight for a wild one. I was named after Jedediah Smith, the fur trapper and explorer who discovered passages over the Rockies and died at the hands of the Comanche. As a kid I loved it and then hated it and then loved it again. It sounded like a joke, like an Amish preacher. It was my first encounter with being different. Baby boomers would say, "Oh, like Jed Clampett! You must get that a lot." I'd say, "No, not really." People my age would say, "Like a Jedi! Are you a Jedi? Does everyone call you Jedi Master? I'm going to call you that." They never did. On the whole it's been nice, because people tend to remember it. I have a theory about this. When you have a weird name, one that's uncommon enough to stand out but not a nightmare to pronounce, people remember you. And when they re-member you—especially when you're young—it builds confidence. You feel special, worthy of being remembered. I don't know if this is true, clinically speaking. But I've always felt comfortable in a crowd, and I think it's at least in part because people remember my name. And that I am loved by God and God's friend, I guess.

As I GREW UP, this smiling kid with a weird name was paying at-tention, and making assumptions. I absorbed lessons and language and took them as truth.

If you were a suburban kid like me, you probably grew up in a school system that wants you to go to college and choose a major and go straight into a job and a marriage and a mortgage. It gives you rungs of achievement: a degree, a wife, a house, kids, golf—whatever—and makes you think these things give life meaning. "Collect them all and win!"

But the big fancy adults preach the opposite as well. They say, "fall in line" and then, in the same breath, "think different, take risks!" We are told, "follow your passion" and "stay hungry," at every commencement and graduation speech. This mixture of school and risk is the holy cocktail of American ideals, and for those rare bea-cons of exceptional success, it turns their life stories into fables. But for ordinary folks, it is a difficult road to walk. Be sensible, but be wild. Be ordered, but be free. Be responsible, but take risks.

I took this double-speak to heart like any good kid born in the eighties. "Do what you love" and "follow your passion" became foun-dational virtues. But it's all so slippery. *Do what you love, but stay on the assembly line. There's no time to find what you love, you should be building your credit score. Take risks, but don't be foolish. Believe in yourself, but only if you've proven you should. Haven't you seen those idiots auditioning on* American Idol, *thinking they can sing? Don't be one of them. Don't embarrass yourself. Don't waste time at a job you hate, but magically manifest money to leave that job and chase a dream. Got it? Perfect.*

It didn't help that my parents were examples of this magic American potion. Both of them were raised poor. Both chased their dreams. Both had success. My parents taught me as a kid that I could be whatever I wanted to be. "You can be a lawyer when you grow up, or a movie director, or a marine biologist. You can be anything you want." I remember their sweet encouragements, watching their pale, chubby son with a weird name swim with his T-shirt on. "You don't have to be good at sports, Jed, but it's good to try. We don't care what you do, so long as you give it your all. And don't feel stuck if you choose one thing. You can try it and choose something else later." This practical optimism gave me the worldview that life had many paths, all there in front of me always.

The factor that I overlooked was the finiteness of time. This concept is invisible to a child. Kids may know logically that they will one day be old, but they can't feel it. It sounds like a rumor.

The carefree timelessness of my youth was rattled in my twenties. A kind of panic set in. Time became visible. Each choice I made began to feel more and more final, as if every choice was the death of all the others. Millions of doors were locking behind me as I passed them in the hallway. I felt that age thirty—adulthood—was coming like winter. Am I missing out? Am I making the right decisions? Am I becoming the person I want to be? It often dawns too late that we have only one life, only one path, and the choices we make become the story line of our lives.

This is the story of that panic and my response to it. I'd done everything right. I'd spent my twenties going to college and law school and getting a job and being a good boy. But when I turned thirty, I quit my job and spent a year and a half bicycling from Oregon to Patagonia. It wasn't the job that chased me away, it was mortality. Everything before was exposition. Filling the hero of the story with background and tools. The life before had happened to me as childhood happens to everyone. The mark of adulthood is when we happen to life. Thirty years old. I was now an adult, with or without my consent, and adults are responsible for their lives. I wasn't going to become someone I didn't choose to be.

How I got to the bike really started after law school.

My first lawyer job was working for in-house counsel at a cruise ship company. Not on a cruise ship, unfortunately, but in an office building in the suburbs. I needed money and I needed a job. Any job. The company was huge. Thousands of employees. I spent that entire summer removing duplicates from an employee spreadsheet containing 13,000 names. I reworded memos and sat through hours of HR training about the proper way to shake someone's hand and the appropriate distance one should stand away from a coworker. I remember my supervisor called me into her office and said, "Jed, we need to talk. We have a policy of no more than three exclamation points in any e-mail. And you have five in your greeting of 'hello!!!!!' That's not acceptable."

She wasn't joking. Now, in my more sober adult years, I can see how I don't need to be shouting in my e-mails with so many exclamation points. But in my twenties, this kind of reprimand terrified me. I seemed to be always in trouble. And I hated being in trouble.

I'll die if I work here. If they don't fire me first.

In my moment of despair, my old friend Jason reached out and offered me a job. He had made a documentary about war in northern Uganda, and it had become a big deal.

"Jed. We're turning our documentary into a nonprofit. It's becoming a movement. We're growing like crazy. Thousands of high school and college kids are starting clubs based on the doc. Come work for us. We need an attorney. We don't know what we're doing. Imagine working with your best friends and changing the world. You'll make like no money, but it'll be fun and important."

In that moment, I pictured myself working in the cruise company's office for decades, bowing to the shareholders, hating work and therefore buying things, a house and a nice car, and having kids and sending them to private school. Raising them to chase their dreams, and lying with my life. That frightened me. I told my friend yes. I'd figure out how to make money later. For now, I'd be poor and happy.

I WORKED AT the nonprofit for five years and enjoyed it. We did national tours, setting up clubs in high schools, building fund-raiser campaigns for students each semester—so even though I was out of school, I still felt time pass in semesters.

As thirty approached, and "youth" was passing into "adulthood," the terrible reality of time hit me like a wet rag. I looked back on my twenties and realized that every time there was a crossroads, I took the first and safest path. I did just what was expected of me, or what I needed to do to escape pain or confusion. I was reactive. I didn't feel like an autonomous soul. I felt like a pinball.

Let me add another layer to my thinking at the time: my faith. I loved God and Jesus and believed I was a "friend of God." He had a plan for my life. A plan to make me prosper. A legacy to live in testament to Him. I was raised this way. It added a glaze over every choice. It was God's plan for my life. And with the creator of the universe pulling the strings, how could any of it be mundane? So my fear of thirty, my anxiety over missing my "calling," carried with it a dull guilt. Was I trusting God enough? Were my ambitions self-serving? Was I doing enough in the service of the Kingdom? Was I laying my life on the altar of His will? I didn't know. But I knew I wanted to do right, to live right, to be good.

This confluence of motivations and choices had taken me through a good education and into a bad job and then a good job, and I'd learned a lot and had fun and collected some skills . . . but I couldn't shake the thought: it wasn't really mine. It was happening to me. I was making steps toward myself, just trying things out, as my parents had taught me. Nothing has to last forever, Jed. Try it and then try something else. Sure, that works for a while, but sooner or later, that's not cute anymore. You can't keep jumping ship.

LOOKING BACK NOW, my discomfort with career and time and choices was the smoke of a deeper fire. An important part of me was covered and squirming. It had something to do with my faith. In doubts and questions. There were deep parts of me that were wounded by Christianity. There were also deep parts of me that loved Jesus and gave Him credit for everything good in my life. This created a tension. And because I was taught that salvation rested on belief, on saying the right words and believing the right creeds, doubt was akin to cancer. Treat it or it will kill you.

I couldn't have said it then, but now I know: my soul was afraid of dying. Not simply from loss of salvation, but from loss of self. If I really was "loved by God, a friend of God," I wanted true friendship. Friends do not walk blindly, one behind the other. They walk shoulder-to-shoulder. I wanted clarity from my friend. To hear answers to my questions.

When you don't know what to do, you travel. You go out and see. You have to rattle the bed, shake yourself out.

I wanted to start my thirties like I started life: wide awake. I didn't have kids. I didn't have a mortgage. I felt like this was my last chance to crawl into the driver's seat of my life.

Eventually, an idea took shape. It was 2010, I was twenty-seven years old. I was talking with a coworker who'd been hired to run our nonprofit work in Uganda. I had just met him and I was asking him simple questions. Just really the small talk of getting to know a new hire. His name was Andrew. He was tall and rugged. His skin was brown from loads of sun. His crow's-feet were deep from squinting. I asked him what he was doing before he came on board.

"I came straight to Uganda from Patagonia," he said. "I rode my bicycle to Argentina from New Jersey."

What? A bicycle? Across all those countries? My god. What a man. My face got hot and my eyes got big and my mind filled with questions. Like the clarity of love at first sight, when you spot someone across the room and know they are yours, this idea struck me like Cupid's arrow. *Could I do that? What an adventure. Am I man enough? Could I finish? How long does that take? I can ride a bike, but haven't in ages. I can camp. I can eat almost anything. Does he think I can do it?* He started showing me photos and my insecurities fizzed in my mind. *No, I can't do this.*

As a kid, I'd tried to play soccer and was terrible. I'd tried to run cross-country and I was slow. I was soft and feminine. I wanted to be a tough kid. It was a tender bruise on my identity. So I became the funny kid.

"Hey, Jed, we're gonna play touch football after school if you're interested!" they'd say.

"Ha! Yeah, right. I don't sweat unless I'm running from the cops." They'd laugh and I felt safe for a moment.

My dad was a farmer with calloused hands. Back sweat stained his denim shirts from riding the tractor. My mom was a fearless country girl from Missouri. My best friends in high school were varsity baseball and football players. I'd always been the soft one, reading a comic book or playing in the woods. I wanted to impress them, though if you'd asked me then, I wouldn't have known that. It was buried too deep for me to see.

As Andrew scrolled through incredible photos of Mexico and Peru on his phone, he explained his route. "It took about a year and a half. I did it alone. Met people along the way. I had been teaching high school in New Jersey and felt that the students needed an example. They needed to see what the world had to offer. So I wrote blog posts for them and I would Skype in to tell them stories from the road. It changed my life."

I must've been looking at him like a spooked owl, mouth agape. "Jed, I don't tell this to many people," he said. "But you should do the bike trip. You would love it."

I didn't know this man. I had just met him, and he said this to me. I could do that? This true adventurer thought I could handle it? A man that had cycled 10,000 miles believed I had what it took to do the same. He looked at me and saw an athlete. That felt better than I'd like to admit.

I looked Andrew in the face and said, "I'm going to do it." I paused, staring over his shoulder at nothing. "I swear I am." It felt like prophecy. I would hit the road and find the world. I didn't know what I was to become, but I knew I had to take steps in some direction. I was speaking to myself as much as I was speaking to him. I was speaking to the universe. "I'm going to go on a bike trip like yours when I turn thirty."

"How old are you now?" he asked.

"Twenty-seven."

"Okay," Andrew said, proudly. "You need to tell friends and family about it. That'll help the trip be a part of your daily consciousness from here on out. You'll talk about it and people will expect you to do it. And their social pressure will help prevent you from chickening out of making excuses."

"Okay!" I said, wide-eyed, realizing the bigness of it.

But I had to do it. It felt correct. It felt like a key I'd been looking for. I needed movement. I knew it would answer questions and change me. I didn't know that this trip would free me from shackles I couldn't see. I didn't know it would pry my fingers from the parts of myself that had to go. I was holding tight to the narratives of my youth like treasure. But with hands full, I couldn't receive anything new. And I couldn't see that I was clutching both treasure and poison.

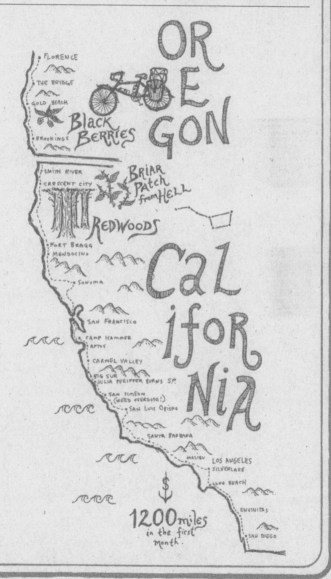

OR
E
GON

FLORENCE
THE BRIDGE
GOLD BEACH
BROOKINGS

Black Berries

SMITH RIVER
CRESCENT CITY

BRIAR Patch from HELL

REDWOODS

FORT BRAGG
MENDOCINO

SONOMA

California

SAN FRANCISCO
CAMP HAMMER
APTOS

CARMEL VALLEY
BIG SUR
JULIA PFEIFFER BURNS S.P.
SAN SIMEON
(WEED OVERDOSE!)
SAN LUIS OBISPO

SANTA BARBARA

MALIBU
LOS ANGELES
SILVERLAKE
LONG BEACH

ENCINITAS

SAN DIEGO

1200 miles in the first month.

Chapter 1

THE PLAN

n early 2011, I told my friends and coworkers. I posted a map of South America on my Instagram. "When I turn thirty, I'm cycling to Patagonia." Some people cheered me on. "Fuck, yeah!! Go get 'em!" Other people laughed. "Isn't it a little early to be telling us your plans three years from now?" "No," I said. "Gotta speak it into existence." Other people shamed me. "Don't be so self-congratulatory. You haven't even done anything yet. Hit us up when you've actually done something."

I soon told my parents. They are divorced, so it was two separate calls. Always my mom first. They were thrilled initially. "Following in our footsteps, I see," my mom said.

I hadn't even considered that fact. My parents walked across America in the '70s. My dad was in his mid-twenties, my mom in her late twenties and early thirties. It took five years, and they wrote about it for *National Geographic*. They were even on the cover— August 1979, if you want to track it down. They were in search of America and themselves in the middle of the cloud Vietnam cast over this country.

They went on their spirit quest. And now I was going on mine. Who was I to think I had come to this idea completely on my own? As my mom began cautioning me to the dangers of cycling across Mexico, my mind was off somewhere else, thinking about destiny and the pre-ordering of things. How so often we *become* our parents, whether we like it or not. I had walked right into Mom and Dad's shadow without noticing.

Let me digress about them for a minute. They became famous from their walk. They wrote best-selling books about it. They traveled the country speaking and doing interviews. They were next-to-household names. They also became famously Christian. My dad's testimony was raw and dramatic: a New England kid from public housing who went to Woodstock and did drugs and never found a rule he couldn't break. He found Jesus on the walk, at a charismatic revival meeting in Mobile, Alabama. He found my mom in a seminary outside of New Orleans—an angel-faced girl from the Ozarks who loved the Lord and knew Scripture better than anyone. Her voice and soft skin gave her the appearance of someone who'd jump at the sight of a mouse. But she was fearless. She'd grab a snake right out of the grass. When my dad met her, he turned on all the charm he could muster and seduced her out of seminary. "Marry me and let's walk to Oregon." Can you imagine? She said yes. I exist because of it.

After the walk and publication of the *National Geographic* story and the subsequent best-selling book, they traveled and enjoyed their fame and worked on new books together. Somehow, they managed to represent both the counterculture of 1970s youth and the wholesome churchgoing middle. They were curious about America. They loved Jesus, but didn't fear the differences of human beings. For a moment in the sun, they were America's dusty sun-kissed sweethearts. They had three kids (I was the middle baby) and bought a farm in Tennessee.

Then, at the height of it all, their marriage fell apart. The perfect couple crashed. Dad was gone a lot. He kept traveling, writing, speaking, and apparently doing other things. My mom was home with the kids. Maybe my dad's charisma got the best of him. I remember him talking to a Waffle House waitress with no teeth for an hour. He's the type of man who sees a dead-end gravel road and turns down it just to know how far it goes. Maybe his best quality was his Achilles' heel. I was a little kid at the time. I don't know what really happened. She told him to quit cheating, and she later kicked him out. Their empire fell. And nothing falls quite like a Christian celebrity.

But through all the mess of divorce and parenting and maintaining public personas, my parents were excellent to us kids. Weekdays with Mom and weekends with Dad. Mom making art projects at night with us. Dad taking us out on the tractor to feed the cows. Whatever storms were happening between them, in their careers and finances, I had no idea. And in spite of it all, they remained explorers to the core. They had walked America's backroads and mountains and deserts, and they would raise their kids to love them the same. Even if they had to do it separately.

We didn't have much money growing up. Writing a couple bestsellers will keep you afloat for a while, but if you can't keep it up, the money runs dry. Add in three kids and an expensive divorce, and it gets hard. But my parents knew how to live on a little. Instead of flying to islands or going on ski trips, we went camping. We took long road trips to see the Grand Canyon, the Badlands, the Wild West. My mom would plug in the camper and I'd disappear to the creek, or down a canyon, and come back hours later with a turtle or a bone.

Mom and Dad never pressured us to become adventurers, and they mentioned "The Walk" only in passing. But they taught me to look around, to explore, and that it didn't cost a whole lot of money to do it. They always told us that we could do whatever we wanted, be whatever we wanted. They had the American dream in the twinkle of their eyes. Both had been rewarded, even if only for a moment, with the fame that comes from taking a chance, risking it all for an idea that awakens the soul.

The point of bringing up their parenting style is this: somehow, my parents had tricked me. They had made me respect them and want to emulate them, all without me realizing it. And comically, I came to the conclusion that I wanted to go on a great adventure in a way that felt completely original to me, and spontaneous. Like I was the first person to ever think of such a thing.

I DIDN'T DO much prep for those next three years. I continued to work at the charity and build campaigns and work on documentaries. But the coloring of those years was different. I knew I'd be leaving as soon as I turned thirty. I knew I had a giant adventure on the horizon. This knowledge changed the way I perceived time. My job felt more important. I took on more responsibility, and worked harder because I only had so much time to get things done. I stopped feeling trapped. I had an escape stomping my way. You might think I would've ridden my bicycle and trained, but nope. I didn't do shit. I guess I was confident that I could ride a bike (I didn't even own one), and that I'd learn as I went. Or maybe training would've made it too real. Too scary.

Thank God I told people about my trip, I thought. If I hadn't, it would be so easy to not do it. I would've changed my mind a hundred times. The inconvenience of uprooting my life, of stepping away from all that I had built, was enormous. But the questions had never ceased. "When do you leave?" "You still doing that crazy trip? I'm so jealous!" "Have you been training?"

Then, quite suddenly, it was 2013, and I was thirty years old, and it was time to leave. Whoa. I had looked down and it was here.

I googled and read cycling blogs. Some had incredibly detailed maps and warnings and packing guides that measured out the weight of this and the weight of that. Some bloggers were so ill prepared, their journals read like Shakespearean tragedies. I thought of my inspiration, Andrew, the one who had done the trip before. I had to talk to him. I e-mailed him. He was off training new employees in Uganda. I needed a pep talk. I was overwhelmed.

"Don't plan too much," he wrote. "You can't assume that a map tells the truth in Central and South America. Just know that you need to make it forty to sixty miles south on each travel day. Trust the locals. Ask the people you meet what's the best way to go. The most beautiful. Let the place tell you where it wants you to go. The worst thing you can do is assume you know now what you'll know then. And don't let anyone else dictate your trip for you. If you want to take a bus sometimes, take a bus. If you need to hitchhike, hitchhike. It's your trip, not anyone else's. If you try to be too fanatical about it, you'll spend more time stressing out and less time seeing a place for what it is."

I liked the sound of that. I picked a date, five months out. I'd start on August 28 in Oregon. I would travel south, mostly along the

Pacific Coast, cross the Darién Gap in Panama, and follow the Andes from Colombia all the way to Patagonia, the very bottom of the inhabited planet. The whole thing would take sixteen months. The timing was important: I needed to follow the dry season. If you hit Central and South America during the rainy season, you're soaked for months. If you hit them in the dry season, you will have only sunshine. And if my pace was correct, I would also hit Patagonia in its spring/summer, which would be November and December 2014. I had to time it right, because Amazon rainy seasons and Patagonian winters would ruin me and possibly send me home.

Two months before launch day, I walked into REI and found the bike guy. The people who work at gear stores usually frighten me. So many times I had tried to buy a sleeping bag, or running shoes, or a tent, and the guy made me feel like an idiot. They can get a tired tone in their voice, exhausted from explaining to so many basic bitches how the forest works. If I had started this trip at twenty years old, I would have trembled as I asked him what kind of bike I should use for a sixteen-month trip through Latin America. But thirty is different. By thirty, I had learned a valuable lesson: You are not an idiot. It's okay if you don't know everything. Don't pretend. Ask all the questions you want. It's fine if you're not prepared for the zombie apocalypse at all times.

So I walked in, told the young guy I needed a bicycle that could get me to Chile. He cocked his head like a dog and asked me if I had been training. When I said no, a confident "nope," he called for some old guy in the back. "Richard's ridden his bike across the U.S. three times," the young guy said. Richard's legs were bowed and his hair was white and thick. His hands were black with grease. He looked me up and down and must have decided it wasn't worth his time to discourage me. "You should go with the Surly Long Haul Trucker," he said.

He motioned to a relatively simple-looking bike hanging on the wall. It looked thick and heavy. It had no fanciness about it. It didn't look fast or sleek. It was just a dark green bicycle.

"If you're headed into South America, you don't want a fancy carbon bike. That thing breaks, you'll be hitchhiking the rest of your trip. You want steel. Any mechanic can weld steel if you get hit by a car or a bus. This Surly is tough as hell. It's heavy, but sturdy. That's the one you want." He showed me the multi-tool I should get, which is basically a Swiss army knife for bikes, and he also said I needed panniers.

"What are panniers?" I said.

He looked at me for a silent beat, certainly thinking, *This boy is going to die.*

"They are saddlebags that you hang from the side of your bike," he said.

I did exactly as Richard said and bought it all. Instead of a tent, I bought a hammock. I wanted to be off the ground, away from critters. The wise man continued, "If you're going to sleep in a hammock, you'll need a reflector pad underneath you to hold in your body heat. Or else you'll freeze. But don't buy one here. It's forty bucks. Go to Wal-Mart and buy one of those dashboard sun reflectors for five bucks. It's the exact same thing." God bless this curmudgeon. Bingo.

The e-mails from my mom never stopped. And the calls. She called me at the office a few months before my last day.

"Jed," she said, which in her southern drawl sounds more like "Jayud," "I just don't know about you going through Mexico. It's too dangerous." I could hear grunting through the phone as she moved her shih tzu off the bed. "Okay, let's get you some food," she mumbled, distracting herself with the dog to minimize the electricity of confrontation.

"Mom, I've been to Mexico many times. Everyone I speak to who's been there says it's misunderstood and beautiful. They say Fox News makes people scared and think that it's only cartels and freeloaders wanting to get here."

"Well, how could Mexico be so great if they all are trying to come here?"

"I don't think that's true. They're not all trying to get here."

"I'm just worried about you. I don't want you cycling alone. I know you're going to say that I walked across America and my parents were worried about me, but it's different. America is different than Mexico."

"Mom, you know I have to go on this trip. I've been telling people for three years now. I have to. You know that feeling. I feel called to it."

"Yes, I know. I know. 'To whom much is given, much is required.' I'll plead the blood of Jesus over you every day. If anything happened to you—"

"Mom, I'll be fine. And it's not the seventies, I'll have a phone and I can text you and get Wi-Fi and call you all the time. When you and Dad did the walk, what did you do?"

"We found pay phones and called our parents once a week," she said. "I know that me being paranoid is ironic because I did this to Meme. And I didn't have a phone then. But that's what happens when you become a mother. You become the things that drove you crazy as a kid. It's the way God made it. To humble us, I think."

"You don't need to worry."

"Well, you can't go alone. I forbid it. Do you hear me, Jedidiah? I forbid it."

I have no rebellion in me. If my mom forbade me from going, I'd be in a bad spot. I never did drugs. Never even tried them. That's what "the bad kids" did, and that wasn't me. Alcohol seemed trashy. Drugs seemed debased. To this day, it's hard for me to break a rule. Especially if I've been told explicitly. This scenario has played out in my life a thousand times: A guard will say, "Sir! You can't be in here. I'm going to need you to leave." My friends will say, "He's not looking, let's go!" And I say, "But he said we can't!" and I slump away.

I wanted to be a good boy, so I agreed to invite someone else along. Well, to be honest, before I had the chance to, he invited himself.

His name was Weston. He was visiting San Diego from New York three months before I was set to leave, and we'd met a handful of times. I was sitting in my office getting through e-mails when he walked in. It was June, three months before I was set to leave. He bounced from desk to desk saying hi to people, and I could hear his voice and the exclamations of people who knew him and were overjoyed to see him. *It's that guy Weston,* I thought. *What's he doing in California?* He came into my office and grabbed me by the shoulder. "I heard you're going on a yearlong bike trip. I need an adventure,

I'm restless. And I want to be a character in a book." He said, "You can write whatever you want. I have nothing to hide."

There was something endearing about Weston's narcissism. Broke and drinking expensive beer. Handy, clever, and tireless. Always on fire for a new idea, a new girl, a new food. He had held a ton of jobs, started businesses, started newer ones in the middle of starting new ones. You never really knew where he lived or where he was. He was tall, muscular, tattooed. Handsome in a way, severe in another. Women loved him. He loved that women loved him.

Why did he want the bike trip? I think he had burned that entrepreneur candle so hard, riding on the fumes of people believing in him, that he got singed. A long ride would be a reset. I thought there was a good chance he might get me in trouble or drive me mad, but maybe I craved that, so I said yes, and told Weston the plan.

We would start the trip at Jessie M. Honeyman State Park, halfway down the Oregon Coast—the same beach where my parents finished their walk across America. I wanted to walk my bicycle into the water where they had finished. I would pick up the baton.

A package came in the mail to my house. It was from my mom. I opened it up and it was a little pocket Bible. Leather-bound. Beaten up, worn, with rounded edges. I opened it up and found red and blue underlining everywhere. Notes in the margins. My mom's handwriting. And some of my dad's, too. I recognized each handwriting style. Inside the flap was a note. "Jed, this was the Bible I carried in my pocket during the whole walk across America. I read it every night. When I was scared, God's word was with me. He is always with you. I love you. He loves you." It was holy to touch. A tangible anchor to my mom in her late twenties, my dad in his mid twenties, the God of the universe with them. Wow. I kept it in my pocket from that day forward.

As the day approached, the trip became the only topic of conversation at the office. My trick of telling everyone had worked a little too well. Everyone asked me about it. Are you ready? Did you learn Spanish? Have you been training? Nope. Nope. Nope. I had meant to learn Spanish. I even bought Rosetta Stone, which is like six hundred bucks. And I'd done it for a grand total of a week. Damn it. So typical. But here it was, the trip was around the corner. The spring and summer of 2013 disappeared, and August popped up like a jack-in-the-box.

By the time Weston and I flew to Portland to start the damn thing, I was sick and tired of talking about the trip and not being on it. I wasn't nervous. I was just ready to get everyone off my back. I was so afraid of being labeled a talker and not a doer. I boxed up my bike and some clothes and left the rest to buy in Portland.

Weston had virtually nothing. A small bag. I thought I was unprepared. Weston was so self-confident, his lack of preparation came off like a deeply considered preparation in itself. "I don't want to have too many things figured out," he said the night before we flew out. "I'll buy a bike on Craigslist when we get there for a couple hundred bucks."

"Are you sure? What if there aren't any?"

"There will be. There's bikes everywhere. And if not, it'll work out. Gotta trust the universe. If one door closes . . . ya know?"

"Well, yeah, that's cool. But we do need to leave on the twenty-eighth."

"Don't worry, brother. I got this. I like that you worry. I like that you have a bike and extra gear and stuff. I got this." He was so confident, it made me wonder if I was the one doing this the wrong way.

We woke at 6:00 a.m., and drove to the San Diego airport to catch a flight for Portland. I checked my bike and watched it disappear on the conveyor belt. I paid fifty bucks because it was overweight. Weston just walked on.

Chapter 2

IT BEGINS

At my friend's house in Portland the night before we left, I laid out everything I was packing. I wanted to put eyes on it and wrap my head around my life-support system of things. The bike sat shiny and unblemished against the fireplace mantel. It had no memories. The rear rack was black and sturdy-looking. Next to my bike were the two panniers, made of black plastic with reflectors painted on both sides. One bag would be for my bike and camping stuff, the other for my clothes. I had five T-shirts, a pair of bike shorts, normal shorts, a pair of swim trunks, jeans, seven pairs of underwear, a sweater, a denim shirt, and a women's rain jacket purchased last-minute from a Goodwill in Portland.

I knew that I wouldn't keep the clothes folded for the whole trip, so I just shoved them into the left pannier, halfway attempting to keep the layers for warmth at the top for access. The right pannier got everything else: a tire pump, extra tubes, my hammock, a little bag of medicine and Band-Aids from my mom, my books, my journal, my multi-tool for fixing and adjusting bike stuff, and my food—almonds, apples, oranges, cans of tuna, crackers. The panniers hung from the sides of the rack, leaving the top of it open. That was where my backpack and sleeping bag went. Also a cheap, giant green tarp.

Weston didn't have money, which he said was intentional. He was experimenting with a form of fundamentalist anticapitalism. He gave hourly dissertations challenging society, the government, the wealthy, the systems of organized humanity. Whenever he was forced to use money, it seemed to be a small defeat. He had a prophet's disposition, always feeling watched and therefore an example to the masses. He differed greatly in one respect from most evangelists, though: he was neither dogmatic nor forceful. He believed nothing was more powerful than example.

That night while I was packing, Weston got on Craigslist just like he'd said he would. He found a road bike for three hundred dollars. It was pink and looked to be at least thirty, forty years old. He had panniers that a friend had made by hand, each one a little larger than a lunch box—which is tiny. My panniers were the size of couch pillows. He had no sleeping bag, either, just a blanket he grabbed from a pile at Goodwill. It wasn't even a quilt or a full-size blanket, but a small, red throw that would only cover your legs. I think it was intended for decoration.

As I fell asleep, I thought of all the things I was leaving behind. My comforts. My expensive coffee and craft beer and back-porch hangs with my friends. My routine and my life. I knew it wasn't forever, but it felt like it. What if my friends went on without me? What if my absence revealed that I was never really necessary? What if no one notices I'm gone?

I said a prayer to myself. "God, keep me safe. Keep Weston safe. Teach me what You want to teach me. Prove my mom wrong. Help me meet the people I'm supposed to meet. Don't let me embarrass myself. Give me the strength to do this whole thing.

"I hope I'm not making a mistake," I thought. "Ugh. Am I? Is this some pride thing? To prove something to people? What if I can't even make it to LA?"

I had, in normal fashion, trailed off from talking to God to simply thinking. Talking to myself. I always scolded myself for doing this. For doing it wrong. For not actually talking to God.

"Amen."

THE NEXT DAY, August 28, was launch day. It was time to go. But we took forever to get ready. We went through each piece of gear, speaking out loud its necessity. "Ten-gallon water bag, for the desert." "Headlamp, for camping." We went to the supermarket that morning and shopped for too long. We bought enough food for a bomb shelter, even though we'd be traveling in the United States for the next thousand miles, and never so remote as to not have a restaurant a few miles away.

Our friends Collin and Stella drove us out. The car ride was charged with energy, with the feeling that we were all part of something important. Maybe it was just me feeling this. I was noticing the curves of the road, the laughter, the Rascal Flatts and Fleet Foxes we blasted on the radio, taking note to remember this drive and this moment. It felt like a slow-motion music video.

I knew that the first thousand miles would be a training ground. I had never been the kind of person who knows how to do things. I had no idea how to work on a bike; how to change a popped tire, fix a slipped chain, raise or lower a seat. But I figured the first leg of the trip would give me the chance to learn what I really needed: how to camp in the wild, how to hide, what food I needed, all of it, before I got to Mexico.

We pulled our bicycles out of the car and hauled them over the dunes that separated the parking lot from the water. I recognized the beach from the grainy photos in *National Geographic* of my parents crying and kissing, walking into this very water after their five years spent crossing the country. A wave of sadness hit me, thinking about 1979 and the joy they felt at seeing this water . . . Knowing that in those photos my mom was already pregnant with my sister, that they had no idea what the future held for them. Deeply in love and freshly accomplishing the impossible. And God rubbing His hands together, laughing.

The start of a big journey makes every detail feel monumental. At least it does for me. The color of the sand on the beach—an off white. The grass on the dunes—sharp and coarse. The breeze from the ocean—cold and smelling like dead fish. And underlying it all, my insecurities. *I don't know how to do anything bike related. I don't even know if my body can do this. What if I have knee problems? What if I have back problems from being hunched over all day and can't finish? Wait, I never even thought of this stuff. What else haven't I thought of?*

I carried my bike into the waves at Honeyman State Park beach in Florence, Oregon. Weston and I dipped our tires into the shallow surf, had Collin and Stella take a few pictures of us standing with the bikes like proud cowboys, and then carried them back over the dunes to the asphalt road.

"I guess this is it," I said. "It's as easy as clipping in and hitting the road." My panniers were heavy and full. My bike didn't have a kickstand, which I found perplexing as I clumsily tried to clip the panniers onto the bike rack. Weston showed me a trick of spinning the bike pedal backward and then using it as a kickstand on a curb. This allowed me to attach my panniers, and then load my sleeping bag and backpack in between them, creating a massive camel hump of stuff on the back of my bike. By the time I got it all tied on, it looked sloppy, wobbly, like a homeless shanty on two wheels.

I took my helmet and sat it on my head. It was big, bulky, and painted in bright, idiotic colors. Red and white and yellow. (It's hard to find a cool bike helmet.) When I snapped it on and looked at myself in the reflection of Stella's car, I gasped. I looked like a ten-year-old kid with a beard. I looked like a nerd. I didn't look like some rugged adventurer. I looked like a kid on a leash.

Weston didn't have a helmet. Didn't even buy one.

When I tried to maneuver my bike around to mount it, I was shocked at the weight. It fell over. It was so heavy I could barely lift it. Shit.

Collin and Stella stood back, arms crossed, laughing as they watched us. Collin was an avid cyclist. Stella wasn't, but reveled in our clumsiness.

"When you clip in, you will fall. Several times," Collin said. "So just expect it. That way it won't hurt your pride when it happens. Everyone falls."

I finally got the bike up and threw my leg over the saddle. Collin's eyes widened.

"Jed, your seat is way too low. Is that how you ride? When you're seated, you should have to stick your leg out straight to touch the ground. No bend. Pedaling down should almost completely extend your leg."

"Really? Oops," I said. "I'm so screwed."

"No, you'll get it. It's fine. Lemme fix your seat and then practice around this parking lot. You haven't practiced with weight yet?"

"No."

Collin looked at Weston.

"Have you?" he said.

"No. But I was a bike messenger in NYC. I'm all good."

Collin raised my bike seat and handled my heavy bike without effort. I was embarrassed, reminded of how bad I am at sports. He kindly and patiently gave it back to me. "Try this."

I got on and tried to clip my ugly bike shoes into the pedals. It didn't make sense. Collin laughed. "You have to twist your foot in, and twist your foot out. Straight down won't work. Wiggle your foot on it till they snap into place."

I did and they snapped in. My feet were now attached to the bike. I felt the bike begin to tip over, and instinctively pulled my foot to brace my fall. But my foot was attached to the goddamn bike. I couldn't. I fell over sideways and hit the pavement, like something out of a cartoon.

"What the hell!? How am I supposed to do this!?" I said, wiggling and still attached to the bike. "I'm gonna tear my ACL and MCL and AT and T!" I shouted.

"It'll become second nature," Collin said, laughing. "Just get some momentum and practice."

I clicked my shoes in and out over and over until I understood how it worked. Then I rode around in a figure eight, cautiously.

At 4:00 p.m., way later in the day than we had hoped, we hugged our friends, said goodbye, and rode away from the beach, with me looking ridiculous in my helmet. My body was an adrenaline whirl-pool. Almost immediately, Weston was riding without hands. Sitting straight up with his perfect posture, stripping his shirt off, and looking free.

That first day we rode toward Reedsport, along the coast and past tall pine trees and the occasional house. The day was sunny and beautiful and full of nervous laughter. Weston rode shirtless with no hands most of the afternoon, which would soon become his general uniform and style. His old cheap bike rattled in its imperfections, but it seemed to work. My new bike was heavy and strong. We were loving it, braiding back and forth as we rode, flowing like happy salmon up a river. Taking up the road, getting honked at, cussing at nothing and cracking up. We found it was fun to swear at the perfect sky and trees. Just shouting curses at them.

I had posted on my Instagram for launch day, "Four years coming, it's coming tomorrow." Friends and family and people I didn't know commented. "So excited to follow along!" "Ahh I feel like I'm doing this with you. I have so much anxiety!" "I just want to pick up and quit my job and join you!" How did these new people find me?

I didn't want to do the normal "travel blog" thing. I had never loved those blogs, as they were long-winded and the formatting was ugly. Writing essays about my trip and assuming anyone would care seemed self-indulgent. I thought, *If everyone is already checking Instagram, I'll just give them little updates and photos as I go. That seems less presumptuous and easier.*

I had never done a long ride. Neither had Weston. Latin America loomed ahead of us. The Southern Hemisphere. So far away. Thoughts crept in while I rode. *I speak almost no Spanish. Weston is the same. What's the word for* bathroom *again?* But when the surge of anxiety would swell up, my optimism would kick in, like it was triggered by a racing heart, and I would be flooded with certainty that it would all work out. I wonder if the old explorers and bold nomads of the past had this chemical nature to their brain. A foolish hope that the other side of the mountain wouldn't kill them.

We cycled down the coast of Oregon. Tall evergreen trees pushed into the clouds like sticks into a pillow. We watched the coastal sand changing from beige to black, the rocks rising sharply out of the ocean like an invading army. Nothing here was smooth, not even the waves. They erupted in jagged rollers of green and blue, lifting knots of seaweed and sticks to smash against the rocks.

I tried listening to music that first day, but it felt wrong and forced. Even with all my natural positivity, I was feeling heavy, dragging behind my bike all the billion unknowns. *When will my tire pop? When will Weston's bike fall apart? Where will we sleep tonight? And the next night? And the next?*

My phone was clipped to a holster at the front of my bike, between my handlebars and right in my line of sight. It was my map. I plotted the day's journey on Google Maps, and then followed my phone as we rode. Later, this became very helpful when towns would have confusing and winding streets. And even without service, my GPS and map would work, so long as I loaded it in the morning.

Weston rode in front of me. His natural pace was stronger than mine. On a long, straight stretch, he pulled back next to me and wanted to talk. "Think we could get our trip sponsored?" he asked.

"By who, like a company?"

"Yeah. You're writing about it. I can write about it, and I think a lot of people want to do what we're doing. We could get a bike company or a camping company to give us money."

"That's not a bad idea. But how? Do you know anyone?"

"I've made pitch decks before, in my New York life. That would be rad."

"I thought you didn't believe in money?" I smiled as I said it.

"It's not that I don't believe in it. I want to dethrone it. Money is a currency, like a current, it should flow through me. Savings is stagnant. Feels wrong."

"Sounds like something Jesus would say."

"I mean, that's why I gave all my shit away. Jesus said to the rich man, give it all up and follow me. Well, here I am. Don't know if I'm following Jesus or just the truth behind what he said."

"Are you calling me Jesus?" I said. We both laughed.

The clouds were fat and lazy on the shore, but sometimes the road would wind into a river valley away from the ocean. The sun would shine just one hill away, and we'd strip off our shirts. My soft white body looked absurd next to Weston's Adonis tan and abs, but for stretches we were alone on these roads, and I felt invisible and free. It was the end of summer, and I'd expected more road-trippers, more tourists. But for whatever reason, we often had the road to ourselves. Sweat would build up in my helmet and, upon a certain turn of my head, it would pour out down the bridge of my nose like a faucet. As the sun started to touch the western hills, it was time to watch for a camping spot.

I had gotten in my mind that I wanted to sleep under a bridge. It seemed like something Kerouac would've done. The romantic tramps and drifters of the past. It also seemed like a smart move in case it rained. We'd cycled over a few, but I didn't know if we'd come up on one as the sun was setting. I told Weston to keep his eyes peeled for a perfect bridge when the day started dimming. I watched the sun move across the sky, and watched the road, and looked at the map on my phone, and hoped for the best.

At one point, I turned my head to see if Weston was still behind me, and he wasn't. I assumed he'd popped a tire or something, so I turned around and backtracked to find him. I couldn't see him. Then I saw his bike, turned over on the side in a hurry. But it didn't look like a crash. Nothing but green bushes flanked the side of the road. Maybe he was peeing? As I pulled up he was shouting.

"These are blackberries!"

The exact same bushes had lined the road for three hours, but I hadn't looked at them. I was staring at the trees and the sky and the road and the trucks passing us. Apparently, late August is blackberry season in Oregon, and the entire state turns into a ripe banquet. Weston ditched his bike and dove into the berries. The thorns tore at his bare skin, but a jackpot fever had come over him. I gingerly laid my bike down, and for half an hour we ate our fill. The bitter sweetness of the berries stung the insides of our cheeks. Our fingers turned purple. By the time we looked up, the sun was getting low. We laughed at our wilderness sweets and pulled ourselves back to our bikes and got back to riding.

I had wanted to get fifty miles in the first day, but we managed only twenty-two. Every mile was a calculation. "Okay, so I made it ten miles in the last hour, so that means if I bike for three more hours that's thirty more miles, that would be forty miles, which means tomorrow if I go sixty miles then I've gone my first hundred miles, and the whole trip is ten thousand miles, I think, which means I'm one percent done. That's not bad." I do this with everything. If I'm at a party, and it's getting late, I calculate exactly how many hours I can sleep if I get to bed in fifteen minutes, or in an hour. The calculation makes me feel like I'm in control.

Finally, as dusk closed in, we crossed a bridge over a little river that wound through a farm. Weston stopped at the far side of the bridge, laid down his bike, and peered over to a clearing below.

I stopped behind him, looked down at the spot, and agreed—this was the place. We pushed our bikes down through weeds and grass till the perfect shelter of the bridge was above us. There were no large trees under the bridge so the hammocks would have to come another day. We would just sleep on our cheap reflectors on the ground. Hopefully around a fire. Time was short; I had to find wood before it was completely dark. Along the river, driftwood had been deposited by flood and tide high on the banks and wedged into trees, messengers of what had been and would be again.

I gathered wood while Weston started our campfire. He loved making the fire. Perfecting his little wooden teepee, talking to himself about how he would like to learn how to do it without matches, without a lighter. Just friction. I had a small Bluetooth speaker. I put on Van Morrison's *Astral Weeks* and cleared away shrubs for the campsite.

Weston made lentils over the fire, stirred in some spices, and we ate our fill. After biking, even just for an afternoon, all food tasted good. I don't know if we were physically tired, or just exhausted from the electric excitement that comes from a long-anticipated launch.

We were full, lying by the tiny fire, falling asleep. *Astral Weeks* played quietly as the embers popped. Then, suddenly, a bright light panned across my eyelids. I sat up like lightning. In the field across the creek was a truck, driving and bouncing through the grass, coming for us. Weston sprung up at the light too.

"Oh fuck!" he said.

"They must've seen our fire. Dang it."

We crouched low and Weston moved like a ninja to pour his water bottle on the fire.

The truck bounced closer, the thick headlight beams flashing in the trees, then across our faces, then in the trees again. We were frozen.

"Where the heck will we sleep? Do you think they have guns?" I said.

Weston was quiet. Watching. The truck got close enough for us to hear music playing inside. The windows were down. Just before it reached the edge of the creek, it made a sharp turn to the left, then kept turning, the headlights spraying around the field and tree line. It kept making the circle. I heard a loud laugh.

It was kids, doing donuts in the field. They hadn't even seen us.

Our cat-stance tenseness subsided, and Weston stood up and went to find more wood. The temperature was dropping fast. I shivered in my sleeping bag.

Day one was done. The sound of the water. I was under a bridge, tired and full, listening to Van Morrison by a creek. I was doing it. Only 9,978 more miles to go.

In the morning, as Weston restarted the fire, I asked how he'd slept.

"I didn't," he said.

"You didn't sleep at all?"

"Maybe thirty minutes. My blanket isn't enough. That was the coldest night I've ever had."

"You need a real sleeping bag."

"I know."

We biked that day through a fine mist to a Wal-Mart, where Weston bought a bulky, cheap sleeping bag. Along the way, the Oregon forest came up to the highway in an impenetrable wall, but we could see that the distant hills had been buzzed bald from logging. I thought about my parents that day. My mom back in Louisiana, agreeing to marry this man and walk across America with him. The first day was probably full of wonder. *What an adventure my life is!* The second day, perhaps less. Maybe more, *What the hell have I done?*

We camped again that night on the side of a hill, just hidden from the road by an embankment. We made it close to fifty miles that day and felt very accomplished. Everything on the ground was soaked through. Rotted logs crumbled like cornbread. Fallen branches were slick with moss. The air was like floating rain, suspended and waiting to wet our faces. But Weston kept his singular focus on getting his fire going. He blackened his thumb with a lighter. He tore pages out of his journal. He blew on tiny bits of damp kindling. Meanwhile, I clumsily tied up my tarp and hammock between two trees. Hammock first, then a string above and my cheap blue tarp draped across it like a Civil War tent.

As soon as Weston got the tiniest fire going, he rolled a joint. I crawled into my hammock to watch, then fell asleep.

Biking south the next day, the highway took us up and over one steep hill after another. We biked up inclines slowly and bombed down long drops that would wind us back to the beach, then away, then back. Long, relentless uphills, and long, cold downhills in what felt like an eternity of dampness.

The next night we stayed with a woman whose son knew a friend of Weston's in San Diego. She put us up in her guest room, and we gladly showered. We played cards with her and her husband. We told war stories of our incredible (two-and-a-half-day) journey. They were impressed and worried and excited for us. She heated up the Jacuzzi. We soaked for hours and she brought us beer.

In the morning she called her friend down the coast. "Tina, these two young boys are bicycling from Florence all the way to South America! They stayed with Bill and me last night and they are just delightful. Such sweet boys. Think they could stay with you tonight? Put 'em up anywhere! They can even camp in your yard." She smiled, put her hand over the phone, and whispered, "She says of course. She says you guys are crazy."

We cycled fifty-five miles the next day, happy to beat our previous day's record. The coast highway took us over steep hills and through small towns and evergreen trees and along cliffs. We reached Tina's house and stayed in her guest room. If this was how the trip would go, people hosting and then calling up their friends down the road, it would be very easy.

After Tina, we had our first sixty-mile day and reached the coast of California. In just those few days, the trip had begun to feel like our whole life. My theory of waking up my senses and slowing down time was proving true. Those days had stretched into ages, my mind so awake that every foot of every mile was noticed and relished.

I kept thinking about my parents. My dad setting out on foot from New York in 1975, curious about what he would see, an America that he would discover for himself. He didn't know that he would meet a girl in Louisiana. That he would marry her. That she would walk with him to Oregon. That they would have three kids and I would be one of them. He had no idea. I bet all he knew was that the trip would change his life. Which it did. And all I knew was that my trip might change mine.

Chapter 3

THE COAST IS CLEAR
(Northern California)

13,726 miles to go

n four days, we'd biked 160 miles. I was proud. How many people did I know who'd biked 160 miles? But I was also tired and uncomfortable. My knees hurt, which I didn't tell Weston. They hurt bad. This was my fear. *What if my body shuts down and I can't even make it to Mexico? Why the holy hell didn't I train?* Already, I felt like I'd been living on this bike forever.

But the pace of biking, even these few days in, was having the intended effect: time crawled. Days were eternal. When it would rain, it rained forever. When the sun came out, it would be hot forever. I was a kid again. It was incredible, too, to watch the land change in slow motion. Riding a bicycle gives the land a realistic scale. You notice every seam and crease. The distances between towns and farms and the height of hills, and the way a road will follow a river or instead cut straight over a hill—you experience it all viscerally. You feel it all fitting together.

I appreciated the accurate map my phone gave me. It alleviated the age-old explorer's fear of getting lost. But I knew, even as I cycled south along the familiar Pacific Coast, that it cost me something else. It cost me a certain amount of wonder. Not only is every map perfectly drawn, but you can zoom your way into any beach cove in the world and practically steal the margarita out of someone's hand. How do we explore a planet without secrets?

I long for the days of lands we didn't know existed, before the uncharted places all disappeared. That's why I love looking at old maps, the ones with misjudged proportions and large sections labeled "UNKNOWN."

A few years back, some scientists were scouring satellite imagery of Mozambique when they noticed a green spot halfway up a mountain that didn't exist on any map. It was the lost forest of Mount Mabu, home to animal species completely unknown to science and forests that had never been logged. No roads. Just a thick jungle sitting halfway up a mile-high mountain, the whole thing surrounded by plains. But of course, places like that are the exception today.

With the Internet connecting us all, the rest of the world feels closer, less alien. But I think that's only true in our minds. The Internet does not bring Argentina one inch closer to me than before. That's part of why I craved this trip. Knowledge alone is like an unearned memory, mostly forgotten. Just facts and two-dimensional images. I wanted to physically discover the world, the old-fashioned way. To cross over mountains to see what was on the other side. To hear languages I'd never heard. To take the photographs from *National Geographic* and put them out in the weather of human imagination.

As we entered California, it looked exactly like Oregon—another reminder of the arbitrariness of most human boundaries. The California I was familiar with was urban sprawl, palm trees, strip malls, stucco, and cracked asphalt. But Northern California swaps the rules. At least along the coast, it's all thick and wet with vegetation. Small towns dot the cold forests, feeling far from anywhere. The first town after the border is Smith River, which was falling apart. It was small and seemed to be choking on its modern irrelevance. The paint had chipped from the small houses. The general stores were closed. Whatever reason this town had to spring up in the wilderness, that reason had gone.

Just south of this tiny town, Weston's back tire popped. The sidewall blew out, meaning that just patching the tube wouldn't be enough to get us back on the road.

We were completely isolated. Our phones had no service. But luckily we were on the only highway along the coast, so any cars had to go this way. We'd have to hitchhike to the next town.

For some reason, hitchhiking embarrassed me. Not the act of hitchhiking itself, but what you have to do to do it. I stood by the highway, leaning out, trying to make eye contact with drivers as they whizzed by, focusing on trucks and big SUVs because of our bicycles. I had fake reading eyeglasses and put them on, to look more approachable. I'd saved up and gotten Lasik surgery before my trip, simply for ease—I was afraid of losing or breaking my glasses somewhere deep in the Amazon and being helpless—but I knew that glasses made me look kinder, softer, and so I put clear lenses in my frames and brought them along, specifically for moments like these.

As I stood there, glasses on and smiling big, car after car drove on by. Each passing car felt like a personal rejection. Weston, who had done a lot of hitching before, said the average wait for a ride is an hour. "And we have bikes, so it might be longer."

"Damn," I said. "I feel so unwanted."

As rejections whizzed by one after another, we had plenty of time to talk.

"People just don't see hitchhikers anymore," Weston offered. "Americans don't have the instinct for it like our parents did."

"Why do you think that is? Isn't it just dangerous? I thought, like, every hitchhiker gets raped and murdered," I said.

"No. Not at all. It's probably safer now than it was in the fifties. The only difference is public perception and national news media," he said, taking the tone he gets when he's about to teach something.

"How so?"

"Back in the forties, fifties, sixties, everyone was hitchhiking everywhere. My dad hitched from Florida to New York and back a bunch of times. What changed was the news cycle. Back in the day, if someone was hurt or attacked in Maine, the people in Los Angeles never heard a word of it, so the sense of safety was only learned organically. National news made people in Boston fear what was happening in Phoenix. It's the same with people locking their doors in their neighborhoods and not letting their kids play in the woods. It's no more dangerous now, it's just the fear has changed."

"Well, if we get abducted and put in a bunker underneath an old white guy's house I'm gonna call bullshit on your theory."

I put on my sad baby-sloth face, accentuated by my fake reading glasses, and thumbed at a few more cars, feeling a renewed sense of righteousness after Weston's lesson on hitchhiking. It felt so stupid that a perfectly good and environmentally beneficial practice like hitchhiking would disappear because of irrational fear. I smiled and made a "pleeeease" face as a large suburban passed. Trucks were better, but we had started trying for anything technically big enough to fit our bikes. The suburban blew past us. I think I might have muttered "asshole." But after a few seconds, I turned around and saw that the suburban, quite a ways down the road, had stopped, turned into a driveway, and was coming back to us. Weston was off in the woods, peeing.

"Whoa! We caught a big one!" I yelled. "Reelin' it in now!"

Weston ran back as the suburban pulled up just ahead of us at a widening in the road. A woman got out. Middle-aged, with brown hair matted close to her head from just showering.

"You guys don't look like you hitchhike much. That's why I pulled over."

"No, ma'am, we don't. We're riding our bicycles to South America and we got a flat tire," Weston said, putting on his theatrical charm.

"Oh my god. Well, I can take you to town. There's a Wal-Mart there and I think they got bike parts. You don't look like the normal people I see on the streets. The gangbangers and crust punks. I'd never pick them up. People aren't trustworthy these days. You never know who's trying to get something from you." She helped us lift the bikes into the back, our gear and bags all disheveled.

"Where you boys from?"

"I'm from Los Angeles and Weston's from all over," I said.

"Well, I never do this. But you boys looked nice so I decided what the hell, I'll pick ya up. Get in."

We climbed into the backseat of her suburban. In the front seat was her daughter. When the girl turned to look at us, I saw the characteristics of Down's syndrome.

"This is Lindsay. She don't talk much. She's retarded."

"Hi, Lindsay," I said, with the gentle tone that people get when speaking to someone they pity.

"Oh, she won't talk to you. She don't talk to strangers. I taught her that. She's real stupid. But I love her. But God, no one prepares you for raising a retarded kid. She is more than anyone can handle. I'd send her back if I could. But she's mine now, I do what I can, isn't that right, Lindsay?"

Lindsay nodded and said nothing.

"I swear I don't pick up hitchhikers ever. But you guys looked like you needed some help, and you don't look like tweakers, so I thought what the hell." She was talking fast, to fill the awkwardness of having strangers in her car. She spoke like life owed her everything, but hadn't yet paid her a dime.

"You can't trust people on the street around here. People don't got jobs, so they're all on meth, or some other drug. I've been on disability for ten years, and I get help from the government for Lindsay. I can't get a job, there aren't none to be had. Stop pickin' at your nails!" She slapped Lindsay's hands. "Goddammit, I told you to stop that."

"iPad," Lindsay said.

"I told you if you behaved I would let you look at the iPad. You can't have it for an hour."

Lindsay started wailing. The cry was low and alien and emerged from a sustained breath. Like a musical grunt off key. I pushed my knee into Weston's and we gave each other a knowing look. He was watching the mother with half-squinted eyes, probably thinking and placing her into categories.

The drive to town took fifteen minutes. The woman argued with Lindsay while we sat quietly in the backseat. By the time she dropped us off in Crescent City, Lindsay was whimpering.

"Sorry about that," the woman said. "She is just terrible. I don't know what God wants from me." We thanked her for the kindness and got our bikes out of the back. Weston and I didn't talk about it. We felt strange and sad.

Crescent City had one main drag and a small harbor. Hills surrounded the town. The Pacific churned beneath beige cliffs.

The only bike shop was closed, so Weston had to improvise. He bought duct tape and began masterfully reinforcing his injured tire.

There were no tubes of the right size, so he bought one that was too big and folded it into his duct-taped mess.

"You can fold a tube like that?" I asked.

"Yeah. I've had to do this before. You just pinch and fold it over itself to make it fit, and then inflate. The pinch will hold. It isn't ideal, but it'll work for a while." I was shaken by my complete ignorance about the workings of a bicycle. I was glad, watching Weston trouble-shoot, knowing that he could solve any problem. A Wal-Mart employee told us that there was a large bike shop seventy miles south in Arcata, a college town. We'd have to make it there.

I stood in the parking lot for a long time while Weston worked his clever magic.

As I went to lean my bike on another pole, I noticed a bee sitting on my handlebar. Just perched there, perfectly still.

This wasn't the first time I'd seen a bee. The week before I left, the *Time* magazine cover story had been "A World Without Bees." The article explained the mysterious "hive collapses" happening to bee colonies all over the United States. Something was killing them. This was bad news for humans, because most of our fruits and nuts are pollinated by bees, and without pollination, there are no fruits or nuts. The article said the bees were dying because of something humans are doing. Perhaps it's pesticides. Perhaps it's our cell phones, or radio waves, or Wi-Fi. No one really knows. When I read this, it hit me that human civilization has managed to get so complex that we cannot trace out the consequences of our actions. So long as the immediate result is what we desire, we are ready to try it—but the threat of long-range danger is harder to feel.

The day after I read the *Time* article, my boss gave me a going-away present. It was a beautiful folding pocket knife, with a polished wood handle and a silver blade as clean as a mirror. And at the joint of the blade and the handle was a silver carved bee. I held it in my hand and looked at my boss in astonishment. He said he didn't know anything about the article or that I had been talking about it.

The next day, I was making the rounds to say goodbye to my friends before the bike trip. I met up with a designer friend of mine at a burrito shop. She was waiting for me when I arrived, sketching on a pad. As I walked up, I realized it was a bee. She was designing an album cover for a friend's band, and they wanted a bee. A fucking bee.

Now, out on the road, I was seeing bees everywhere. They would land on me and just ride along for miles. I swear.

WE CAMPED that night, our fifth, in a thicket of blackberries halfway to Arcata and awoke at 6:30 a.m., at first light. Rain had dripped into our hammocks and we saw that we'd been sleeping in puddles. Shivering, we packed up our hammocks and bikes, still clumsy at the task but improving. Once our cargo was piled high, we pushed with much grunting back toward the road. My feet slipped in the wet leaves.

We dried ourselves the best we could and were blessed by midday sunshine. We rode down to Arcata, a town known for its Victorian houses and famous for its celebration of weed. The many coffee shops and cafés had bright colorful murals of mushrooms and psychedelic fantasies. We tracked down a well-stocked bike shop and got Weston a proper tire and new tubes. We stayed with a friend of a friend in a crowded college house and we smoked weed with some well-flanneled college guys. Weston showed me how a gravity bong works in the kitchen sink, using half of a two-liter Pepsi bottle sawed in two. I took a long hit and felt nothing. But I didn't push my luck.

We woke the next day and committed to a full day of riding in the light. We cycled through decently sized towns, which now felt like bustling cities. We finished the day with hours of riding through dark forest and camped again. The next day, it seemed that there was a gas station just a mile down the road, tucked in the tiny dirt patch between the only highway and a wall of evergreens. I needed coffee. We found the Exxon market bustling with people—truckers, passersby, locals—getting their coffee and prepackaged gooey pastries or a decent breakfast wrap for $2.50. Apparently it was the only business for miles. I got my coffee and sat down in the haphazard seating area in the corner of the gas station.

Next to me, an old man hovered over his cup of coffee and a

Snickers bar. He wore a dirty thick plaid flannel shirt, with layers underneath, and a thick beanie. His pants were brown and dirty. His clothes looked three sizes too big. He wasn't reading, or saying anything, or looking around. He was only sitting. He reminded me of the kid in high school, forever picked on, who had retreated into his mind, always a time zone away.

I drank my coffee and read the news on my phone. I felt him sitting next to me. Ten minutes later, the old man stood up and picked up a bicycle helmet. I hadn't noticed it sitting on the counter next to him. It was pink-trimmed and certainly meant for a preteen girl. He removed his beanie, smoothed out his thin white hair, and strapped on the helmet before walking outside. Through the large windows, I saw him walking up to a child's mountain bike. The neon paint had chipped away, but the remains of a lightning bolt remained. Onto the rusted rack on the back, he had tied a ratty flannel blanket and two Gatorade bottles, each half-full of water. He adjusted his helmet and rode away.

I wondered if he lived in the woods nearby. I wondered if this was his morning routine.

We finished our coffees and shitty breakfast food and I surveyed the map on my phone. We were headed toward the alien world of the redwoods. The giant groves of Northern California. The guardians. As if the redwoods protected the perfect weather and fertile fields of central California from a northern invasion. As the Sierras defended her from the east. And the desert defended her from the south.

Two hours into the giant trees, we saw the old man again, pumping up a hill on his tiny bicycle. He stopped as we approached, turned to us, the first time I had seen his face, and asked "Which is the best way to get to San Francisco?" I almost didn't hear him, his voice was so small.

Weston answered, "The 101 here will take you there, but you should take the Redwood Highway. It's more scenic and has fewer cars. You'll see the turnoff just ahead."

"Are there hills?"

"I don't know, but probably," Weston said.

"Okay."

He got back on his bike and continued grinding up the hill toward the turnoff for the Redwood Highway. Weston and I looked at each other. This old man was cycling alone to San Francisco, 250 miles away—and who knows where he'd started. He had no tent. Only a blanket, the clothes he was wearing, and the child's helmet on his head.

We soon caught up with him. And as we passed, we cheered. "You got this! Woo-hoo! San Francisco, here we come!" But he didn't seem to notice. A few hours later, we stopped for a break. We were eating snacks and resting in a moment of sunshine when he came riding up and put a leg down.

"Well, hello!" I said with delight.

"I should have stayed on the main road," he mumbled. "Bigger hills. I like bigger hills. This is too flat."

"You want the hills? Aren't they too much?" Weston said.

"No." No eye contact. "I need to get to San Francisco."

He climbed back on his bike and left without any more conversation, his little legs pedaling much too quickly, his oversized pants flapping like a joke. We sat there, eating granola bars and drinking our water, wondering what was in San Francisco for him. I wonder now if he ever made it. We never saw him again.

RIDING THE Redwood Highway, I felt like a pauper sneaking into the castle. The trees began to tower above us, like a convention of gods, either speaking so far above that we couldn't hear, or waiting for us to leave so they could begin again. We stopped a few times for hours at a time, hiding our bikes behind felled redwoods the size of shipping containers, and traipsing into the forest with our paperback books in search of a reading spot by a stream or in a sunbeam meadow. We found it. And we read.

Along the way, the flora and landforms would change magically and suddenly in a fascinating smashup of microclimates. Dense forest became a golden hillside became a clot of oak trees in the cleavage of two hills became a rocky cliff down to the sea, all within a few miles of one another. Riding through each, we never tired of wonder, and we loved camping in the woods. The practice of hanging hammocks and unpacking and packing our bikes became quick and easy. The rain stopped. When we pulled away from the ocean, the heat became intense. We bathed in creeks and gas station bathrooms. We stayed with a woman we'd met hours before. We drank beer and slowly my tailbone stopped aching.

As we got closer to the Bay Area, rustic villages and makeshift living transformed into the semi-rural escapes of the wealthy. Second homes, high gates, vineyards, glass castles standing on rocky cliffs commanding the ocean to be beautiful. The coastal roads above San Francisco are some of the most beautiful I have ever seen. Every turn is a bluff, a farm, cows grazing with a view of the ocean.

Our individual styles of riding had formed by now. Weston rode in front. Unable to cruise or simply look around, he attacked each mile as though it were a race. He focused on his leg muscles, his form, his speed. I was not like that. I looked around and admired, meandered and felt pangs of love. When we stopped, usually at the crest of long inclines, I asked, "Weston, how amazing was that barn?"

"What barn?"

"How did you miss it? It was huge and right on the road. So amazing, falling apart, leaning to its left. I can't believe it's still standing!"

"I didn't see it."

In the evening, we would buy bottles of beer and sit around the campfire and talk. Weston was always talking. "I am pushing myself more each day," he'd say. "I am a student of my own body. If I ride upright, with no hands, and hold my core constricted, I can work my whole body as I pedal, and if you focus on the glutes, they engage and do the pushing."

As we approached the Golden Gate Bridge, so did the fog. It pushed on and around the bridge like milk pouring into coffee, swirling and taking over. When we rode on the giant red structure, we could not see the water below. Only gray. Cars would appear out of nowhere and disappear behind us. It was cold. We stopped. We were out-of-body present, observing ourselves on the bridge, as if from outside. As I stared at the bay below, a boat that looked like a spaceship came into view. It was a catamaran, adorned with the word *Oracle* across its red and white sail. It moved silently, and by watching its wake, I finally grasped how far down the water was.

Riding into San Francisco was fun but ridiculously stressful. We hadn't seen a metropolis yet, and I had never biked in one. Cars felt like enemies, and we were trespassers in their city, on their streets. And the famously steep hills? They are not an exaggeration. For the first time, I had to walk my bike. Weston just powered through.

Winding through those streets, I couldn't help but imagine the hills around the bay before the people showed up. How they were once full of shrubs and grass, and now hardly an inch of original nature is left. Almost the entire peninsula is blanketed by cement and bricks and wood and foreign trees and foreign grass. I could feel the heavy human yoke. I found myself wondering, "How can the earth hold up all this stuff?"

We stayed with an old friend of mine for three days, and in no time, I slipped back into the comfortable urban life I had enjoyed before the trip started. The comforts of Southern California were all here. Coffee, craft beer, window-shopping as we strolled for blocks and blocks. But Weston and I couldn't stay. We were heading into unknown worlds that, perhaps, had none of those things. I would be stripped of what made me feel safe to make room for something else.

One morning Weston checked his e-mail and sat up straight. "Oooh! They want to meet us for coffee!"

"Who?" I asked.

"One of the top guys at Instagram!"

"Excuse me?"

"Yeah. A buddy of mine from my New York days knows him, and reached out and said he should meet with us."

"Oh my gosh, it's that easy?"

"I mean, I guess when you're doing something badass like riding bikes to South America, people will meet with you," Weston said.

"You sneaky man . . . setting up meetings. What does that mean? Do they want to sponsor us or something?"

"I'm not sure, but we should meet them, no? They're down to meet us at a spot called Trouble Coffee tomorrow."

The next morning we took an Uber to Trouble Coffee, though we debated riding our bikes for effect. But it was across town and too early and too cold.

Josh and Matt were there, waiting for us. We didn't know what they looked like, but they had looked us up and spotted us right when we arrived. They ordered us coffee and cinnamon toast and we sat outside in the misty cold San Francisco air.

"Nice to meet you guys," Josh said. He was tall, late twenties, and soft spoken. He was very calm—so calm that he seemed uninterested. He wore a black hoodie and jeans. He was a Silicon Valley heavy hitter, and looked exactly as I expected. Matt was a little more animated, but not by much.

"Tell us about your trip," Josh said, almost inaudibly. Weston and I told them about the excitement of starting out, about my parents walking across America, about camping under bridges and by the side of the road. At a certain point, I felt like this was a job interview, where they had all the power and maybe they were humoring us as a favor for a friend, and not actually interested. I felt stupid. They almost didn't seem to be listening.

I was telling a story from Northern California. ". . . So we finally reached the redwoods, and riding bikes through them is the most—"

"How do you like that cinnamon toast? It's famous in SF. Toast is a thing here," Josh said.

"Oh, yeah, it's really good. I love it," I said. I felt stupid. Why were we here selling ourselves? To get some huge company to feature us? These guys were clearly doing someone I didn't know a favor. They bought us coffee and toast but I was feeling like a schmuck. I quit telling stories. We talked about the toast some more. About the neighborhood of Outer Sunset. About how the fog was nicknamed Karl. That Karl even had a Twitter account.

"Well, that was embarrassing," I said when we'd parted.

"No, it was fine. They're just tech guys. They don't communicate like us."

"They hated us," I said.

WE SPENT ONE more night in San Francisco and then headed south—past Monterey and Carmel. I had driven Highway 1 many times, and the Central Coast of California is one of my favorite places in the world. The landscape south of San Francisco quickly transforms from tightly packed city to suburbs to farms and forest. Redwood trees huddle in the moist mountain creases, leaving groves of eucalyptus to climb the drier hillsides. And the little towns on the Central Coast always send my mind soaring, imagining other lives, ones where I would grow up in the eucalyptus forests, building forts.

We camped and stayed with friends and acquaintances along the coast, but my real dream was to reach Big Sur, the little town about two hours by car south of San Francisco, famous for attracting writers and artists. Jack Kerouac. Henry Miller. Robinson Jeffers. The draw comes from its remoteness and grandeur. A lot of the California coast has cliffs and coves, but Big Sur has giant mountains and no easy ingress or egress. It is remote because it is hard to get to. The cliffs are too steep, the water raging into the rocks. The summits are too high and the canyons too narrow for wide roads. It is a coastal ecosystem separated from the rest of California by the scale of its barriers. Biking through Big Sur means miles and miles high above the water, each foot of pavement delivering you to the best ocean view you've ever seen. Big Sur is also famous for a thick and heavy fog. Some people make the drive from Santa Cruz to Morro Bay and are lucky to see the red taillights of the car in front of them. But if you know Big Sur well, you know that you can almost always beat the fog. You need only go up. Gain some elevation on one of the many switchback roads branching off from Highway 1, and you will find yourself above the blanket, with the sun shining and rolling across the cotton lumps of clouds. The mountains push up from the fog, cooking in the sun and feeding their cold and damp roots at the ocean beneath.

On the day we rode up the first inclines into Big Sur, we had hot sun. I felt chosen by God.

I had always wanted to camp above McWay Falls, a waterfall in Big Sur that spills directly onto the beach. It is a thin stream when seen from the designated overlook point, but it's a lot of water, if only one could get below it. There seems to be no way down the cliff to see it up close. "Area closed, no trespassing" signs lined the other side of the fences down the cliff. Droves of tourists park along Highway 1 and walk to the overlook to take pictures, and it is very difficult to get a spot to camp there. A few of my friends had managed to get a booking, and they said we could crash next to them. Perfect. Again, the serendipity of some of this was not lost on me. It was just like the bees. Was God sending me signs to make me feel safe and good? I don't know. But it felt like it.

I had been posting about the trip every day on Instagram, and it was fun to have people follow along virtually. "Oh my gosh, you're really doing it?" "How do you charge your phone?" "How is your phone working?" But the feedback added an element of performance to the trip. I had an audience. So many people were worried about how I charged my phone. This amused me. I would charge it in coffee shops and cafés, of course. It wasn't so hard. But people imagined me in the woods.

We camped with our friends above the waterfall, and over beers that night concocted a plan.

"We should wake up at dawn and shower in the waterfall!" my friend said.

"We're doing that," Weston said.

But Jed the Rule Follower panicked.

"Oh my gosh," I protested. "Y'all, there is no way down. And won't rangers check in the morning?" I asked. "That's probably like a thousand-dollar ticket."

"Don't be a baby," my friend said. "You're biking to Patagonia, you gotta be bold. We'll go at first light, no chubby ranger is up and checking then. We'll be fine. I'll wake you up."

"Okay, we'll be up," Weston said.

I was nervous about the idea but fine with being pressured. If we got a ticket, it wouldn't be my fault, and I could say "I told you so."

I awoke to my friend leaning over me. "Wake up, it's time." Weston and I sprung out of our sleeping bags and headed to the overlook. We climbed down the flaky cliff, sliding and hanging on the ice plants and shrubs. With scrapes and scratches and big rocks giving way, tumbling down and breaking into pieces, we made it down the waterfall. Up close, it looked huge. The water fell in clumps and looked heavy. We stripped naked and got under the water. The illegality of it felt liberating. The naughtiness added to the fun. The water was fresh and cold and clean. It was the best shower you could imagine.

Back at the campsite, and feeling refreshed and scandalous, we started packing up.

I checked my phone and saw that I had 10,000 new followers on Instagram. What?! What was going on? I refreshed, in one second I'd grown another 100. What happened? Wait, did they? I checked my feed and there it was, a photo I had taken of my bicycle by the ocean . . . featured on Instagram's official account. "Follow this guy," the message said. "He's riding his bike from Oregon to Patagonia and Instagramming the whole thing." Posted two hours ago. It had 20,000 likes. Oh my god. Josh and Matt had posted us to 60 million people. Oh my god. They didn't hate us.

"Weston! They posted!"

"They did!? Show me." I showed him the post. By then it was 21,000 likes.

"Hell, yeah! This is brilliant. I always knew they'd post," he said.

"You did not. Wow, this is crazy. Like, thousands of people we don't know are going to watch us bike. Is that good?"

"Absolutely, Jed! Think about it. If we have followers from all over, we can ask Instagram for people to stay with in Mexico and South America! People will let us stay with them," Weston said.

"Oh wow, that's a great idea."

Now that we were going to be watched by thousands of strangers, I felt the affectation of having an audience. I felt that I would speak differently. See things differently. So many people. I began to worry. Would I care more about the post than the actual experience? Would I have to be fake or sanitize my posts?

No. My mom already followed me, so I was already censoring myself a bit. Which I think is okay. Saying everything you think or do in public isn't appropriate at a dinner party or online. So that shouldn't be an issue. No, I'm just going to post what I would post if I were talking to my friends in mixed company. That's effortless and still me.

Everything is okay and good, I thought.

Then, *Fuck. I guess I can't get hurt and quit now.*

THE SOUTHERN PART of Big Sur served up wind and dense mist. I had never really feared for my safety on the road, but on the tight turns, chubby-faced white retirees in RVs carved the road up with sharp turns and new rigs. They would slide by so close, my depth perception failed, and I was certain I had passed through them like a ghost.

Big Sur ends abruptly in the south. The mountains that guard the land from the sea fall away, and softer green hills make room for cow fields and farmland. We stopped at a pullout where elephant seals congregated on the beach, and a parking lot had been erected for tourists to stop and stare at these obese wonders. I leaned on the wooden fence to stare at the massive seals below. Most of them were sleeping, and a few were hump-flopping their way across the beach. None seemed to be in the water. A huge male, with his disgusting spongy nose, was chasing a smaller male across the beach. Back on the bikes, evening came on faster than it seemed it should have. We passed Hearst Castle, high on the golden hills to our left, and grabbed dinner at an overpriced diner. I ate chicken chimichangas (which will be important to know later) and was miserably full. We stopped at a gas station to buy some water and toilet paper for our imminent camping.

Parked just outside was another touring bike, with a trailer hitched to the back. When I looked at it more closely, I realized it wasn't actually a trailer, but a kid's seat that gets pulled behind. The seat held a big, overflowing backpack and was so overfilled that bungee cords strained to hold the contents together. Weston had already found the rider and was talking to him.

His name was Johnny Jones. He was very tan and overweight and had bad teeth and a huge smile. He had no hair but wore a bandana on his head. He looked almost Samoan, like a giant baby. I went inside and bought some supplies. I returned to my bike and passed

Weston and Johnny, chatting away, entering the gas station. I packed my panniers with snacks and water and toilet paper.

After some time, Weston came up to me holding a lunch bag.

"Where'd you get that? Is that food?" I said.

"Johnny gave it to me!" He opened it up and it was absolutely full of weed.

"Whoa!" I said.

"He is traveling the country by bicycle as a way to deal with his depression. He said, 'Who can be sad on a bike?' He talks to offices and construction sites and asks for one-dollar donations. He used to be on all kinds of meds and prescription shit and gave it all up for the bike. After he told me his story, I offered to buy him a Gatorade . . . I don't even really have money for Gatorade, but I just felt like doing something nice for this guy. His story is amazing. Let whatever money I have flow through me. So I bought it for him . . . and he said he wanted to repay me, and dug this out of his bag, and gave it all to me. He said weed is real medicine. Not that man-made crap. Holy shit."

It was so much weed.

"You're going to die from that," I said.

"I know. I'm so excited. Feels like a sign from the universe. From God. I think Johnny Jones was an angel. And he has your same initials. Wow."

JUST SOUTH OF the gas station we found a campground in the small tourist outpost that exists only to serve Hearst Castle. The campground wasn't full and there was no one at the entrance, so we rode in and set up shop in a far corner spot, hoping we could wake at sunrise and be out of there without paying.

As the sun set, we threw our bikes down, hung our hammocks, and walked out at twilight to the beach. We sat on the sand and listened to the waves. Weston pulled out his rolling papers and an enormous handful of weed.

"Jed, you don't like weed, right?"

"No. It makes me sick."

"Come on. Tonight, on this beach, in this place, it's worth giving it another try. You always say you're waiting for the right moment. What if tonight is the right moment?" Weston said.

I'll admit, I believe in giving things multiple tries, and not holding a person or an experience or a thing to one bad memory, or three. Especially things that people love. And the trip itself had an exploratory spirit about it. What was a bike trip like this for if not trying things? Saying yes to anything.

"Okay," I said finally, "but I'm not going to smoke much. Just enough to feel something." Weston seemed to inflate with triumph. Smiling, he rolled a very fat joint, lit it, and took a long drag. He passed it to me. "Wait, so what is the proper way?" I asked.

"Pull in the smoke, and hold it for as long as you can, deep in your lungs, let it go all the way to the bottom, you'll probably cough but that's okay," Weston said. I inhaled deep, held it, and coughed.

"Good. Okay, puff puff pass." Weston reached for it and took another long toke. "Johnny said this weed was given to him in Humboldt County, and was grown outdoors. So it's more harsh than the candy-looking, medical-grade stuff you see in dispensaries. But it's good, you'll be good." He would speak with that flattened stoner voice that comes from holding your palate closed as you let the smoke sit in your lungs. I didn't feel anything.

"Here, let me try again." I reached for it and inhaled again. I held it in and only made the smallest chirp of a cough.

"Okay, I think that's enough," I said.

"Well, maybe one more, then you're done."

I wasn't feeling anything so I took another long large pull. Then Weston finished it off for several puffs. I studied my feelings to see if anything was happening.

Weston began doing yoga in the almost darkness. "Just feel your body," he said. "Every inch, just move slowly."

By now, I was definitely feeling something. My head felt like it was filling with water, or jelly, and my eyes would drag the image when I turned my head. My arms began to feel very heavy. This was it. It was happening. *Quick, do yoga,* I thought. I am remarkably inflexible, so yoga meant waving my arms around repeatedly and bending over ever so slightly. My mouth became very dry, so dry I thought something was wrong. I don't know how long we sat there, Weston doing yoga, me pretending to be okay while overanalyzing everything happening to me.

When I stood up, I felt like the connection to my body had a satellite delay. I was sinking. It was like trying to walk on the bottom of a pool. My stomach began to ache. How could this be what everyone loves about being high? I was not relaxed, or giggly, or hungry. I thought my mouth was going to crack off. My whole body felt like cement.

"I'll be right back, I have to use the bathroom," I said. My stomach hurt. It was such an odd feeling—a pressure in my gut, a knot, an ache. *If I sit on the toilet, maybe something will happen and it'll help.* I stumbled through the campground to the bathroom, which was a cinder-block structure with six or seven doors all in a row, each stall with its own mirror and a sink. My stomach felt bloated, like maybe I'd swallowed a baby. Maybe the chicken chimichangas I had eaten earlier at the overpriced tourist restaurant near Hearst Castle were bad. Maybe getting high screws with your digestion. I wished Weston had come with me to the bathroom, so I could ask him which one was the culprit.

I thought if I took a shit, the pressure would go away and maybe the high, too, so I pulled my pants down around my ankles and sat on the toilet. I was breathing heavy and strange, slow, long breaths like a woman giving birth. Nothing was happening. I looked around the room, trying to count how many white-painted cinder blocks were stacked from floor to ceiling. I pushed to try to make something happen. Nothing. Even sitting there, with my pants down, my arms folded in my lap, my body hunched over, my stomach wasn't improving. It was getting worse. I felt the pressure in my stomach expand, grow, and suddenly my saliva was warm and flowing. *Oh God.* I lunged forward, still sitting, and threw up on the floor in front of me, into my underwear, all over my shoes and shins and bare knees. The entire chicken chimichanga lunch.

The shock of this should have sobered me up. It did not. I was still high, still sluggish, sitting with my bare ass on a toilet, a lava field of puke all over the floor. Often when I am alone, and especially when I am drunk, I talk out loud to myself. Apparently I also do this when I am high. "Well, this is tragic," I said. "You have to clean this up, right now. Can you imagine a poor park ranger coming in here and seeing this? He'd quit." I was trying to make myself laugh. I think I was smiling.

I looked around for any kind of help. There was a sink. And a paper towel dispenser. It was empty. I stood up, stepped out of my shorts and underwear, and walked over to the sink. I lifted first one leg into the sink, and washed it off, then the other. I threw my underwear away. I rinsed out my shorts. I scrubbed my shoes. I got massive wads of toilet paper, the thin kind that disintegrates when wet, and began scooping the chimichanga mountain into the toilet, one double-handed scoop at a time. I was still so high. I don't know how long I was there, on all fours, scrubbing and scooping, ass in the air, soaking my shorts and shoes in the sink. It could have been three hours or twenty minutes. Once the floor was clean, I spent God knows how long wringing out my shorts to get them dry. I put them on. I put my shoes on. I looked around the room, slowly, blurry, proud of my cleaning job, ashamed of my chimichanga. I opened the door and thought, "No one will know what just happened behind this closed door."

I did feel better, still high as a satellite, but my stomach didn't hurt anymore. I floated through the dark toward our campsite. Weston was standing out in the road, away from our hammocks, visibly upset.

"Where've you been!?" he demanded.

"In the bathroom," I said. "I didn't feel well."

"There's something in our campsite!" Weston said, with the truest tone of fear. "There's a man walking around our hammocks in the dark." Weston's knees were bent and he was bobbing, ready to run or fight.

I was too high and tired for this. "You're sure it isn't a raccoon? You think there's a man crawling around in the bushes around our hammocks? I doubt that."

"DUDE, I heard it!" he exclaimed. "It was too big to be a raccoon.

Maybe five raccoons. What if it's a serial killer on the loose, or a homeless guy on meth!?" He was sincerely scared.

"You are high. So am I. I didn't hear anything, so I don't care," I said. "I hope it kills me."

I walked with determination into our campsite and crawled into my hammock. My sleeping bag was crumpled underneath me, and I fought for what felt like forever to get my feet in it. Weston watched for a while, then, seeing that I wasn't scared, crawled in his hammock and went to sleep.

I woke up rested and sober and hoping that the chimichanga incident had been a dream. But I saw that I wasn't wearing underwear, my shorts were still wet, my shoes still soaked.

Over instant coffee in lukewarm water, I informed Weston that my weed days were over.

Chapter 4

THE TEMPTATION OF HOME
(Southern California)

13,162 miles to go

We biked into San Luis Obispo and stayed a day there. The next day, we would ride to Pismo Beach and meet up with Weston's mom, who'd decided to come out and visit us. I'd never met her before. Weston was excited for the reunion, but apprehensive. He had a charged way of talking about his family and his childhood. A lack of stability. Lack of security. But love, too. We biked into Pismo and along the beach to a narrow house on the sand. Their family friend or some uncle owned it, I can't remember. As we pulled into the driveway, Weston's mom and stepdad stood waiting to greet us.

"Boys! You've made it!" his mom shouted. "Jed, it is so nice to meet you. I'm Linda. I've heard so much about you. If my boy is going to go off and do something crazy like this, I'm glad it's with you."

"Linda, so nice to meet you! Thank you," I said. "I've heard so much about you, too." That wasn't true. But I always say that.

"Come in, we've already cooked up a feast."

We chained up our bikes and carried our panniers inside the house. There was a guest room on the first floor by the garage. Then upstairs was a big long room with windows facing the ocean and the broad beach.

She had pizza boxes open on the table. Weston made eyes at me, as if referencing the junk food. We ate ravenously and drank our Cokes with the TV on, and they asked us questions about camping and sleeping and bikes and charging our phones.

"Has Weston tried any of his theories on you yet?" Linda asked.

"What do you mean?" I asked.

"Well, he's always into some new idea. I just quit listening. You can't take it too seriously. He'll be on to the next thing in a few days. He's just so passionate," she said.

I already knew this about Weston's personality, but it was different to hear it from his mother. Weston didn't protest. She was performing in front of him for me, speaking to me, but effectively speaking to him.

"In high school he was so Christian, which I didn't like. Then he was atheist. Now he's what? What are you, honey, vegan?"

"No, Mom."

She picked up on his frustration. "Oh baby, you know I love you, and I'll support you whatever you believe. I just get whiplash is all."

I thought about Weston in a new way after seeing him with his mom. He wasn't a caricature, no matter what his antics. He was a whole person, shaped by nature and circumstances.

Later, while Weston read *Siddhartha* and his parents watched TV, I tried to get more intentional with my journaling. It hurts to write by hand if I do it for too long, which pushes me to keep my language tight and right. The permanence of pen on paper means something. You say it, and it's there, and if you change your mind, the scribbled-out words are still there—no pretending you're perfect. For me, thoughts and emotions stay cloudy until I put them into words, give them bodies to walk around in and be their own thing. That's when they become knowable.

I also tried to draw maps of my trips. Old-timey ones that looked like a field guide Darwin would carry. I love old drawings and the sketches of cities and animals from ancient field guides. I like timeless things, old things. They've made it to the modern age and taken on a meaning larger than their intention. I wanted my journal to be like that. There is a weird paradox in trying to live a meaningful life, one you will talk about and tell about. There is the present experience of the living, but also the separate eye, watching from above, already seeing the living from the outside. Darwin and Steinbeck wrote alone by hand in leather-bound books that only later found an audience. Still, they wrote as if to an audience, with the presumption that someone, one day, would read their private work. Is this so different from what I was doing on Instagram? It feels cheap to make the comparison, but maybe it's not.

We stayed just one night, all Weston could seem to handle, and packed up to head out in the morning. Out in the driveway again, and ready to roll, Weston's mom said, "Okay, boys, be safe. Weston, I love you. Jed, take care of him, okay?" Weston hugged her loosely and pulled away before her hug was finished, kissed her on the cheek, and we biked away.

From Pismo, we biked away from the coast, into the golden hills of central California. The farms and dusty oak trees and gentleman farmer ranches sprawled on both sides of us. Born and raised in Tennessee, I have always wanted hills and trees. I trust land like that. Flat land and barren desert threaten my sense of understanding. I cannot get my bearings. I have no point of reference, and can't wait to leave. But around hills, trees, streams, and valleys, I want to linger. This part of California does that to me. I want to know every streambed and hill. I want to climb into the rafters of every barn. But I think it must matter where you were raised. I have friends from the Mississippi Delta who can't stand land like this. Because they can't see the sky behind the hill, they don't trust it. They need the sky and land to be wide open. And I have friends from Palm Springs who feel claustrophobic around too many trees. They want the land to be naked and honest, with no secrets.

We cycled over the mountain pass on Highway 154 and down into Santa Barbara. Behind us, mountain ramparts, too steep and wild to be developed, protected it from the hot dry interior. And the smaller hills, dotted with perfect Spanish homes, seemed to crawl on all fours down to the ocean.

Santa Barbara is one of those places that's so beautiful it can feel like you've wandered into a European postcard. The Santa Ynez mountains are steep and green behind the coastal hills of town. They push the city right up on the Pacific Ocean, with mansions and Spanish cottages covering the hills. From the coast, you can see the Channel Islands, long and large, a jagged sleeping dragon in the water, some twenty miles off shore. The place is so picturesque, the Mediterranean climate so pleasant, that it gives me pause. This kind of perfection can breed something like arrogance in those who live there. I have met many lovely people from Santa Barbara, but I don't think I would raise my children there. I'm not sure any of us are at our best living in paradise.

From Santa Barbara to Los Angeles, the wild coast of California that feels too mean and holy to belong to anyone lost some of its agency. This was the manicured, bought, sold, developed, regulated coast of Southern California. Still beautiful—still wild in many ways—but it felt more like real estate than nature. The best beach houses, the best cliffs, the best coves—but owned by someone else. And the public beaches are covered in signs and controlled by rules.

We spent a full week in Los Angeles. It was a welcome home and a sendoff at the same time, an "Oh my god, you're actually doing it" week of celebrations. It felt good. The muscle that knows routine takes time to be reprogrammed, and being in the city with my friends, going to our old restaurants, sitting on the same old couches, watching the same shows and laughing, it felt like our trip had only been a weekend excursion and not a real, life-altering choice.

All week, my mind flirted dangerously with this comfort. I was at my friend Willow's house, on the couch, watching old episodes of *Breaking Bad* and feeling incredibly normal. I sat on the couch I'd sat on a thousand times, drank the same Trader Joe's wine I'd always drunk, and made the same jokes with my friends.

"So you're actually doing it, you've already biked a thousand miles!" my friend Jenny said. "Feels so weird having you back on the couch. Like it's not real."

"I know. I feel like I haven't started yet, though. I have nine thousand more miles. It feels fake."

She laughed. "You aren't on some epic adventure. You're the same asshole who dances to Sia with me in the kitchen. You're a scam."

"I won't be a scam when I bike out of Los Angeles in two days."

"That's not happening. You can't leave us. Just google some photos of South America and post them to Instagram and make shit up. No one will ever know."

Weston and I stayed on the east side of LA, in a hilly neighborhood called Los Feliz. It is composed of old houses restored and preserved by artists and actors. It feels like the kind of place Joan Didion would have lived, smoking cigarettes, and watching musicians and actors experimenting in excess. The surrounding neighborhoods play host to the culture makers of Los Angeles, from Beachwood Canyon to Los Feliz, Atwater Village to Silverlake, Highland Park to Echo Park, to Lincoln Heights, to the Arts District downtown. The key to living happily in LA is localization. Newcomers try to have lunch in Venice and dinner in Studio City, and end up losing their minds. The traffic turns visiting these towns, only ten or fifteen miles apart, into day trips.

People love to blame a place for their own failures. Los Angeles is the king of this. So many people move here to chase a dream, or to escape the cold, or to escape their family. The city is supposed to be the answer to their discontent, to whatever it was that rejected them at home, and in their mind, simply having the bravery to get out west deserves fanfare. But once here, they find that no one cares about them as much as they do. If vanity drove them to this city, they discover that vanity doesn't like peers. It likes followers. In a city that feeds off the big-fish-small-pond kids, they discover a big pond swarming with over-the-top talent and perfect bone structure.

The moment I got to USC, I was humbled by the caliber of human beings. Back in Nashville, I thought I was the next Spielberg, but in LA, I was just another wannabe. I discovered this when a friend of mine was directing a short film for class, and I offered to help. On set, there were fifteen people, lists and lists, rented equipment, lights, a boom, walkie-talkies. I stood on the tiny set and thought, "This looks terrible. All that pressure. My god."

I felt a spinning sense of loss when I realized I wouldn't be a director, but it was the first time in my life where I learned the difference between dreams and goals. Each of us has a mash-up of talents and experiences and potential that plants something in us, and becomes a dream. A dream of being a creative, or an executive, or a father. A dream is the myriad ways we could be fulfilled in life using our talents to make beautiful things. But then there are goals. Goals are specific guesses at what we could do or become to fulfill our dream. Dreams are like a compass that points in a general direction, and goals are the islands in the ocean along the way. Goals are just guesses at where to make a home, and when they aren't right, we try another. It isn't a death, and it doesn't negate the dream. I had mistaken the goal for the dream at USC, and in that moment, Los Angeles could have eaten me up. Instead, my confusion eventually led me to law school, which led to my charity work, which led me to this bike trip. You could say I was saved from misdirection by not being too handsome or too talented or too ambitious.

After a dangerously comfortable week in LA, eating tacos and telling stories like we'd been on our bike tour for a year, we headed south on a hot sunny day. We pedaled along Santa Monica Boulevard, where cars choked the roads and we needed to be agile and all-seeing. But my bike was so heavy, I couldn't turn on a dime or make a quick decision. Weston, who packed virtually nothing and rode shirtless, moved as if weightless. I made a wide left turn onto La Cienega and a car screeched its tires to avoid me and honked. It was that sustained angry honk when the person holds it many seconds too long, to signal to you and the world how sinful you are—not just your action, but your whole being.

Fortunately, Weston had mapped a way to bike along the cement canyons of the Los Angeles River and its tributaries. Once we made our way into a canal bike path, the world slowed down. I felt safe again, cruising through a part of Los Angeles I'd never seen. As if layered on top of my familiar streets, or maybe beneath, was a highway for cyclists, a parallel universe of ways to get from A to B. I felt like a stranger in my own city.

In the beach cities of the South Bay, an area in the southern part of Los Angeles County, the cycle path emptied out onto the Pacific Coast Highway. From there we made the easy ride through Orange County, stayed with Weston's cousin, and then on to the coastal military base of Camp Pendleton. We tried to bike through the base but the soldier wouldn't let Weston in. "You have to wear a helmet on a military base if you're riding a bicycle," the soldier said.

"Okay, but come on, we just have to get to San Diego, and we're riding to South America, you can let us through," Weston said.

"No, you'll have to turn around and ride down Interstate Five."

"You're joking," Weston protested with attitude.

"You'll have to turn around and ride down Interstate Five."

Weston fumed as we rode on the shoulder of the interstate. Apart from this military base, Southern California's coast is one giant connected suburb. This makes it feel easier to bike across. The ride to San Diego took two days.

Once in San Diego, Weston and I felt something new, ominous, and exciting: the gravitational pull of the Mexican border. The crossing point from known to unknown. From my language to their language. From trusting myself to trusting God. From me being right to my mom's worst fears coming true.

We were drinking craft beer around a fire in a friend's backyard. A law school buddy named Michael Gonzales joined us. We called him Tank. He grew up in a Mexican community outside LA, and he'd made so many jokes about imagining my scrawny white ass in Mexico that I invited him over to teach me how to make it down there.

"Tank, so, I know I was supposed to learn Spanish. But I got busy. Whatever, I suck," I laughed. The anxiety of crossing the border into another world had wiped my brain's hard drive, and I had lost what little Spanish I'd picked up from my single week of using Rosetta Stone. "At least I tried," I said. "Weston doesn't know shit."

"Hey!" objected Weston. "I am good with my hands. And that includes hand gestures and also smiling."

"Boys," Tank said, taking on an uncharacteristic fatherly tone, "you'll be fine. No one is nicer than Mexicans. When your food's that good, you're nicer."

"Okay, so, tell me some music to listen to so I can connect with people," I said.

"Like modern music?"

"No, like what is so classic Mexico that anyone in any village will like me more for knowing it?"

"Oh, I know. Vicente Fernández!" he said, springing up in his chair. "He is El Rey de la Música Ranchera! The king of ranchera music. He's like a cowboy Sinatra. Just go around singing 'Volver, Volver.' You'll make friends everywhere you go."

Tank taught me some other phrases in Spanish. *Excuse me, sir, my bicycle is broken, do you know the closest bike shop? I am lost, which way is town? Do you have any water?* I couldn't count to twenty. I was frozen. Sure, I was excited to discover Mexico, and I led with that emotion. But beneath that, my animal brain was terrified. Ahead, 760 miles of desert. Hot sun. Cacti. Hardly any people, hardly any towns. Could I carry enough water? Would a rattlesnake get me too far from town?

We drank more beers, and the fire crackled as I stared off in thought. I was scared. I felt the weight of the duty too much to enjoy everything that was ahead of me. What if I hated it? What if it didn't give me the revelations I asked for? What if I failed? What if risking it all was a scam, a selfish worship of the grass being greener everywhere but here?

But that's not what I said to Tank.

"I'm so excited! Ahh! I just want to be on the road sleeping with the coyotes," I said, my eyes a bit glazed. We cheersed our beers and Weston took a long drag of his joint. Tank was speaking to me in Spanish. He said something about tarantulas. That would have to do for now.

Chapter 5

CROSSING INTO BAJA

12,765 miles to go

The final night in San Diego we slept on the floor of my friend's house. We wanted to cross the border pretty early. I was tired and thought I'd fall right asleep. I didn't. I just lay on the carpet, staring at the ceiling fan above me, my stomach in knots.

We had been on the road for five weeks. I'd learned how to change a popped tire, and my tailbone had grown immune to the ache of the bike seat. I knew how to find a camping spot during the golden hour. I knew how to hide my bike from the road. I knew how to ride sixty miles a day, and how much water and food to replenish each day. I knew where to put the food in my pannier so I could reach back and pull it out as I cycled. But tomorrow we would cross the border and ride through Tijuana to Rosarito, Mexico.

I woke up with the sun. I got up and rubbed my eyes and walked with heavy, sleepy legs into the kitchen, where Weston was making pour-over coffee. He turned to me, bright as Bo Peep. "Good morning, you pale Mexican! We gotta get to our home country!" I shook my head and laughed and yawned all at once.

"You excited?" he asked.

"I am. But a bit numb to it, too. Doesn't feel real," I said.

"Yeah. I wish I'd learned a little Spanish right about now. I mean, I did take it in high school. But where did all those words go? Oh well. That's the adventure. I'll just mime my way to Patagonia."

Our friends woke up and we made eggs and dragged our feet. I kept unpacking and repacking. I kept worrying about water. "Oh shoot! Do I need to run by REI and get another water bag? I don't know if I have enough," I said.

"Dude, you have a ten-gallon bladder. That is insane. People live in Baja, and they drink water. We'll be fine," Weston said. His tiny panniers seemed ludicrous. I wondered if I'd have to provide water for both of us. He was so confident we'd be okay. I appreciated that, and hated it.

Finally, we put our bikes in the back of a friend's truck, and he drove us to the border.

I've read that the San Diego–Tijuana border runs down the middle of the largest wealth gap in the world. On the American side, the stucco tract homes with Spanish-tile roofs of San Diego, with green lawns and flowers and wide, clean roads. Then a barren stretch of swamp and brush about half a mile wide that touches the border. Then begin the fences. Our side has fences made of tall cement tubes layered together like a zipper and driven into the earth like an alien art installation. The tubes are separated by enough space for a fox or a cat to slip through, but not a person. On the Mexican side, they have a fence too—rusted and brown and flaking, nailed together like a hippie quilt.

San Diego's cliffs are made lush and green by water piped in from faraway mountains. In Tijuana, the same cliffs are parched and flaky.

Passing from the United States into Mexico is very easy. If you go by car, they don't even stop you. Weston and I walked our bikes across a cement bridge and down a winding zigzag ramp and found the passport check. There was virtually no line, maybe fifteen people in front of us. The signs led us into a small room with aging white walls, yellowing at the top. The fluorescent lights above were tired. We were causing quite the inconvenience, wheeling our fat bikes with us in the cramped hallway. But there was nowhere to lock them. And we were cautious about Mexico already, words from my mother sneaking in. *Mexico is dangerous. They behead tourists if you're in the wrong place at the wrong time. Look at these headlines—it's a war zone down there. Why don't you bike across Canada?*

At the front of the line, the woman at the desk asked how long we were staying. "We're taking our bikes from here to the southern border. So about sixty days, I think," I said.

She looked up. "Really?" she said, with consternation.

"Yeah! Wanna come?" Weston said.

She let herself smile and then laughed. "Absolutely not." And stamped our passports.

We walked our bikes over one more bridge and into Tijuana. Weston was barefoot, which he noted out loud as we entered Mexico. We got on our bikes and rode into immediate chaos. No shoulder, no sidewalk, roads and overpasses and busy cars everywhere. Everyone driving like they're racing to the ER with their wife in labor. Some of the buildings looked new. Others, right beside the new buildings, were falling apart. There seemed to be no plan, no uniformity, no grid. Without a shoulder to the road, we tried to stay as far to the right in the lane as possible, but this only made things more danger-ous. Rusted trucks tumbled past just inches away, and drivers got honking furious at us when, unable to find a pattern or direction, we had to cross lanes at the last minute. I counted three dead dogs, mangled from being run over dozens of times. It is one of the few times in my life I have feared death. The sound of screeching tires and honking horns followed us the entire two hours from the center of the city to the quieter beach road.

The final exit out of town and toward the beach required a dash across four heavily trafficked lanes to an exit ramp that wrapped around to the quiet coastal road. Weston made it over fast and easy, and I tried to follow. But as I crossed, a truck speeding toward me slammed on its brakes. It skidded and fishtailed before coming to a complete stop only five feet away. The man never honked. Actually, he looked as terrified as I did.

"Holy shit!" Weston said when I'd made it across. "You almost died!"

"I know!" I said. But the adrenaline pumped so thickly through my veins that death could only feel like a joke.

Once outside Tijuana, the road turned into a two-lane highway, freshly paved, smooth and beautiful all the way through Rosarito.

This beach town caters to college kids who want to party, in beach clubs with thatched-roof bars and tattooed DJs. The hills above Rosarito and the cliffs over the ocean are dotted with pretty houses, similar to ones you'd see in San Diego or Orange County, but here, tucked between the mansions, you can see shacks and tiny box homes, some resembling a turned-over Dumpster. But even many of these seem to sit right above the surf, with laundry hung out to dry and a few plastic chairs to enjoy the view.

Our plan for the day was to make it halfway to Ensenada, a city sixty miles down the coast, where a few friends had rented a beach house for the weekend. They had invited us to crash with them. By the time we were riding out of Rosarito, I had worked off the adrenaline rush, and my muscles had turned shaky and then very tired. South of town, the landscape gave way to brown and gold hills against the ocean with white stucco houses haphazardly dotted up the hillsides. Folks here enjoyed the exact same climate as San Diego, but with a tenth of the trees. That's because most of Southern California's trees are imported and kept alive by imported water. It took me years to figure out why Los Angeles looked so verdant, and yet so strange. Tijuana and Rosarito showed me the answer. In its natural state, the land is nearly treeless. Save for the oaks that hide in canyons, Southern California is a man-made garden. Finally, we were seeing what the land is supposed to look like.

We met up with our friends by golden hour, and they were an excited welcoming committee. They poured us margaritas and we cooked dinner and told the story of cycling through Tijuana. "Those roads are crazy, you guys are crazy," one friend said, inspecting our heavy bikes and gear. "Everything you have is on these bikes? That's all you have?"

"Yep. This is it, trying to simplify. Take only what I need," Weston said.

"Wow."

We felt cool and rugged, but the adrenaline come-down had us asleep on the couch by 9 p.m., while our friends played beer pong just feet away.

The next day, we woke up early, said our goodbyes, and headed

out. We cycled south along the beautiful two-lane road, passing by
the several toll booths that paid for the paved road. The path looked
similar to the coastal route above Santa Barbara, and it felt familiar
and comforting. Maybe Mexico wouldn't be as wild as we thought.

BY MIDAFTERNOON, we made it to my old roommate's dad's house
in Ensenada. This was the last stop in the chain of homes we had
been offered by friends, the southernmost point of connections with
the familiar. It was a nice house that sat above town on a hill overlooking the main drag of restaurants and tourist shops. We had the
place to ourselves. We stayed a week, eating tacos and practicing our
dismal Spanish, thinking it would help us adjust to Mexico before
heading south into the Baja Peninsula, the thousand-mile stretch of
scattered towns and hateful sunshine. We were at the last stop sign
before the wilderness.

In my blog-reading, I had found several detailed accounts of cycling Baja. "Bring lots of water." "Hammocks won't work because
there aren't trees." "Tarantulas." "There is no shoulder so trucks will
get very close and blow you off the road." Yikes.

The Baja Peninsula is a long leg of land, like Florida, but thinner—
and almost twice as long. She is as dry as a million-year drought.
Crispy mountains run down her spine, splaying out in the direction
of the two coasts. The desert is unbroken and natural water is scarce.
The unforgiving land prevents many people from calling the peninsula home. And yet archaeologists have discovered caves with paintings of deer, dated at 10,000 years old. Humans have been scrappy,
tough bastards for so long.

Baja is the sinister cousin of Southern California, with similar
sunshine, waves, and mountains—but California has water, bled
from the snowmelt of faraway mountains. We funnel it into our valleys and turn California into a garden. Baja, on the other hand, is
surrounded by ocean, and doesn't have distant mountains to catch
moisture. This turns the peninsula into a thorny, rocky, angry thigh-
bone with almost zero fresh water. Baja would be our first true test.
Were we cyclists, adventurers, or just fragile tourists?

On the third day, after reading every blog, I made a shopping list. Beans to cook. Lots of water. I bought ten extra tire tubes, which is too many. Cans of tuna and almonds and peanut butter.

On our fourth night in Ensenada, after reading all the blogs and buying gallons of water and watching *Back to the Future* on VHS, Weston and I found a pool hall on a back road far from the tourist zone. The place had twenty tables. The ceiling was low and black, and people at the bar were smoking. A few exposed lightbulbs hung from the ceiling over the tables, and one of them had a green chandelier, intact from a more ornate time. From the moment we walked in, we were under the watch of the locals. Clearly this place was not a spot where tourists often showed up, which made it perfect. We bought Tecate beers and started playing pool.

Weston and I had now been together a month. I felt safe with him. He cooked and fixed tires and could do anything with duct tape. He never complained, unless it was about society at large. We'd become the type of comrades who can spend the day in silence, existing together, thinking independently, then spring into conversation out of seeming nowhere.

"I like the heat," Weston said, as we worked our way around the table.

"What heat?" I said.

"The heat of the desert. But I don't like the cold nights. What do the blogs say about what's ahead?"

"That we need to bring lots of water. And that there isn't any shoulder on the road, but that the truck drivers are nice, and the people in RVs aren't."

"Like Big Sur. Those fuckers. Old white Republicans." After his shot, Weston gave a nod to some guys at the bar that were watching us.

"I can't believe how many dead dogs we've already seen," I said. "The blogs say to expect more. Remember that huge bloated elk in Oregon we biked past? It looked like a hippo."

"No, I didn't see it."

"You were probably high."

"Is that judgment I hear in your voice?" Weston asked, smiling.

"No. No. I love cigarettes, but I don't think I fiend for them the way you fiend for weed."

"I'm not addicted," Weston replied. "I feel called to it. When I smoke, it's like saying my prayers. Makes me present. There's a difference. One is a need. The other is a desire. A commitment."

"Thou doth protest too much," I said, laughing. It was my turn to shoot.

"Well, I'm no more addicted to this than you are to your phone. That little computer represents the world we're leaving. Friends back home and screens. This flower is my connection to the present. To the unknown. To not planning. To letting life and this trip happen. Whatever." Weston chuckled, feeling like he was getting too intense. "I'll run out in this desert if I'm not careful. Might have to wait for Cabo or La Paz or wherever at the end. You'll see, it's a practice. Not a need."

"Touché," I said, not sure what I meant by it, but wanting to concede.

Later that night, our last in Ensenada, we watched *Jurassic Park* on VHS. Pushing the tape into the player felt nostalgic and comforting. The movie did, too. After five days spent avoiding the unknown, we were antsy to hit the road early.

THE NEXT MORNING, a Thursday, brought blue skies. People were heading to work and the city was waking up, and none of those people knew we were headed south to Patagonia.

We cycled out of town and the landscape abruptly turned rugged and rural. Tomato plantations stretched across the desert coast. Rows and rows of plants, of white tarps like tubes protecting the plants from bugs or birds or dry heat. These farms were massive operations. They resembled what I could only imagine as terraforming, the apocalyptic future hope of colonizing Mars. The land looked dead and hostile, yet rows of planted green bushes bordered huge fields of tomatoes, as if to block them from view. As if to make the craziness look more lovely. The white plastic greenhouse alien structures numbered in the thousands. Trucks carried millions of tomatoes out onto Highway 1—headed to California, to the port of Tijuana, to the world.

Highway 1 is the main thoroughfare of Baja, crisscrossing down the long desert arm all the way to Cabo. It is almost always paved, except for certain short stretches of construction, maybe a mile at a time, where the road is diverted to the lumpy ribbed dirt on the shoulder, and biking becomes an organ-jostling nightmare. Every giant semitruck and busted, rusted work truck, every sleek American RV, and a host of ancient vehicles takes this same road, basically the only road, each one zooming past us on our bikes. The potholes take their toll, and the side of the road is littered with rusty nails, bits of metal, wires, coils, and even more roadkill than we saw in Tijuana.

We biked in the beating sun and the heat began to feel different from California's. Maybe it was the absence of trees. Maybe it was the heat-scorched dusty roads. On the unpaved portions, the trucks would kick up blizzards of brown dust, which would cake our bodies and lips, and force us to close our eyes and hold our breath until it was safe to breathe again. Travel felt different now. This felt like navigating a developing country. This reminded me of my time in Africa. I was no longer home. And this, or something a lot like it, was what we could expect for the next fourteen months.

The dust-blown, nail-dodging, pothole-hitting routine became the norm for a few days. And then as the cruel sun finished its business, the worry would set in. Where to sleep? The rule of hiding from the road felt even more imperative here, because we would be trying to camp on people's farms. On Mexican ranchers' farms. I had never met a Mexican rancher, but somehow a stereotype had formed in my imagination. They were mean.

We looked for boulders to set up behind, for trees or cacti to hang our hammocks from. The only trees grew in riverbeds, and often in thickets. When we could find them, they were great for hiding in. We needed trees with strong branches or trunks to hold us up, and at a perfect distance of eight to twelve feet across. Too close and we'd sleep like a closed clam, which is impossible. Too far and the ropes wouldn't reach.

The idea was to be invisible: no one should see us leave the road, or be able to see our camp from a distance. And so, as the sun went down, we would ride with our eyes peeled for the right spot, hoping that whoever was riding in the front saw it, too.

Then, a possibility. A bridge with a dry riverbed, some oak trees crowding by the edge waiting for the rainy season, maybe even a patch of green grass living off secret water below the sand. Or a pile of boulders with a sandy nook between them, just a few feet from the highway, but hidden from sight. We would set up, hang our hammocks, and crawl in with twilight still glowing. The thrill of trespassing every day, moving like tramps and ghosts, made us feel like cowboys delivering letters to an outpost a thousand miles away and a hundred years ago. A few mornings in and two hundred miles down Baja, we woke to unbelievable cold. The afternoon before, without noticing, we had moved away from the ocean and its moderating influence. I could see my breath in the morning light as I peeked out of my sleeping bag and the taco of my hammock. I shuffled in my hammock to signal to Weston that I was awake. He was, too. "You get out first," he said.

"No, you. Make a fire," I said.

"Fuck, no," he said.

I acquiesced and slid like a worm out of my hammock in my sleeping bag, and stood in the cold. This is hard. I knew it would be hard. But my muscles hurt. And it's cold. I hate this.

"We need to dress quick and hit the road to get our blood going," Weston said.

"I'm the one out of my hammock. Come on," I said.

We ate a few cookies and I drank coffee made in my water bottle from instant Nescafé powder and cold water, then we took off.

As I rode, I noticed my bicycle was taking the road well, its tires new and wide. We'd hit gravel bits and dirt bits, but mostly we rode on asphalt. But the asphalt wasn't the smooth black kind. It was the bumpy gray kind, and tightly packed with small stones. Weston's bike didn't do so well, its tires too thin, too bald. He would shake terribly and eventually an item—a shoe, say—would get knocked loose from his belongings and bounce away behind him, or the whole pack would slide off. In the beginning, he had stopped to fix his old bike and jury-rigged cargo without complaining. It was part of his message and mission, to show that a cheap old bike could make it if you were willing to be patient and work with it. Now he would curse as he fixed things.

The cold morning quickly turned oven-hot. The sun was heavy on us, pushing my skin like an iron. I wore sunscreen but, as the hours went on, I worried I wasn't reapplying enough. My skin was red. I put on long sleeves and accepted the sweat just to avoid the burn.

We spent the day bumping and shaking our way through dusty towns and unpaved roads. The semitrucks left grooves in the dirt road, like ripples in water. This made biking terrible. Our hands went numb from the battering.

The towns we biked through mostly seemed to be hubs of the tomato plantations and places where workers lived. Cinder blocks were piled up and made into a store or a house. We went through lots of these towns, many without any sign of their names. But I mapped the route on Google Maps, so the names scrolled past as we did. Camalú. Colonia Lomas de San Ramón. Colonia Nueva Era.

The end of our fourth day biking was signaled by the sun getting close to the ocean. We needed a canyon or grove of oaks to camp beneath, but every spot we found was too close to human beings. Too close to a farm or a shack or a busy walking path. We couldn't hide. We couldn't find a hotel, either. Well, I found one, but when I asked if they had a vacancy, the blank-eyed woman at the counter said, without looking up, "No." But the moment we got back on the road, as I swerved to miss a nail, and Weston swerved to miss me, his front wheel bent in half. He tumbled hard from the bike. Weston was fine, he always is, but the wheel was beyond repair. He couldn't even roll the bike. He had to carry it on his shoulder. There was nothing to do but walk ourselves back to a gas station near that mean-spirited hotel.

Of course, I thought. We just make it into the desert, finally into the hard part of the trip. And we're failing. I'm completely roasted from the sun. My skin hurts and my legs hurt, and already we have nowhere to sleep. We can't even make it halfway down Baja. What if Weston's bike is impossible to replace? The only bikes I've seen down here are recycled mountain bikes. And where are we going to sleep? Is this a bad neighborhood? "God, help us. Please help us. Show us a place to sleep, or send us help."

We sat at the gas station for thirty minutes, hoping to hitchhike with any truck that could fit our bikes. But drivers shook their heads or pretended not to hear us. One guy listened to Weston for a minute, but when Weston slipped into English, he drove off. Weston went back to fooling with his tire. I watched some ants, wondering how they lived in a world without water. Then I smelled weed. Weston had rolled a joint.

"I just realized this is my last one," he said.

"Well, this situation sucks, so I suppose it's as good a time as any. Can't you get seriously in trouble with weed in Mexico?"

"Yeah. But people are obviously ignoring us. And I can hide it quick."

"I think maybe we should walk back toward town. This place is dead. And there's more people actually walking on the street."

"Okay. Lemme finish this."

The sun was very low now. As we walked in the deep gold that comes just before twilight, more vehicles and walkers crowded onto the road. The shacks and homes along this stretch of road all looked built in a hurry. Weston was frustrated but holding his tongue. He had bought the cheapest bicycle he could, to prove that this trip could be done on a real budget. Now we were paying the real price, a mounting pile of inconveniences. I was mad at him, and he knew it.

Suddenly, we heard someone speak English behind us. "Where are you going? Need some help?" in a thick Mexican accent. We turned around to see a short man with a broad smile and a baby face walking behind us. He wore dirty jeans and a loose-fitting T-shirt.

"Do you know where a hotel is?" I asked.

"The only one is right here but they are full. They have only three rooms because the others are broken," he said.

"Oh. There are no others?"

"No," he said. "But you are travelers?"

"Yes, we're biking down to South America," I said, hoping it would impress him.

"You are welcome in my home. I am Miguel. I like helping people. And I see this bicycle is broken. We can wait for the shop right here to open tomorrow, and then I take you in the morning on my way to work." He motioned his hand to a street just out of sight, implying that just out of view was a bike shop.

This was our first invitation into the home of a stranger. I thought about my mom's warnings. Her e-mails of beheadings. I think I would've been hesitant with a lot of men, for fear of theft or worse. But Miguel had a sweet face and excellent English. And I had just prayed for a place to stay. Was this the universe answering? It never made sense that God would be so transactional—"prayer works" implies the harder you pray, the more you get what you ask for.

But this prayer had worked, hadn't it?

We said yes, and Miguel walked us off the road down into the neighborhood. Leading away from the one paved road was a grid of dirt roads. Only they weren't dirt. Our bike tires sunk immediately into soft white sand. As soft as powder. The bikes couldn't roll at all, and loaded down with all the weight of our bags and panniers, they simply dug into the earth like a shovel. Which is when Miguel, without hesitation, took Weston's bike and hoisted it onto his shoulders. People stared at us as if Area 51 had released its aliens: two gringos flanking the small Mexican man like a pelican V formation. Kids began trailing us, laughing and talking too fast to be understood. They stared at our strange bikes, so much shinier than the rusted and duct-taped mountain bikes they had.

We passed flat-roofed houses that were little more than stucco boxes, flaking and cracked by the sun. Stray dogs ran around everywhere. It was almost dark when we got to Miguel's house—another box in a line of similar structures. Strung between the bare or dead trees out front were six or seven heavily laden clotheslines.

Miguel asked us to wait for a moment while he talked to his wife. When she came to the door, she looked us up and down sternly. She was dark skinned, regal, and severe. I saw a little girl peeking out from behind her. Then a lanky boy of about twelve sporting crooked eyeglasses came out to talk.

"Very nice to meet you," he said. "Sorry for my English, I am still learning."

Miguel was thrilled. "Maybe tonight you can help my son with his homework? He has to write a speech in English and he needs help to make sure it is right. Is that okay? You will sleep in his room, he can sleep with us."

We entered the house, which consisted of two rooms. Miguel gave us the grand tour. "In this room we cook and my wife and I sleep, and our daughter sleeps with us here. We sleep here." He gestured to a double bed in the corner. A Spanish-language game show was playing on the small TV. Next to the bed, a stained couch, a stove, a sink, and a few plastic chairs. Miguel led us into the second room. A small mattress with stained sheets and exposed springs lay on the floor, surrounded by tools, old toys, a stack of broken plastic lawn chairs, metal poles—possibly shower-curtain rods—and empty beer boxes.

A naked lightbulb hung in the center of each room. A shared bathroom had a toilet and a showerhead, but no curtains.

Gesturing to the bed, Miguel asked, "Is this okay? You will have to be very close. I know this is very different than America." He looked at us with a humbly furrowed brow and sweetness in his eyes.

"Yes, of course. Yes, oh my god, of course, this is amazing!" I said.

"My wife wants to make you a good dinner. I must run to the market to get some supplies, but I will be right back," Miguel said.

"Oh, we will go with you and pay for everything. It's the least we can do," Weston said. He looked at me for confirmation, and I said, "Of course!"

"Oh! Thank you!" Miguel said. He laughed and slapped us on the back as if we were old friends.

We crammed our bikes into the son's room and followed Miguel out the front door, followed him to the market, and bought everything he asked for. Meat. Onions. Cilantro. Weston asked him if he wanted ice cream and Miguel didn't seem to hear. "I don't know if they have a freezer," I whispered. Weston's eyes got wide, shaken by his assumption, and nodded. Miguel asked gingerly if we could buy some beer, and we picked up a twenty-four-pack of Tecate. He was thrilled.

As we walked home, he told us about his family. "My son Alejandro is very smart. He is the top at his school. He will work in the U.S. No question. He is studying English and, you saw, it's pretty good. He will get better. I am proud of him. My daughter, Litian, she is smart, but I don't know. She is light skinned, that is very good, not like her mother. Alejandro has the dark skin like his mother, but he is smart, so he will be okay. My wife, her skin is too dark. Here, it is a bad thing to be so dark skinned. People don't like her in this town because of it. It is racist here. She has indigenous in her. She is a beautiful woman, but she is very dark. I'm glad Litian is light skinned. It will help her if she is not as smart as Alejandro.'

He asked if we wanted to smoke, meaning weed, and Weston said yes. Miguel took us down a different sandy street in the dark, found a man who seemed to just exist underneath a tree, and told us to wait by the wall. When he returned, he said he needed twenty dollars. Weston, who always seemed to manifest money from thin air for these moments, pulled out a twenty and handed it to him. Miguel slipped into the shadows for twenty minutes, but when he returned with a paper bag, he was grinning.

By the time we got back to Miguel's home, his taciturn wife had finished frying the perfect hand-shaped tortillas. I looked at her differently now. I noticed her skin and thought about people being rude to her. About how she didn't speak much, and perhaps that was to stay invisible. She accepted the meat we'd bought and instructed us to sit on the couch. Alejandro appeared with his speech written in English and asked me in a crisp rehearsed sentence, "Excuse me. Do you mind if I practice my speech in English with you, if you please?" I obliged happily, and he fixed his glasses and began reciting. He was holding the paper and his hand was shaking. He stopped after one sentence. "Please do tell me if my English has mistakes."

"Okay, I will," I said, smiling with my whole face in that way you do when you want to encourage someone in a tender moment.

He read his work, which had a few misplaced or misconjugated words, but it was wonderful. I made some edits, and Alejandro was very pleased. He sat down beside me to scrutinize what I'd written. Miguel explained to me how important it was to him for his children to learn English. It was their ticket to a better life. He bragged how his son was the best in his school, the best English-speaker in the entire town. How English could get him jobs in hotels and tourism and restaurants around here—or better yet, help him thrive when he made it to the United States.

Miguel got me thinking about how strange it is to be born in a country whose influence has spread around the world like an infestation. The world's hunger to speak English is emblematic of this. Some cultures welcome our films, television, and music, or feel drawn by the prospect of money and power. Others resist. Either way, my culture is the most dominant on the planet, and I benefit from that. Sitting there watching Alejandro studying my markup like it was holy scripture made me wonder, what moral weight does being the beneficiary of my dominant culture place on my shoulders?

Miguel's wife made us fried tortillas and meat with cheese and beans, and it was delicious. She merely nodded as we lavished her with compliments in horrible Spanish. "*Incrediblé comida!*" We got very full and laughed and Miguel told more stories. After a while, the fatigue of riding bikes all day caught up to us, compounded by social exhaustion from being guests on exhibit in such a tiny space. But Miguel kept handing us one beer after another. "Maybe we should sleep soon," I proposed finally. "We biked very hard today. We are so grateful . . ."

"Oh yes, we will go into the other room!" He leaped up and led us into Alejandro's room. We said our thank-yous to the lady of the house and the kids. Miguel now sat down on the floor with a fresh six-pack of beer. "You aren't too tired, are you?" he asked with the eagerness of a kid afraid of being sent to bed. "Can we keep talking?"

"We are really tired, but yes!"

Miguel handed out beers and went on talking. He was getting visibly drunk, and Weston and I had a "what-have-we-done" moment of eye contact with each other. But when Miguel started rolling joints, Weston perked up. Miguel stumbled up to open a window.

"I was in Nebraska for eleven years," he said. "You know Nebraska?"

"Yes, I've been there—" I was about to say how boring it is.

"It is so beautiful," Miguel said between puffs. "Such nice streets. Nice people. So much work. I want to go back." He described it like it was paradise. "I had another wife then. With her, two sons. My boys. They are with her still in the U.S. I had a problem and was deported. A bad problem. I can never go back legally. They will put me in jail for the rest of my life," he said. I wondered if he would tell us what he'd done. He didn't.

"I did try to sneak back in after they deported me the last time. You pay these guys three thousand dollars in Tijuana to sneak you over. They hide you in trucks or sometime they will pay you to take drugs through the tunnels in the desert between San Diego and Arizona. There are many tunnels. My friend signed up right before me and paid the three thousand dollars, but then he went missing after he came to the meeting place and paid the money. They found his head a week later in a trash can in Tijuana." Miguel shook his head as he spoke, telling the story as if to admonish us, to teach us a lesson about the dangers of trusting crooked people.

He cracked open another beer. "I will get back to Nebraska. My sons are there. I just have to be patient. These tomato farmers are crooks and they work us like animals. I can't stay here. I have to be patient. But I have hope. You will see me in the U.S., no question. My son is smart," he said, motioning to the kitchen, where his son had been before.

He was slurring now, saying half-words and mumbling, and he kept slipping into Spanish. I wondered what would happen to his current wife when he left. If he would bring her with him. He didn't say, and I was too sleepy to ask.

"Miguel, don't be offended," I said, "but I am about to fall asleep from being so tired. Keep talking and hanging out, but I might fall asleep."

"Oh, of course, I am being rude. Yes. Sleep. Weston, do you want to smoke more outside?"

"Yeah, sure," he said.

Weston and Miguel walked outside and left me in the dark. It would be Weston and me on this mattress. I huddled to one side and closed my eyes, but instead of drifting off, I fumed. Mad at Weston's bike, mad at his choices and his philosophies. But I also thought of Miguel's kindness, his son, his wife and daughter. I was sleeping in a man's house who saved our butts when we needed it most. I would've passed through this alien tomato farm world without ever really knowing anything about it, but Weston's bike broke. His frustrating choices slowed us down and led us to Miguel. This shitty situation had given us the opportunity to receive the kindness of a stranger, to see the life and home of a person we'd have never known. I lay there thinking back through my life—how much energy I put into planning, trying to guarantee my independence, but how so many of my best memories have come from the times where I needed help and received it.

In the morning, we woke to find that Miguel had gone to work at dawn and left us a note scribbled with well-wishes. His wife made us eggs, rice, and coffee. And his son informed us he was going to skip school to help Weston fix his bike.

Alejandro took us to the closest bike shop, but they only had old mountain bike wheels, nothing that could fit Weston's frame. He needed a new rim, hub, new spokes—the whole wheel. A task we thought would take an hour turned into a daylong quest. We took the bus to a bigger town, where Weston left me at a little restaurant. It had Wi-FI, so I checked Instagram and FaceTimed my mom. I didn't tell her anything about Miguel's scary stories. I told her we'd stayed with a kind man and his family. I told her all her prejudices about Mexico were wrong. I told her it was safe and perfect.

Around 3 p.m., Weston finally returned with a brand-new front wheel and tire, though it was 20 percent smaller than his back wheel.

"Thank goodness for Alejandro. He saved me. He translated my haggling," Weston said.

Alejandro blushed. Weston leaned in. "Do you have twenty dollars to give him as a tip? I don't have any more money." When I handed Alejandro twenty dollars, he shyly tried to refuse, but I insisted and shoved it in his pocket. "Little dude, you're smart and you speak incredible English and you're going to make a great life. Thank you," I said.

OUTSIDE OF TOWN, the tomato farms stopped abruptly and left us with cliffs and coastline—not quite desolate desert, but not as shrub-covered as California's hills. In some of the fields between us and the beach, we saw a red grass of some kind that looked like pools of blood, like we were gazing at the world through a color filter. For the final hour before twilight, we climbed away from the beach, up into steep, treeless hills, and at last light rolled down a long, thrilling grade into a small town nestled in a canyon with a hotel.

We got a room and ate Baja lobster for dinner in the attached restaurant. Baja lobster looks similar to the kind found off the coast of Maine, but without large claws, as if the claws have been removed, but the crustaceans themselves can grow to be gigantic. At the restaurant, they had one mounted on the wall, a prize from the past. It was the size of a duffel bag. We ordered two large ones and ate till we were full. We felt we deserved it.

We slept hard, woke up, stocked up on snack food and cookies at a tiny market, and headed up the mountains again, away from the ocean.

We cycled and baked on hot roads. The mountains leveled off and we were clocking fifty- and sixty-mile days. The heat created mirage waves over every dip in the road. Highway 1 crisscrosses Baja all the way down to La Paz, and it is the only main road. I had studied the map obsessively: the incredible thinness of the giant peninsula; the way it looks from a satellite, like gold, with almost no vegetation visible. The eastern boundary is the elongated, crystal blue Sea of Cortez, a breeding ground for manta rays and whale sharks. At the northernmost point of the narrow sea, the Colorado River empties into it. Or used to. For millions of years it spilled water from the Rocky Mountains into the sea, but California, Arizona, and Mexico rerouted nearly all of the river, so now the mouth of the Colorado is a dried-up and apocalyptic marsh.

All day and night, semitrucks roared past us, their loud Jake brakes rattling down the hills like machine guns. *Ga-ga-ga-ga-ga-ga-ga.* But these truckers are also the caretakers of the road. When we approached a rig that had pulled over for the driver to check his load, he saw us, scrambled into the cab, and emerged smiling, with cold water.

Somewhere in all those miles of heat and nothingness, I noticed time had changed. "Meetings" and "dates" and "days of the week" used to mean so much to me. They were necessary frames for my life, for the passing of time. Now I never knew what day it was. My alarm was the sun. I woke up when the light was too bright to keep sleeping, or when the desert heat forced me out of my hammock. The work day was movement, making it farther south. Any forward progress felt like work well done. The end of the day came when the sun approached the horizon and golden light signaled the coming darkness. Compensation for my labors simplified, too. After climbing a hill, I had earned a cookie or an orange. I would stop at the top, enjoy a snack and some water, and then glide downhill. This was my work. This was my new occupation.

I enjoyed feeling like this. But it wasn't pure. It wasn't contemplative. It was survival. It was heat and simplicity.

For days, we rode down the barren central spine of the peninsula. My knees were killing me. I ran out of water and drank Coca-Cola. The thought of California made me sad. It was behind me, full of happiness and people I knew. The only thing before me was my front wheel and the god-forsaken desert. Where had my optimism gone?

Halfway down the peninsula, we did our first hundred-mile day. Riding at night was dangerous, but making a hundred miles during daylight wasn't realistic: it took us almost all day to cover sixty. One morning, the map tempted us with a sizable town, Guerrero Negro, a hundred miles away. We talked through the options, then Weston and I decided to go for it—even though we'd certainly have to bike after dark. A hotel and a restaurant and maybe even Wi-Fi were worth risking our lives in the darkness.

A relentless sun beat down on us from above, and the road radiated heat up as we cycled down the long straightaways between tan rock mountains on both sides. I drank lots of water. The day passed with almost no talking. We stopped to rest very few times.

We found one café for lunch, inside a woman's house, where we got Coca-Colas in glass bottles and ate tortillas wrapped around rice, beans, and chicken. Then we got back to the road. We pedaled in grim determination.

We made it to the coast at dusk, with twenty miles left. More cars and houses appeared along the road. As it got dark, we hugged the narrow shoulder so as not to get hit. Weston's bike had no reflectors and no lights. My bike had both. So I rode in the back, where cars would see me as they sped past. We rode slowly and deliberately. At the crest of a small hill, with sand dunes to either side of us, we saw the lights of town maybe five miles away.

Guerrero Negro. Mecca.

My legs were hurting me so badly I told Weston I needed a break. We sat on a sand dune and watched the cars ride by while we ate all of the food from our bags. All the snacks. The cookies and all of it. The pain had kept me from realizing how hungry I was. The inside of my knees felt like grinding metal on metal. My ankles were sore and my tailbone was raw. It was dark, so we didn't feel rushed; it couldn't get darker than black. Finally, Weston took charge. "We're almost there, Jed. You can do this. Did you notice we've gone over a hundred miles today already! We'll reach a hundred and eight by the time we get to town."

Weston was being kind, but I got up and hobbled back to the bikes. Fifteen minutes later, we rolled down the town's main street, lit only sporadically by yellow lights. Bars and a few restaurants were open. Huge whale murals adorned the walls of the two hotels we checked out. We chose the second one, because it seemed to be the cleanest, with the most lights on. I was so delirious and in pain that I didn't care what it cost.

We rolled our bikes into the little room, and I collapsed onto my rock-hard bed. Weston turned on the TV. We were giddy at having made it, and the prospect of a hot shower and the novelty of sleeping with a roof over our heads. Just seeing humans walking around felt like some deep reward.

But fifteen minutes into lying there, my stomach started to twist. Then the bloated feeling moved lower. I thought it was diarrhea, so

I started to walk to the bathroom. Before I was through the door, my spit got hot and my stomach wrenched like it had been sucker punched. I barely made it to the toilet before I threw up every last bit of food I had eaten—chunks of salami and cracker and cheese, each heave feeling like it would be my last breath. After my belly emptied, I just kept on throwing up, or trying to. Weston ran out to buy some water bottles.

"If you're heaving, it's better to throw something up rather than just to dry heave. That's the worst," Weston said.

He stayed up most of the night watching over me and lightly scratching my back. Mothering me. By the time the sun came up, I was asleep with my cheek on the toilet seat, holding the bowl like my best friend. But when I woke up in the bathroom, I felt better. Better but weak. Even standing up and walking back to the bed felt like lifting three hundred pounds.

I was too weak to ride, so we decided to stay another day. The hotel was more expensive than we could really afford, so Weston found some Wi-Fi in the hotel lobby and looked on Warm Showers. It's an app that lets bike enthusiasts around the world offer couches or floor space and a shower—not necessarily warm—to people on trips like ours. Weston found just one user in the town—Erika—and messaged her. She replied almost instantly, and said she was excited to host us.

An hour later, Erika met us at the bank across the street and led us to her house. The main road's pavement quickly ended, as nearly all the gridded side streets of Guerrero Negro were sand. The sand was too soft to ride over, so we walked our bikes behind her rattled old minivan. Erika was in her forties, and told us in soft, broken English that she worked in the office at the local high school. We were intrigued by her nonchalance at welcoming two strange men into her home.

After pushing the bikes through sand for what felt like an hour, we reached her small house to the fanfare of barking mutts. Then one, two, three teenaged sons walked out to greet us. Then her husband. Even though they lived in a desert outpost surrounded by salt flats, the boys dressed like they were from San Diego: skater-brand shirts, flat-brimmed hats, sneakers, two with baggy jeans and one with skinny jeans.

As we walked into the house, I asked Erika why she had accepted us for a stay. "I try at my English," she said. "It is very bad. It is good Americans at my house from U.S., I practice my English. My sons, too. You want food?"

The house consisted of a living room with an old PC crammed into the corner, a kitchen, and two bedrooms closed off by sheets hung from shower rods. After the niceties of meeting her three sons and husband, I started looking around outside for a place to sleep while Weston carried on with our hosts. There were no trees to hang our hammocks from. I spread out my rain tarp in a shed and lay down for a second, fully aware of how rude I was being, but unable to do anything but sleep.

I don't know how long it was, maybe one second, maybe an hour, but when I opened my eyes it was 2 p.m., and the father was standing over me, telling me in Spanish to come inside. It's true what sociologists say: only about 40 percent of communication is in the words, and the rest is in the tone, gestures, facial movements. Once inside, he showed me that the couch pulled out into a bed. All I wanted to do was lie down on that bed and sleep until dawn, but with classic Mexican hospitality, the minivan was already running and he gestured to us to get in. He was taking us on a tour of Guerrero Negro and the miles of salt flats that support the town's main business. My mind was numb and my body was ruined, but when he spoke I smiled, looking toward whatever he was excitedly pointing at.

The salt flats are huge pools of dehydrating seawater, lined with white crystal mounds separating them from each other. Everywhere, heaps of crystalized salt. In my hand, the crystals looked like jewels. He took us from there to town, where we saw a party going on with dancing horses, trotting and doing tricks with master cowboys. We saw a large aboveground cemetery with brightly painted mausoleums. My weakness dominated my thoughts. Weston did a good job of picking up my slack. I could hardly fake delight at all these things. My eyes were half crossed.

When we got back to the house, I crumpled onto the couch. Nearby, the thirteen-year-old son sat at their PC with a Casio keyboard, watching a piano-lesson video on YouTube. He had headphones on, and his playing made no sound. The other two boys sat cross-legged a few inches from the TV, watching soccer, but I was hypnotized watching the boy learn piano all by himself. I remembered my own piano lessons as a kid, and how begrudgingly I practiced for fifteen minutes a day, with my mother watching me like a hawk to make sure I didn't sneak off to watch TV or eat BBQ potato chips. How inconvenienced I was in my roomy house with so many entertaining distractions. And here was this boy, a lover of music, using the free music lessons posted by some random person in Ohio to learn to play on his busted-up Casio, in the middle of a desert town with one paved road. What if he becomes a great musician? I bet he will. I can still see him sitting there, focusing harder on that YouTube video than I've ever been focused on anything in my life. One of life's secrets is tucked away in that moment. I know it is. It has something to do with contrast.

I slept well and felt better in the morning. The kids were up and off to school, and after breakfast, we said our sweet goodbyes and reluctantly got back on the road.

BY NOW, the charm of being in the wilderness was completely gone. My clothes were stiff with sweat and my white T-shirts would never be white again. My bike felt heavier than before. Weston's bike seemed more tattered, flimsier. The new wheel squeaked, and I saw it as a warning siren for the next breakdown in the middle of nowhere.

Cutting inland from Guerrero Negro, we lost sight of the Pacific for good. While plunging ever southward, we had to cross Baja to reach the coast of the Sea of Cortez. I was constantly nervous about running out of water, rationing and taking tiny sips. We went full days without seeing a town or hardly a human, all the while steeping in the anxiety of not knowing what lay ahead. Ride. Keep riding. Don't complain. Stay positive. Don't snap at Weston. You're not mean. You're just hungry and tired.

I fantasized about a real town, with real stores. A place where I could buy fresh T-shirts and underwear. I would stare at the map and see hundreds of miles in all directions with no civilization, and I'd meditate on misery. On my stupid choice to be here. I started plotting a guilt-free escape. What if I claimed I had terrible knee pain and couldn't go on? No one expects me to bike in pain, right? Or maybe I could just do the trip in doses. I'd go home for a month, and hit the road for a month, come back home and write about it, and then hit the road again for another month—all the way down to South America. I could do that, and never be gone long enough to hate myself or the trip.

But if I did that, wouldn't people think I'm a pussy? A fraud? Not a real adventurer?

But the true despair came from my head. California was gone. My home and my friends—the community I had built for a decade— were gone. I wouldn't see any of them for the next year and then some. Maybe a twenty-one-year-old could take this trip and explore the world without worrying about what's happening without him at home. But by thirty, I had built a life good enough to miss. To fill the time, I spun fantasies about being back home in LA with my friends, with a beer and a good laugh and a TV show marathon. I could marinate on that one image for hours, the way being in love fills your thoughts with the beloved. I was in love with the thought of home.

In central Baja, alien-looking trees began showing up on the barren landscape. Trees or cactuses or Dr. Seuss creations. I came to find out they were called boojums. They grow mainly in central Baja and reach up into the sky fifteen feet or more. They look like tall, spiny green road cones and often have no real branches—the kind of plant you could imagine populating Mars—or like the tails of cute dragons sticking straight in the air, burying their bodies to beat the heat. At night, we lit fires by burning the bones of dead boojums. We hung our hammocks from them. Weston would cook in his single crusty pan while I played episodes of our favorite podcasts, *Radiolab*, *This American Life*, *Freakonomics*, on my portable speaker.

One night it got so cold I couldn't sleep. We had found an uncharacteristically lush river meadow in the midst of the dry and barren landscape, and made camp there at sunset. The ground was green, covered in tiny white wildflowers. I changed my clothes, hung my hammock, got in my sleeping bag, and fell right asleep—but by 1 a.m., the temperature had dropped from 100 to 45 degrees. The air beneath my hammock chilled my core and I couldn't get warm again. I just lay there for hours, cursing the world. After unpacking every piece of clothing I had and layering it, I gave up. I thought the ground must hold more heat than the air. I put my Wal-Mart windshield reflector on the grass, stuffed my sleeping bag with my clothes, and finally fell asleep on the ground, either because it truly was warmer or just from total exhaustion.

The next morning, I awoke stiff as a fossil, and we packed up.

"Wow, that was one of the worst sleeps of my life," I said, going for commiseration.

"I slept fine. I was cold, yeah, but I was out."

Ugh. Damn him. Sometimes it hit me that his "man-of-the-earth" schtick wasn't a schtick. He really was tough and principled and strong. I think the fact that he wasn't flawless in this gave me ammunition to poke holes. To disregard him. I remembered what his mother said. This happens a lot with people who espouse idealism. We want to feel better about our mediocrity, so we look for the holes.

That day, we had another forever ride through nothingness. Hoping for a tienda where we could buy a cold Coca-Cola. For a place where we could buy lunch. For shade.

It was October, and it killed me to think I'd still be on this trip in October a year from now, only so much farther from home. Each time we crested a hill and saw yet another vast valley of emptiness, this feeling hit me with more force.

This is what you wanted, I told myself. To be free. Out here. Living the dream at thirty. And for what? To be uncomfortable? Well. You got that. But who cares? What are you really here for?

Through all that relentless heat and emptiness, my thoughts were cursing me. Nostalgia for my life in California progressed to the point where all of the imperfections, all of the things that sent me on this trip—my dream of a free life, of self-discovery and adventure, of doing hard things and writing about them, of bucking the system and being wild—evaporated. Home seemed like paradise, so fulfilling and lush. How foolish was I to want to leave it? All to go on some stupid, vacuous, self-absorbed man adventure.

I thought about my boyhood in green suburban comfort, about how I got to California in the first place. And, eventually, had a moment of clarity.

I am on this bike, on my spirit quest, in the desert wilderness, I thought. *This is where people have revelations. This is where I must learn.*

Chapter 6

SOME BACKGROUND AS I LOSE MY MIND
(Baja and My Childhood)

As I cycled, Weston ahead of me, I stared at my tires. I worried they were deflating. But as they spun, I couldn't make out if they were getting flatter. My eyes played tricks on me. Too much movement, and you can't see minor changes. Until it's too late.

I had changed in little bits my whole life. Never all at once. I thought about growing up, about what got me to California, about my mom, my faith. Weston was far enough ahead of me. Some absurd notion of him overhearing my thoughts was quieted by his distance.

My mind left the desert. It reached all the way back. For comfort and understanding.

I GREW UP IN Nashville, Tennessee, a place with almost more churches than houses. I realized I was gay at twelve years old. At least, that was when I discovered there was a word for it.

In third grade, I guess I was eight, I learned something was off. I was sitting on the school bus one day, all the way in the back, and the fifth graders in the next row were laughing and talking about something called a "boner." They were huddled three in the seat and laughing. Gregarious and friendly as a kid, I leaned in to their hushed conversation and spoke up: "What is a boner?" They cackled at my question and, excited, turned to me. "It's when your penis gets bigger." I exclaimed, "Oh my gosh, I get those, too!" I was so excited to share something with the older kids. They said, "Yeah, so what makes you get them?"

"I do from my dad's *Sports Illustrated* swimsuit magazine," one kid said.

"I do from magazines, too. Girls in bikinis," another kid said. I thought I was getting the picture. Yes, I know exactly when they happen. They asked me, "What makes you get a boner?" I blurted out with joy and zero hesitation, "Body builder guys on ESPN!"

They pulled their heads back like confused birds and furrowed their brows for what felt like a minute, but must've been two seconds, and then burst into laughter. "That is so weird!" They laughed and laughed. They never called me "gay" or "fag," they didn't call me anything. They just laughed and then turned back to their own conversation. I think I laughed, too. I can picture myself, my eyes panicked, my mouth pushing out a laugh. I didn't talk about it again.

Nashville in the nineties was a tricky place to be gay. Evangelical Christianity was the dominant culture, although it was so insular and convinced of its rightness that it didn't see itself as a culture. It saw itself as normal, the way things were. I knew my desires were weird, but I didn't know they were gay. I didn't know the word. I'm sure I heard sermons and saw things on television about it, but it went right over my head. It was such a private embarrassment, such a shadow I was afraid to examine, that I truly didn't. I gave my stuffed animals girl names. I cuddled them and thought I was doing the right thing.

In church I would draw spaceships and battles and dragons and monsters on the bulletin. Never looking up, never listening. If I made sound effects as the lasers hit an enemy spacecraft, my mom would shush me, or sometimes lean over and ask, "Why can't you draw something nicer than demons?" I didn't have a good answer.

In fourth grade my friend Ryan slept over. He said, "Have you ever seen people having sex on TV? It's like this—" He crawled on top of me, both of us in our pajamas, and wiggled around. Something like butterflies and fireflies and the thrill of the roller-coaster drop rushed through me. I loved his weight on me. He laughed as he crawled off. "Can you do that again? That was so funny," I said. He did it again. I may have asked for a third go-around.

I discovered my "condition" had a name when I changed schools in seventh grade. The new school brought new faces and new boys. I noticed their butts in their khakis, and I noticed that I noticed. Then, on some television show, I heard someone talking about being "gay," and the whole universe rushed through my mind at once. I thought back on everything I'd heard in church, and realized I was the thing they had warned against. I was immoral and bad.

This is a wild thing to conclude as a kid. It's not like the moral lessons everyone learns in the course of growing up—like when you call someone a name, see them get hurt, and your conscience teaches you the power of words. Those lessons sting then move you to better behavior. This revelation was different. I hadn't done something bad. I was something bad. The only you that you know—everything you're becoming—is bad, and there's nothing you can do about it. It's a horrible and complicated headspace to grow up in. (This, in my opinion, is why so many gay people turn to art, music, fashion, or comedy. As the world around them grows hostile, their spirit becomes obsessed with the meaning of it all. Straight people, finding the world designed to suit them, don't need to explore its meaning in quite the same way. But gay people don't have that luxury. We must study it, dissect it, reject it, or reshape it. We do this with the thing that was rejected: our heart.)

When I realized this in seventh grade, I decided that it must be a phase and that I would never speak of it. In that moment, I traded total honest self-expression for observation, for social anthropology. What I mean is, I knew I couldn't be myself, so I had to watch and figure out how to be. On my first day at the new school, a kid picked on me. My voice was too high, and he said that I was a girl. I was so angry at him. His name was Timothy Rogers. (You always remember moments like these, the kind that put into words some private fear, and the full name of the person who made you feel that way.) I remember standing in the hall, in one of those zoom-out sequences from a John Hughes movie, and seeing an angel on one shoulder and a demon on the other. The demon said, "Just call him out, yell at him, hate him, be mean, scare him. You're bad now, you're a bad person, embrace it . . ." But the angel said, "He doesn't know you. You're a nice guy. Make him see that there is no reason to be mean to you, because you are a good person."

I know I just said that I felt bad for my feelings, that my desires made me bad. But therein lies the war I fought inside me. I was told that I was bad, but I felt like a good kid. I didn't feel the sin in me, I just recognized that I was supposed to. Existing in this tension became my normal. So it came down to feeling. I am not mean, I said to myself, so being mean will be acting, and acting makes me tired. So I decided to win Timothy over by being friendly. I decided to be a nice person because it felt easier.

Between the ages of thirteen and fifteen, I got good at fending off the insults of other people with my sense of humor. I could cut someone off before they'd finished their basic joke about my voice, my limp wrists, or my hands waving in the air. I'd have their friends cackling. I remember a big kid named Geoff Warner stood over me in eighth grade and said, "You're a faggot." In retrospect, I kind of like the way kids insult one another. There is rarely any cleverness. Just raw reportage. I think I shot back something existential like, "Well, that came out of nowhere. Yes, I know I talk like a girl. But girls love it. I speak their secret language. All I know is that all the cheerleaders like me, and I'm going to Meredith's birthday party on Saturday. If you were nicer, you would be, too." That's probably revisionist history, but I just remember him being surprised by my answer. From then on, I beat them to the punch. I made fun of myself. I mocked my own voice. I exaggerated my silliness to show that I did it on purpose.

The deepest hurt was the surprise insult, when some kid I didn't know would ask me if I was gay. What? Why did he ask me that? Shoot, what did I do to give it away? "No, I just talk like this. I'm over here trying to get attention. I'm weird. I don't want to be like everyone else." I'd felt found out. That was what I had to avoid. So I acted weirder in every way possible. I obsessed over *Star Wars* and anime and comic books and science. I said weird things that didn't make sense just to throw people off. I raised my hand in Mrs. Shackleford's English class and asked, with the intrigue of a journal-

SOME BACKGROUND AS I LOSE MY MIND   95

ist, "Mrs. Shackleford, do you wear a thong?" This, of course, had no relation to anything. It just came to my mind. The class gasped and held in their chuckles and shot their eyes in unison to her. She fought her smile, because she liked me. "Jed, uhm, you aren't allowed to ask me that," she said. "I'm going to have to give you detention."

Leading with my weirdness, I took the ammunition right out of their lips. Or gave them words that didn't sting as much. "You're such a nerd." "You're such a freak." "You're such a weirdo." Mmm, those felt nice. Insulation from the other words.

And I was friendly. Very friendly. I made friends easily, even if they were simply kids who knew my name and liked to see what I would say next. I made it through middle school and kept my sexuality mostly hidden, from my friends and from myself, all the while collecting new friends and a reputation.

My weirdness got me weird friends. Not quite outcasts, but a solid group of five guys who didn't care to fit in. They didn't take church seriously. They made fun of their stupid parents. They were into Stanley Kubrick films and ranking the best movies of all time. But our wit was sharpened on one another, and primarily on me. My few friends made fun of me constantly. They mocked my sunny disposition. They mocked my voice and my body. Sarcasm was God. There was no time to be kind to one another. We were constantly ranking the best movies of all time, and agreed that *The Shawshank Redemption* was number one. But after that, it was all arguing. Arguing over how terrible the new Spielberg movie was, or how genius it was, or whether or not the score was up to par with older John Williams work.

As high school came, my weirdness faded. I discovered that I could turn the dial on my comedy just a little and make the cool kids laugh. If I was clever instead of weird, if I was smart instead of crazy, I was interesting to them. And slowly but surely, they invited me to things. "Hey, Jed, wanna go to the Metallica concert?" "Me? Uhm. Yes. I love Metallica." I'd never listened to one song by Metallica.

They liked the way I made them laugh. But more than that, they didn't mock me. I was used to people laughing at me. These kids were laughing *with* me. And they were Christians.

I gave the Bible a chance in my senior year of high school. I'd been dragged to church my whole life and never given that huge stupid book an actual chance. I had disregarded Christianity as mythology in a reactionary attempt to find my own identity in the shadow of my mother. But my new best friends were Christians in high school and I wanted to speak their language. I would like whatever they liked.

Everything changed, though, when I read the book of Ecclesiastes. My youth group was dedicating the summer to reading and studying it. Normally I sat through the teaching with my mind turned off and my pen out, doodling on whatever paper I could find. But the youth leader was reading passages.

"There is no remembrance of people of old, and even those who are yet to come will not be remembered by those who follow them."

"For the living know that they will die, but the dead know nothing; they have no further reward, and even their name is forgotten."

"Meaningless! Meaningless!" says the teacher. "Utterly meaningless! Everything is meaningless."

Damn! That is some dark shit. It was dismal, an almost nihilistic sequence of wise sayings and rules to live by. It was from the perspective of an ancient king who received all the luxuries of opulent living, and found them empty.

Later that week, some of the coolest guys in my grade asked if I wanted to join a Bible study group with them. I said yes. Not because I wanted to study the Bible, but because I no longer hated the Bible and I wanted to belong to something. These Christians were nice to me. And these guys were baseball players, football players. Those types of guys hardly ever noticed me, and now they were inviting me to spend time with them. To talk about life and God and this newly interesting book. I relished every meeting, every hang.

My weirdness faded into the background. I stopped talking with my hands so much. My voice got deeper. Maybe it was puberty. Maybe it was performance.

The Bible study worked on my mind, kneading it in new ways. I believed in these guys, and through them, started to believe in the Bible. For one, as a teenager, knowing I was gay but not sure what that meant, the feeling of normalcy and acceptance into the dominant cul-

tural clique was an incredible relief. Humans want few things more
than to belong. And nothing unites people like a common enemy.
Faith gave me that. A community of people united against evil, the
devil, sin, the secular world, Democrats, sex, drugs, gays. The sense of
purpose was incredible. We were on a journey together.

That was the crack in my armor. A slight change in perspective,
an angle by which belief could sneak in and change my life. There is
a reason why organized religion has billions of human beings—the
majority of us—under its spell. It is because it benefits us. And if it
benefits us, it must have truth in it, some clues to the workings of the
universe. If it didn't, it would be unspreadable. And its best trick is to
hook you with its beauty, and demand you drag with it all the rest.
You come for the sound of the choir, and go home with the weight of
the bricks and the golden cross.

It was tiring, though, to know that my very existence was a problem. When you carry a secret for as long as you can remember, years
of offhand comments pile up like a CIA case file. One friend would
say, "Gay people are so gross," while watching a pride parade on
television. Another would say, "Fags, like real fags, are so annoying.
Why do they have to talk like that?" I'd file these comments away.
And the fear. I'd double-check my voice for difference.

Television was my only window into a world where people spoke
differently about my secret. In school, in church, in every avenue of
my real-world life, I felt alone and burdened by my shameful desires.
But the characters on TV were not like anyone I knew. They showed
me options that didn't seem to exist in my surroundings. The main
show for me was *Will & Grace*. I saw the character of Will as a gay
man who wasn't hypersexual, wasn't the caricature of femininity I
had been trained to hate, didn't seem to be overcompensating. This
was huge. The model of another way to be what I was. My own
curiosity helped, too. I have always been motivated by understanding the workings of things, and the vast majority of "sins" as talked
about by Christianity made sense. Gossip is hurtful and untrue.
Greed is unjust and destructive. Promiscuous sex poisons intimacy
and emotional strength. But a committed relationship with someone
I love? That didn't compute.

———

WESTON AND I were cycling all day, talking very little. I was excavating my past, thinking over the years and my pain and my fragile masculinity. I came across so confident, so sure-footed. We set up camp each night and ate our salami and cheese and Weston made lentils over a fire and we drank boxed wine and Coca-Cola. I didn't talk to him about my cycling thoughts. Not because I didn't trust him, but because I didn't know what to do with it all. I was homesick, but also leaning into the lessons I knew I wanted from this bicycle. I was unpacking the bags of my life, spreading the contents on the floor to have a look.

Until the summer before I went to college, I kept my sexuality a secret. I never kissed a boy. I never had a secret behind-the-barn makeout. In the privacy of Internet searches and library sneak sessions, I would read all I could about being gay. The causes. Was it a disease?

I told my friend Carla first. Early senior year, I overheard her watching a reality show on Bravo and mutter, "I wish I had a gay best friend. It seems like the best thing." I made a mental note: *If I can tell anyone, it will be her.* She was best friends with all my best friends, too, so I thought she could help me figure out how to minimize the damage.

I told Carla on her couch. I cried.

"Carla, you know how I've never had a girlfriend?"

"Yeah."

"I, I don't exactly like girls. Like in that way."

"Oh, really? Do you mean you like boys?"

"Yes." I couldn't say the word *gay*. It stung too much. It felt too covered in blood and fire.

"Really!?" she said. "I suspected when we were freshmen. But I stopped thinking about it."

"You did?"

"Yeah. You weren't gay or straight. You were just Jed."

I felt relieved that Carla was surprised at all. I carried shame at being perceivably gay. Anytime someone asked me, a stranger or a friend, I recoiled in failure that I had not hidden it better.

Carla and I planned which friends to tell next. Whit would be next. Then Rob. Then Kyle.

I told them one by one. Sobbing. Hands over my face. But none of them got up and walked out. None of them called me disgusting or a moral failure. They all said, as if they'd had a secret meeting to get their stories straight, "Jed, I love you, man. This doesn't change anything. Who cares?" It took me hearing that from all of them to believe any one of them.

I felt emboldened to move to California for college at USC. The love of my friends, the acceptance, hadn't pushed me away from the faith I knew. It pulled me closer. I wasn't rejected by the church for being the way I was. I was loved. My community loved me. I wasn't the stereotype my church had been taught to fear and reject. I was their friend first. And they couldn't kick out their friend.

I loved Jesus for not taking my friends from me. The least I could do for Him was keep my lips and hands and penis to myself.

THE DEEPER I GOT lost in my past, the farther I rode behind Weston. I wasn't watching the road, I was looking through glazed eyes. When I would stand to pump the pedals up a hill, the bike wobbled hard back and forth. I went through my twenties in California. My love of God. Tall hundred-year-old cacti rolled by. I sat up straight and leaned back and felt the wind on my face with a good downhill coast. Sweat poured from my helmet. I was cooking in the sun, but my thoughts remained in Los Angeles. My mind was ticking through the last decade, what had come of it, what it meant.

The wager I had made with God as I drove out to California from Nashville in 2001: I will stay celibate, I won't throw my body around without Your blessing. I feel like it is okay to be gay, but I know that's not what Your Word says. So I'll let You make the call. If You bring a boy into my life that loves God, loves the Bible, and loves me, I'll know it's from You. If You don't, I won't risk being wrong just to feel good. This I promise You.

I became a leader in my college youth group. I went to Christian retreats and camping trips. I had a great time. And God never sent me a godly man. Or a woman. Or anyone. Just lots of friends.

By the time I turned twenty-seven, the same telescoping of time and the future that sent me on this trip shone its light on my romantic retardation. *I am almost thirty, and I've never touched anyone. Is this my life?*

Back in California, I knew of a guy at my church who was happily married to a woman. He had a daughter. I had been open with some of the leaders about my sexuality, about "my struggle," and they told me about Derek and his triumph over the deception of homosexuality. He had "overcome his struggle and been freed." I asked if he knew of any meetings. He told me about an organization called Exodus International and said he'd be glad to take me to their weekly meeting.

Two weeks later, I met him at his house to go. I was so tired of the theological acrobatics, so ready to be done with it. I wanted a wife. I wanted a kid like he had. I wanted his nice house in Long Beach with an Audi in the driveway and no good Christians breathing down his neck to change. I didn't know him well, but I had made up his healed life as a dream. His wife and daughter were home. His house was beautifully decorated. He was sweet and spoke to me about freedom and loving his wife. He said he had been with boys before his wife, and never figured out how to shake the shame. He said being with his wife made him feel whole and accepted in the sight of God. He spoke quietly and with great calm. He showed me some photos of him in his twenties, when he was "active in the gay lifestyle." His eyes were alive. His smile was ear to ear. Maybe it's because he was younger then.

He drove me to the meeting and hardly said a word. He put on worship music. The image of an uncle driving his niece to get an abortion came into my mind. A heaviness. A necessity.

The meeting was held in a church on Venice Boulevard in Mar Vista. I sat with my friend near the back. This was a free meeting. There were weekend seminars you could pay for that were more in depth. Tonight was just an intro. When we showed up there was a guy on stage singing and playing a guitar. He was in his fifties, thick and muscular, with a buzzed head, and had the look of a motorcycle gang member. He had a high voice and his "s"s held. He wore the guitar on his hip softly, and sang "How Great Is Our God!" over and over. I surveyed the crowd. Probably sixty people, mostly older than me, in their late thirties, forties, and fifties. Mostly men but some women. Most were singing. A few stayed seated, looking at their hands or the back of the pew before them.

When the singing ended, a small bald white man came to the stage. He had electric eyes, as if animated only by caffeine or speed, but aggressively so. Around his eyes were tired wrinkles. His face was red and flushed.

"Welcome, everyone. For those of you here for the first time, you are especially welcome. For those returning, welcome back to a place where you can feel safe, loved, and accepted in the arms of Jesus." He spoke with conviction, but an odd one. An urgency, almost a controlled anger reciting kind words.

He spoke about the freedom of Christ. The lies our desire tells us. How "the heart is deceitful above all things, Jeremiah 17:9." He said our culture is lying to us. That the shame we feel is God calling us home.

I surveyed the room and felt such a heaviness. I noticed the man next to me. Mid-forties, handsome. A little too tan and clothes well-chosen and fitted. He listened to the sermon squinting, almost wincing. He worked his lips, thinking. It looked like he was arguing with someone unseen.

"Now I want everyone struggling with homosexuality to stand up. You're safe here. Stand up. We're going to have Kyle come back up and play some music. And here's what I want you to do. Forgive whoever touched you, whoever abused you, whoever molested you. Was your mother overbearing? Did your father abandon you? Who did this to you? Were you molested, raped? Don't let them have power over you. Give it to God. He wants to take it from you. Put it on Jesus. He is the man you're meant to love. Men, He will free you to love women, and women, He will free you to love men. So now, say the name of whoever did this to you, shout it out, set them free and set yourself free."

The music began playing and names flew. People were shouting. The first one came awkwardly, like an out-of-tune trumpet. "Michael Green. I forgive you! Michael! Michael! Jesus forgives you!" Then the others came all at once. One man said, "Ryan, Ryan, Ryan, Ryan . . ." Another said, "Mother, mother, mother." Another said, "Uncle Daryl, Uncle Daryl . . ."

I stood in silence and looked around the room. People held their hands high and shouted. The music was loud. I have never been molested. I have great parents. Sure, they got divorced. Maybe that made me gay? Did my dad abandon me? No. Did he neglect me? Not to my knowledge. Maybe I've blocked something. Maybe I was molested? Was I? Am I traumatized and I've blocked it out?

No. I had no one to forgive. No one made me this way. Nothing I can trace made me this way. I just like boys. As the man on stage continued the forgiveness session, a Bible verse came into my head, John 10:10: "The thief comes only to steal and kill and destroy. I came that they may have life and have it abundantly." I looked around the room. Where was the life and life abundant? These people were zombies. Another verse came to me, Matthew 7:15: "Beware of false prophets, who come to you in sheep's clothing, but inwardly they are ravenous wolves. You will know them by their fruits. Do men gather grapes from thorn bushes or figs from thistles? Even so, every good tree bears good fruit, but a bad tree bears bad fruit."

This was good fruit? This was life abundant?

I looked at my friend sitting next to me. His face was tired. He seemed like a broken horse, saddled and roped to a fence. He drove me back to my car, I told him thank you, and I felt worse, like the healing was a scam.

I met a guy a few days later and kissed him. I was twenty-eight and let him lead. And in the two years leading up to my trip, I kissed a few other boys and dated my first boyfriend. We had sex. I said, "I don't know what I'm doing." He said he would show me. He was tender and kind.

I went on this bike trip to chase adventure and avoid the assembly-line life of routine and expectations . . . right? That is why I ran off from my twenties to South America? But unpacking my childhood, my faith, my sexuality, walking through the building blocks of my mind, I could see I had a lot of things pulling strings in the shadows, making decisions for me just outside my view.

I was thirty years old, a rugged adventurer and a sexual infant.

I JUST KEPT PEDALING, talking to God, not Weston. And by that I mean thinking, staring at the ground, at the mountains, feeling my smallness in the bigness of the world. Feeling how ancient and powerful the desert was, how disinterested it all was in my life and in whether I touched my lips to someone else's. How entire mountain ranges could disappear, and I wouldn't care, but if I kissed someone, or didn't, I would be elated or devastated. I made a lot of miles boiling in thoughts like this.

We made it down the rest of Baja without much incident. In spite of the gruesome tales about Mexico and drug cartels and beheadings . . . we only met kindness. The police at the many checkpoints laughed as we approached on bikes and offered us water and advice on our route. Truckers continued to pull over to hand us more water. Even the tarantulas and scorpions moved over as we passed, as if saying, *After you, good sir.* I rode many miles with only my mind as the enemy, missing home, missing my friends. I was tired of thinking and tired of the desert. Tired of forcing meaning and pretending to be tough on this stupid road. I didn't want to voice my despair—I thought it would discourage Weston—but I also felt so weak and alone in my loss of wonder and desire for the trip.

"Dude, this has been hard for me," I finally confessed to Weston the night before we got to La Paz. We had camped for the night in a dusty riverbed, and as we were drifting to sleep, with the promise of a city the next day and some kind of escape, I told the truth. "I've been trying to stay positive, but damn, I'm ready for La Paz, for a city, for that ferry, and to get off this peninsula."

"Shit, I'm so glad you've hated it, too. I want tropical beaches and warm water, any water. I can't drink one more Coca-Cola or eat one more cracker and salami. I'm so fucking over it. Dude, I thought you were so okay with all of this."

"Fuck, no. I've hated this hell since I got sick in Guerrero Negro."

"Really!? Me, too!" he said, feeling sudden companionship. "I didn't want to say anything because I thought it would bum you out, or change the energy. I wanted to be positive."

"Me, too," I said. "I feel like we're so lucky to be on this trip and people wish they were doing it and not stuck at a desk job, but damn, the adventure wears off, doesn't it? I mean, I'm not ready to quit right now or anything. But it feels good to admit it isn't one long string of euphoria."

"Fuck, it feels good to admit that," Weston said in the darkness of his hammock.

"Let's drink all the beer in La Paz, live it up for a minute, and catch the ferry out of this shit box of desert hell." We both laughed hard at the release of being allowed to hate the adventure we were on.

The next day we cycled into La Paz and celebrated the miracle of civilization. We stayed with a Christian woman named Lucinda that we found on Warm Showers. She was excited to share Jesus and her church with us. We slept on the couch in her small house. Her hot shower and stocked refrigerator and soft voice felt so welcoming. We went to a movie theater—an IMAX, even—and downed enough popcorn and soda to make us nearly puke. We saw the movie *Gravity*, and felt that we'd been transported to the future. The air-conditioned theater. The soft seats. The special effects. I felt very close to Weston, having survived the desert, sleeping by fires and hunting water and relishing cold Coca-Colas and the conversations with locals, both strange and sweet. We were comrades. Brothers already.

WHILE IN LA PAZ, homesick but encouraged, contemplating how I was going to stay sane for the next year on this bike trip, my friend Adam e-mailed. "A crew of homies is going surfing in Nexpa, Mexico. Is that on your way? It's tropical and tiny and perfect. You'll love it. Come hang with us! November 2nd!" I checked the map. Nexpa was indeed on our course. We'd ferry from La Paz, near the tip of Baja, to the mainland, to a city called Mazatlán. Then we'd head south to

Puerta Vallarta, then down below that was Nexpa. To get there by November 2 would require a push, but to see our friends would be worth it. When I ran the idea by Weston, he was ecstatic, so I told Adam that we'd meet them there, no matter what it took.

We stayed a couple more nights in La Paz, relishing the creature comforts, laughing and getting drunk, then bought tickets for the overnight ferry to Mazatlán and the mainland.

It was a thirteen-hour crossing. We couldn't afford the private cabins, so we had to sleep on the deck of the ship. There were probably a hundred people, maybe more, bodies in every corner hiding from the cold and wet wind. Weston met an eccentric old white man who had left the United States because he thought it was too corrupt. They started swapping conspiracy theories. The guy told us he had a private cabin with three empty beds and said we could sleep in his room. I crawled into the top bunk and tried to sleep while the old man kept telling Weston about contrails and the falsification of the moon landing and Obama's secret mission to buy Cuba. Weston was endlessly fascinated. I was happy to be off the deck of the boat. I fell asleep as they were discussing the fact that fossil fuel comes from dead dinosaurs, and how it is impossible that there were that many dead dinosaurs to provide enough oil for the world, and that therefore petroleum was a chemical made up by the Russians to control the world.

Chapter 7

CARTELS AND COCONUTS

11,834 miles to go

Crossing that slip of ocean was like sliding down a wormhole to another kind of Earth. Immediately the mountains of Mexico turned from dust brown to jungle green. The rivers here swelled with muddy water, and I had never been so happy to see chubby tourists and traffic.

Mazatlán is a tourist destination, with hotels and restaurants lining the beach, bicycles for rent, families splashing in the waves, and everywhere signs for beer and tacos and happy hours and margaritas. It felt familiar, like Florida.

Weston got high and we rode our bikes in the humid hot night air without shirts on. True to form, Weston's tire popped on the boardwalk and we had to fix it and it took forever, so we found a shitty hostel down the road and slept in a bunk room full of snorers. Still, we were incapable of being frustrated, so inflated with joy that we floated like parade animals over a marching band.

The next day under a hot, wet sun, we started south to Puerta Vallarta. The city quickly turned into coastal farms and fields. We hadn't ridden in humidity yet, and sweat poured from our bodies. My helmet filled with sweat that dripped in my eyes. Over the next few days, farms gave way to tree-covered mountains and now it looked like Hawaii. In Puerta Vallarta, the scene changed to expensive boat docks and condos and high-rises. We stayed at a hostel and walked around town. Halloween was in the air. We got drinks with strangers and people were in elaborate costumes, and lots of gay guys were out in Speedos and boas. "Jed, you might just get some tonight!" Weston said.

"Uhm, I don't think so. I am not in a Speedo, nor do I intend to be. I look like a scrawny hippie rat from this bike trip. I ain't getting no buff beach boy," I said, deflecting.

"Well, you're not with that attitude," Weston said.

We had so much fun in Puerta Vallarta that we stayed for several days. We should've left, because Nexpa was several days' ride away, and we had to get there by the second, but we met some French girls and Weston was trying to kiss one and we loved the beach and our hostel was cheap. The town had great restaurants, narrow cobblestone streets, and steep mountains all around. I read on the beach. Watched a parade. Drank good coffee and bought coconuts from street vendors for a dollar. We knew we were staying too long, but we wanted to have fun anyway. We knew it would mean hitch-hiking south. We didn't care. Fuck expectations.

Early on the second, we packed up our things and biked out of town. We figured if we could get on the southern highway, some truck or farmer might take us the rest of the way. At a promising spot, we turned our bikes upside down and I managed to find a piece of cardboard to make a sign. "Nexpa." I added a smiley face.

No ride materialized. Every truck that came around the corner only sped on by. After several miserable hours of standing in the sun, a local bus stopped and the driver made an offer we couldn't refuse.

It took the rest of the day to reach Nexpa. Turns out we had badly miscalculated. We learned the hard way that three hundred miles by bus on a narrow, winding road in Latin America is likely to take a life-time. We drove through forested hills and shoulder-high grass along the road. Cows stood almost invisible in the fields, eating their fill. At dusk, when the bus finally pulled into Nexpa, we felt like cheaters but we didn't care. Who were we cheating? We made the rules.

Nexpa is just a romantic blip on the coast where the waves are perfect and a lazy river pours into the Pacific. Almost no Internet, no supermarkets, no stores. We showed up to the one-street town and went looking for our friends. They'd mentioned that they were at the main hostel right by the beach. As we walked our bikes down the little street we saw hammocks and people on the balcony of the only obvious hostel, and I heard English, and then I heard Adam's voice. We ditched our bikes without locking them and ran up the rickety stairs. It was a riot of cheers and hugs and "Holy shit, you found us" and "Get these men some beers!" I felt like a soldier coming home from war. We laughed uncontrollably and hugged and touched their faces and made foolish jokes about getting shit-faced and partying just to laugh more.

The hostel was a series of beach huts and shacks owned by a British woman named Susan who'd married a Mexican man and was raising her kids in this outpost of paradise. The beach curved around a crescent bay to the mouth of a river, where the flow of fresh water had pushed sand into a bar that made for excellent surfing waves. Huts topped with thatched roofs studded the sand, and the air was warm and pleasant. We surfed and got sunburned and drank beers and befriended the owner of the only bar on the beach. His name was Stewart, and he spoke English with an American accent. I asked him his story.

Stewart told us he was born in Mexico but had raised a family in Florida until "some bullshit" happened between him and his wife. She called the police and claimed he "hit her and messed her up," and he got deported. He said she was a crazy bitch, that he just wants to see his kids and that he's not a bad guy.

"It's a wild thing to think," he said, "you're building a whole life in the U.S., with a wife and American-born kids, and then you get sent to live in Mexico again. I had never really lived in Mexico. So I opened this bar. It's pretty cool. But I meet a lot of American surfers, and it makes me want to get back to the U.S. It's pretty fucked up."

As he talked, I would drift between good cheer and observation. This often happens to me when I'm listening to someone tell a story they've rehearsed a hundred times with a hundred different visitors. Their face is not astonished by their own words; they're not reading your face as they go, to tell if their sentences are landing. They're bored at the injustice of having to make their case again and again to a deaf universe.

The days drifted by with big beers and big waves and sitting in the back of rented trucks and beat-up local trucks as we hunted not just remote beaches, but beaches that seemed to be lost to humanity. I half expected a velociraptor to stalk me as I napped under the palm trees.

Then, on the morning of November 4, the town started scrambling around, gossip traveling with lightning speed. All roads in every direction had been blockaded. The military was staging an overthrow of the Knights Templar, the main cartel here in the state of Michoacán. An hour down the coast in Lázaro Cárdenas, the largest town on this part of the coast, the Knights Templar had taken control of the port for the past few years. They'd slowly bribed and muscled their way into controlling trade in and out. Component chemicals for methamphetamine production came into the port from Asia, and then from there, they could make the meth in the nearby jungles, then put it right on trains and trucks bound for the United States. They'd made millions as a result. The military was retaking the port and pushing the Knights Templar into the jungle and up the coast, back toward us. We had no idea what was going on—only that the people of Nexpa seemed to be stressed. "The mafia is pissed," they told us. "They run this state." The last time the Knights Templar fought the military, Nexpa was stranded without food or water for two months. "Every kid and grandma comes out to the street with their guns."

Black military helicopters buzzed overhead all day. Humvees loaded down with local vigilantes, supported by the military, roared past the surf shacks. We couldn't even get to a supermarket two miles down the road.

Shaken up, we went to Stewart's bar to drink and dull our nerves and listen to the gossip. He explained that the Knights Templar got their name from medieval warriors who protected Christian pilgrims during the Crusades. They'd become the de facto government in Michoacán. They patrolled the state's steep forests and chaotic network of dirt roads in lifted four-wheel-drive trucks. They moved like ghosts, nowhere and everywhere. Recently, they had been trying to diversify their income. They'd made a fortune selling meth to the U.S., and had seized iron ore mines in Michoacán to sell the mineral to hungry Chinese companies. They were also illegally selling rare Mexican timber to the Chinese, Stewart said. They'd bribed and conned their way into control of the massive industrial port in Lázaro Cárdenas, which had a direct line to China and was poised to become the biggest Pacific port outside of Los Angeles. In retaliation, the military had been secretly preparing an attack.

Today was the day. Today they choked every road in the state.

When men entered the bar, "You can always tell cartel boys," Stewart whispered. "They show up in lifted trucks and carry huge walkie-talkies." The men couldn't have been older than nineteen, and it was clear that the far corner table was theirs and always theirs. They seemed calm and wound up at the same time, like pit bulls.

For an hour, the cartel boys set the tone of the room, ordering beers and talking among themselves, watching football on the television and occasionally mumbling into their walkie-talkies. At one point, one of the teams scored and they were visibly pleased. They looked over at us—the nervous gringos at the bar, pretending to be oblivious to their presence—and raised their glasses in muted cheers. We cheered back. They smiled, downed the last gulps, and walked out.

Stories of life in cartel country kept flowing with the beer. Susan, the British surf goddess who owned the hostel shack we were renting, talked about a Texas family that had come down in their brand-new white F-150 truck. They entered Michoacán, and within the hour, cartel boys in Jeeps had pulled them over at gunpoint. The boys politely escorted the startled Texans out of their truck, said "Gracias for the donation," and left them on the side of the road.

"You have to drive a beat-up piece-of-shit car," Susan explained, "and you'll be left perfectly alone. Show up in an all-wheel-drive anything and it'll be gone in a week." She had built a life on this beach, minding her own business and making it a point to own nothing the cartels could want.

We spent the next few days at that bar, thirsty for news. In this place, the Internet, where it even existed, offered no answers or updates. We only had word of mouth.

The sense of being stranded in paradise was kind of nice. Susan kept ensuring us that everything was fine, that the cartels would never bother tourists. But there was a forced confidence in her words. We all knew that drunk, money-hungry teenagers with guns could lead to unfortunate events. Our buddies from California stayed up through the night debating whether or not to tell their girlfriends and wives about the roadblocks. And by roadblocks, I mean the cartel. In the United States, the dominant story about Mexico is cartel violence. I had told my mom that reports were overblown, that Mexico was wonderful, that she was xenophobic. But here I was, surrounded by teenagers with guns and Humvees and military helicopters. My friends were deciding not to tell their wives. I was not going to tell my mother.

I couldn't give up on my global optimism. I've always believed that the world is far friendlier than it is not, far more loving than hateful. Fear is like a thorn in your foot. It may be proportionally small in relation to the body, but it hurts and demands attention and everything halts until the thorn gets pulled. But dammit, I felt stupid, feigning my optimism here in Nexpa. Playing it cool. Wondering if I'd be shot by accident or on purpose. There is truth in a mother's worry. There is also exaggeration and unfairness. If I die, she wins, I thought. If I live, I win.

The truth is, violence is the exception—not the rule—in almost all places on this planet. There's a saying in journalism: "If it bleeds, it leads." Humanity fixates on violence. We're fascinated by its abnormality; we want to understand it and learn how to avoid it. But the truth lies somewhere in between blood and peace. Most of us will move through life without experiencing the abnormalities of violence, but that doesn't mean those abnormalities don't exist.

It was strange, watching the waves crash, feeling the cool breeze on our faces. Nothing had changed, except the news, and the goings-on of humans. A coup was under way, and paradise didn't seem to notice.

We went surfing, my California buddies talking nonstop about their wives and girlfriends. "Melissa did not want me to come," one guy said. "But she's always worried about nothing. Fuck." Now that the roadblocks had sprung up and the locals were nervous, they seemed shaken; perhaps more shaken by proving their ladies right than by the possibility of injury. To hear them talk, this wrongness would come at a great cost down the road. "I told you so" is a weapon that can be deployed for years. Weston and I listened as our friends anxiously calculated how to get home, but we knew we weren't going anywhere. They heard the government was letting people through the roadblocks to the airport, so they decided to hop in the rental car and chance it.

We woke up early to say goodbye. They were leaving just a day early from their scheduled trip, but the debates and planning of escape routes consumed so many hours the day before, it felt like we had all been stranded and trapped in the tiny town for weeks.

Later in the morning, Susan gave us stand-up paddle boards, and her thirteen-year-old daughter took us out on the river. As we slid them into the warm water, she warned us against paddling across the river's wide mouth, because that's where the crocodiles liked to hang out. We said okay and laughed. Teenagers with guns. Now crocs. But as the three of us paddled upstream, we weren't thinking of war. Tall palm trees and thick jungle leaned out over the water, and I watched the muddy banks for logs that could be crocodiles. Paddling was easy in the lazy current. In the distance, we saw cliffs covered in vines and flowers. Birds spooked and flew from the trees. Weston paddled alongside me, and Susan's daughter slid ahead of us as if not paddling at all.

We got to talking about explorers and Indiana Jones and Steven Spielberg and movies from the eighties. Weston said, "Can I tell you something that will make you hate me?"

I said, "Of course. I already hate you."

"There are two things I don't like, and every time I say these things, people hate me afterwards."

"This is a safe place. On this river, we can speak truth without judgment," I said.

"Okay, well, here we go: I don't like *Star Wars*, and I think I hate the Beatles." He paddled forward and didn't look at me. He grinned at this scandal.

"WHAT?" I shouted. "You have got to be kidding me. *Star Wars*? How can you be a stable human being without loving *Star Wars*!? Do you hate sunsets, too? What about food? Do you hate food?" I shouted.

"See, I told you," he said, laughing. "This river is not a safe place. I've made a huge mistake."

For an exercise in empathy, I tried to argue his point of view. "Okay, okay, I mean, the Beatles, I don't love some of their songs," I said. "And I must admit I get annoyed when music snobs demand I like something because it was groundbreaking. But the Beatles sound changed so many times, there has to be SOME song of theirs you like. Like 'Eleanor Rigby.' Come on! You have to love that song!"

"I'm not sure I know it," Weston said.

"Okay, thank God, there's hope," I said.

It's remarkable how normal moments live on in the middle of chaos and tragedy. People still play chess and drink tea in the middle of war. New inside jokes are born at funerals. Stranded in Nexpa, I saw the locals laughing over beers. Making jokes about the military, about the cartels, about resorting to powdered milk the last time this happened. Human beings have little capacity for sustained horror. I think our minds need to play to survive. Permanently serious people always look so tired, maybe because they are fighting an emotional battle that eats the body alive. To laugh and play while the bombs drop is one way to survive a war, even to win it.

As we paddled up the river we came to the big bridge on the coastal highway. It loomed over us, tall and cracked. We heard a loud engine and looked up as a Humvee boomed down from the bridge. We paused for a minute to make eye contact and acknowledge the wildness of what was happening around us. Weston broke our silence. "Do you think me hating *Star Wars* is worse than being the leader of a cartel?"

"Absolutely."

Beyond the bridge, we came upon a huddle of crocs floating in the middle of the river. In a tight-chested instant, we turned around and paddled furiously, laughing and feeling exposed on the boards. Once downriver, we dragged the boards up onto the grass to watch

Susan's daughter shimmy like a spider up a tree to knock down some coconuts with her machete. The giant rusted knife looked half as long as she was tall. Back on the ground, she slashed off the tops of the coconuts, revealing the milky meat inside, tender and delicious.

The next day, Humvees buzzed across the bridge and kicked up dust, and black helicopters patrolled the beaches. I lay in the hammock. I did push-ups. I sliced more coconuts. I found a stack of old *National Geographic*s in Susan's hostel. One of them from 1986 had a story about Leo Tolstoy, about his hometown in Russia, about the man behind the legend. I grabbed it and walked out to the river. I sat against a palm tree facing upriver, where I could see the bridge and the Humvees and the mountains. Behind me I could hear the waves of the ocean.

I read that when Tolstoy was young he wrote in his journal, "I am twenty-four years old and I have still done nothing . . . I am sure it's not for nothing that I have been struggling with all my doubts and passions for the past eight years. But what am I destined for? Only time will tell." I was thirty years old reading this, sitting by a river in Mexico, wondering what I had done with my life. I knew it wasn't for nothing that I'd been struggling with all my doubts and passions for the past twenty years. I had dipped so deeply and completely into my faith, into my love of God, or who I made God to be, and what the people around me said He must think about everything. I knew it was not for nothing, but what, I didn't know. I just knew it was somewhere in me, and I needed travel to shake it out. I needed to see different things to remind me what I was, in contrast to what I already knew. To see clearly what I had become.

Days passed trapped on that riverbank, beside that beach, with nowhere to possibly go, all tangled up in my head. We lounged and played in paradise and spent many hours at the bar. To Weston's delight Stewart would always walk out and hand us free joints. Stewart had news on the cartel war, too. He explained that the Knights Templar were losing their fight with the military and getting pushed into the jungle. But the rule of law wouldn't follow in their wake. Stewart's uncle was high up in another cartel (I think it was called La Familia) based in Morelia, Michoacán's capital city—one that had more members and sway with the government. Once this fight was done, they would move into the region and pick up where their predecessors left off.

Ten days in, we woke to the new normal of coffee and toast and waiting for any news of the fighting. Susan was not in the hostel when we got up. As we were making the coffee, she ran in, excited. "It's over! The military pushed the mafia out last night and they retreated. The roadblocks came down this morning!"

The weight of the air suddenly lifted. The beach town was no longer a prison. We were, it seemed, free. Nothing around me had changed. The river flowed just as it had minutes ago. The waves were still pumping. The coconuts grew in silence just the same. But the whole world looked different. Our internment camp had morphed back into a beach town.

WE SPENT A final day with Susan in Nexpa. It was a vacation again, but with our new freedom, we felt the time we'd lost. We should've been in Morelia by now. Susan had whetted our appetites for the colonial beauty of the city, the cobblestone streets, the cathedrals. But she wasn't confident that the cartel nonsense was over, so she insisted on driving us south to Lázaro Cárdenas. That way we'd be through the epicenter of the fighting and on the highway that led up the mountains to Morelia. We gratefully accepted. She dropped us by the highway and we hugged and she waved as we cycled away.

We made it one day up the mountain, slept terribly in a bug-infested grove of trees, and early the next day, Weston's wheel broke. After trying for three hours to get a truck to rescue us, we asked a passerby with a phone to let us make a call. I had written down Susan's number (thank God) and we called her. She seemed relieved to hear from us, as if she hoped we'd call, to check in or to need her again. "I don't like driving the truck up in the mountains, because the mafia loves to steal trucks," she said, "but this is Ricardo's truck . . . I hope it gets stolen. He deserves to have his truck fucking stolen. Here I come!"

To get out of the sun, we waited under a bridge until she pulled up honking and waving and laughing. We were sweaty and so happy to see her. She reiterated her fear of driving, so Weston drove. We threw our bikes in the back and traveled from sea level to over six thousand feet, from hills covered in jungle and palm trees to farmland, to pine trees, to cooler air. The humidity quickly dropped as we drove higher. As I sat in the truck and watched the land whiz by, I felt how my trip was changing. I was having fun, and I wasn't. This wasn't a weekend camping trip; there would be no quick return. My bed wasn't waiting for me. Not long ago, I was thinking how brave I was to go on this trip and do this difficult thing. I reveled in people's astonishment. Now their astonishment made sense. They knew something I hadn't. What was I doing here?

But I held this feeling of dread in one hand. The other hand was holding love. Love for Mexico. For the land and the ocean. For the freedom of seeing new things and not knowing what was next. Have you ever felt two things at once? Two opposite things?

Farms became little villages became the outskirts of Morelia. Fields gave way to a tightly packed Spanish Colonial grid, with cobblestone streets and walls and the spires of cathedrals reaching high above the grid. Morelia looked more like the photos I'd seen of Spain than what I knew of Mexico.

Susan was going to stay with a friend in town, so she dropped us at our hostel. Later, we met up at the cathedral to find dinner. As we walked up, a full symphony was playing in the square and there was a fireworks show at the entrance to the cathedral, set to shoot off as the orchestra crescendoed. It was all part of a music festival taking place in town.

Morelia felt every bit as cosmopolitan and savvy as an artists' town in Germany or Park City, Utah. We couldn't believe the contrast here to the feeling of lawlessness on the coast. The streets of Morelia were stone, the buildings European. I stood, frozen in front of the two giant cathedral bell towers as the orchestra played. Women in big Victorian dresses, fully in costume, waltzed around in front of the violinists. Thousands of people milled about and were mostly quiet to respect the musicians.

Weston and I felt safe again.

For the next two days, we explored Morelia by eating at cafés and

walking the streets. Thanks to the music festival, parades of musicians from all over the world shocked us at every turn. Bagpipes
from Scotland. Jazz. Tubas and cellos. Walking in clumps, playing
their music over flower petals strewn in the streets.

Morelia had a well-stocked bike shop, and an oily mechanic to fix
Weston's bike. We bought lots of new tubes. I had my bike checked
out and cleaned and lubed. When both were shiny and ready to roll,
we mapped our route to Mexico City. The next day, we rode out of
Morelia. The town ended abruptly, from thick Spanish stone to rolling hills and farms. Then, as quick as a page turn, we were winding
up into the green mountains. It was gaspworthy beautiful. The air
was crisp, the sky sunny and blue, the world inviting. The trees were
tall and the cows by the side of the road were fat and pleasant. We
rode for several days. We started seeing monarch butterflies. Lots
of them. On weeds by the road and in the air. We camped in abandoned barns and thick forests. We took a shower in a waterfall.

The Baja desert had worn me down. Mainland Mexico was showing me something new. This was the Altiplano, the giant spine of
Mexico, floating more than 5,000 feet above sea level, cooling the air,
reducing humidity, and making the world as pleasant as paradise. A
natural kindness.

Three days into the ride, the sky changed. It was full of specks.
Birds too high to make out? Millions. Pepper raining across the sky.
"What is that?" Weston asked.

"I don't know." I stared into the sky as we stood by the side of the
road, squinting up.

"Jed, look!" Weston said, pointing to a bush. It had several monarch butterflies on it. "Dude, they're butterflies!"

The great monarch butterfly migration was under way just as we
approached the town of Zitácuaro. A local told us that we were near
the forest where they arrive every fall, by the millions and millions.

We ditched our bikes at a cheap motel and took a bus to the forest. The mountains here were covered in evergreen trees. The air
was chilly and garnished in mist. We booked a horseback ride into
the forest. Our guide took us over a ridge and down into a gully
where we saw that the trees looked strange, as if they were dipped

in chocolate and dripping. "Can you tell us about why they're here?" Weston asked.

"Sure," he said with a proud smile. I remember his English being excellent. He'd done this tour many times before. "Monarch butterflies born in the fall are different than all the other monarchs. They are a super generation. They can live up to eight months as they travel from Canada all the way down to our forest. Then, after waiting out winter here, they'll head up to warmer places like Louisiana and breed. Their children will live for only six weeks. It can take five generations of their children, who live so much shorter lives, to get back to Canada. Then those born at the beginning of fall, they become the super ones again. Then those ones begin the great journey. They can fly from Michigan all the way here, to Zitácuaro."

As we got closer, we saw that every single inch of each tree was covered in butterflies. "Look up," our guide said, and in the holes of blue sky between the trees, we saw a blizzard of butterflies. "This is early, and more butterflies will come. But now too many butterflies don't come back. Five years ago, we had ten times more."

The monarch, too? I thought of the bees, and what it must mean, we humans ruining everything. We don't have any way to process how everything we do touches everything else.

"It is probably climate change," the guide said. "Or technology. The cell phones. Something that people are doing is confusing them or causing them to die. It is very sad. We do not care for the beautiful things of this world." His voice was heavy and pensive as he worried out loud about the future of this forest and his region's claim to fame.

We returned to our bikes thrilled at the majesty of the butterflies and thrown by the confusing science of their decline. When we got back to our motel, a parade was noisily clanging down Zitácuaro's main street. So many parades.

Cycling through the mountains of central Mexico, we would camp and find tiny hotels for less than ten dollars a night. On one rainy night in the woods we used our tarps and hammock string to make a simple A-frame ground tent. It got very cold up in the mountains at night, so we hoped we could make a tent to stay dry and warm, side by side. We were at close to 9,000 feet. It rained and we got wet, but not soaked. As I was falling asleep on my back, something fell onto my closed eye. I reached up and felt a squirming fuzzy creature. I flicked it off and found my phone for some light. My eye was already on fire, as were my fingers. Weston heard me scream "DAMMIT!" and sat up.

"What?" he asked.

"Something stung the shit out of my eye!" The flashlight revealed a fuzzy brown caterpillar crawling on my sleeping bag. Apparently, its fuzz was a swarm of stinging needles, and it had fallen right onto my eyelid.

I fell asleep with my hand pressing on my eye, wondering if I'd been poisoned and doomed to blindness. I woke up the next day soggy and okay, but determined to sleep in hotels for a few days.

We passed Christmas tree farms and white-tarp greenhouses of poinsettias. We saw vendors selling stick sculptures, with Santa Clauses and reindeer shaped from bundled sticks and vines. It was mid-November, and the Christmas decorations made me feel happy.

A FEW DAYS LATER, the road dropped out of the mountains and into Toluca, a big town west of Mexico City. We found a family to stay with on Warm Showers and met a group of three brothers. They took us to dinner and practiced their impeccable English. They loved pop-punk music and Quentin Tarantino movies. They said they were perfecting their English through watching television and movies. They said that this would get them good jobs in the hotel industry. They said we shouldn't bike from their house into Mexico City because it is too crowded and only freeways. We said warm goodbyes and cycled to the edge of town. From there, we hitchhiked in the bed of a truck into Mexico City.

I began to sense the scale of Mexico City, more sprawling and populous by far than New York City. But what did it look like? I couldn't picture a skyline. Or even a building. I conjured up the grimy streets from *Man on Fire*, the Denzel Washington movie with child kidnapping and car chases racing through the city. It is strange to know a place's name so well, to know something about it, and to have almost no image of it in your mind.

The Mexican Altiplano had changed my tune about this country. The baking misery of Baja was a memory. This was a paradise. As an American, my assumptions about Mexico were formed in ignorance. I assumed the country was a dry, dusty desert populated by cacti and big hats and U-shaped horses and sun-baked clay homes. And then maybe Cancún—jungles, white sand, and embarrassing tourist traps. It never crossed my mind that the center of the country could possibly look different or have its own benefits. I didn't think about it. I just filled in the blanks with drug cartels and heads in bags. And yes, I had been stranded by a cartel, sure, but somehow I couldn't agree with my mom.

Take, for example, the chain of towns called Pueblos Mágicos, one-time colonial settlements that run through the mountains of central Mexico and elsewhere. Each town is Spanish by design, built to remind the colonists of their homeland and paid for by the king's gold (much of it heisted from the Aztecs and Mayas). At the center of each town is a massive cathedral and square. These beautiful relics, still very much alive and bustling with life, are far older than anything in the United States. They feel so completely European that their proximity to the United States comes as a shock. You look up at one of those buildings, and some subconscious association between European architecture and distance causes your mind to assume jet lag and time-zone adjustments. But all of these towns are in the same time zones as the United States. When I walked the streets of Morelia, I thought of how absurd it was that no one I know had ever been there.

In Toluca, I called my mom. I told her that my extended stay in Nexpa was simply a desire to soak up the sun. Now that I was safe and far from the coast, the cartel felt fake. I gloated to her about the butterflies. The cathedrals. The music festival. The colors and flowers. The constant parades. The food. It was as if Mexico had tortured me with that desert, testing me to see if I was worthy. Now she was showing me all her riches. I was falling in love with a country I'd never really considered. Sometimes love sneaks up on you, doesn't it.

But then, perhaps we had only been lucky.

Chapter 8

THE CATHEDRAL SITS ON THE TEMPLE
(Mexico City)

10,740 miles to go

Mexico City is a beast, the second-largest city in the world, spreading out in every direction. Not too many skyscrapers. Just apartment buildings and homes and flat rooftops and satellites sticking out of windows and clothes on lines and honking cars. Originally the city was the capital of the Aztec empire, and the city's very existence is a testament to Aztec genius. This high-elevation valley had been a shallow lake, but the Aztecs made their own land by packing mud and grass to create ever-expanding islands. When the Spanish conquistadors showed up in the 1500s, they set out to erase that empire. Today, ancient trade routes lie buried under freeways. The massive cathedral at the city's center rises on the foundation of the destroyed temple and pyramids beneath it. In some kind of karmic justice, the cathedral leans right, sinking further into the mud year after year.

I thought about how the church of my youth had built a cathedral on top of me. On top of my sexuality. Burying my desires. Trying to erase an insurrection. I knew that the Gospel was true, and therefore it was worth spreading it at any cost. Right? For the saving of my soul. For the saving of the Aztecs. Right?

We got our bikes out of the truck right outside the giant plaza in front of the massive cathedral. Its proper name is the Metropolitan Cathedral of the Assumption of the Most Blessed Virgin Mary into Heaven. Whoa. It's the largest cathedral in the Americas. We gawked at it for a few minutes but quickly strapped our things back on our bikes. We walked over to a park bench and sat down. We had to bike to some suburb to meet our host, and I needed to study the map. City biking. Dear God.

We had found a girl on Instagram who offered to host us. She had messaged me:

> If you need a place to crash in southern Mexico City in the area of Coyoacan (you will love) as we say in Mexico, my house is your house :), also, I can show the city or whatever you need in their days in the city.
> Good life forever!
> —Beatriz

She sounded great. We had no idea who she was, of course, but when we checked her photos on Instagram and tags to see if she had friends, if she had weird tastes or any red flags, she seemed normal enough. She liked coffee shops and getting drinks with friends and the occasional museum. Instagram stalking felt oddly trustworthy. Studying how people represented themselves said a lot about who they were. At least, that was our hope.

Looking at my map, I had forgotten to click the button for turn-by-turn directions. Google Maps could show me the streets, but without Wi-Fi it couldn't show the route. Shit! I checked for open Wi-Fi. "DF WiFi Gratis" came up immediately. I clicked it. There were some directions in Spanish I didn't understand, but a box to check. I checked it. Then I had Wi-Fi. Full bars. This entire plaza had free Wi-Fi. Los Angeles had nothing like this.

Weston had lost his phone again. "I think I left it in the truck," he said casually. Classic. So I navigated for us, which was normal. I stuck my phone in the little clip between my handlebars and let the map tell me where to go through a maze of turns. This would be the most confusing navigation I'd done. Usually, we were on country roads or two-lane highways in the middle of nowhere. This route was a mess. Turn after turn and roundabouts and alleys. While I scrolled around the map and cursed under my breath, Weston rolled a joint and took a couple of puffs. He was looking around and soaking up the plaza. I was sweating over my phone. The sun was out and sharp and hot. At 7,300 feet, the elevation of Mexico City made the sun feel closer.

We started biking, with Weston right behind me. Cars were everywhere. Honking. Speeding. Mirrors whizzing by and clipping my panniers. Meanwhile, Weston was taking puffs on his joint and riding gleefully, zigzagging and taking his time. Many of the intersections were clotted and chaotic. I'd pump as quickly as I could through them, only to stop on the other side and see him looking in the other direction. I'd call his name and he'd see me, and grin, and take his time to cross. "Sorry, man. I'm coming. This place is awesome."

At a few of the intersections, we had to carry our bikes over one of the caged-in walkways above the street. The act of lifting my bike with all its gear up the stairs, one step at a time, felt like moving a refrigerator—but a bony, sharp, floppy refrigerator that rolls out of your grip and tears at your shins.

In thirty minutes, we made it about halfway to Beatriz's. Then I lost Weston. I had crossed a bridge, and then an on-ramp, and stopped on the other side. Weston was a bit behind me but in clear view. He was leisurely crossing the bridge, humming and bopping his head. He wasn't looking at me, or anything really, just grinning and bopping. As he was about to cross the on-ramp, maybe twenty feet from me, he veered right, following the natural curve of the road. I shouted his name. I shouted again. He didn't look up at all. He was vibing to unheard music without a care in the world. He merged onto the freeway and disappeared under a bridge and into the flow of 65 m.p.h. traffic.

I stopped yelling his name. I stood there with my mouth wide open. Surely Weston would instantly get struck and killed. He didn't know where we were going. He didn't have a phone. My phone didn't work to make a call in Mexico. Anyway, who would I call?

Crossing back to the bridge, I looked down onto the freeway. He was gone. How the hell would we find each other? But Weston is scrappy. He's fine. Right? He doesn't know where we're headed, but he'll know to find a computer somewhere and e-mail me or Facebook message me. He's not an idiot. Okay, I'll just get to this girl's house and then I can message him. Ugh.

I pushed on, imagining Weston high as hell and finding his way to God knows where. An hour later, I arrived at Beatriz's apartment building and followed the instructions she'd e-mailed me. She lived in a big concrete building with a call box at the front door. The neighborhood seemed quieter, more suburban. A place for families. I buzzed her and she answered right away. "I am coming!" she said, and appeared moments later. Beatriz was short, with black hair and a kind face. She wore ripped jeans and a sweater and was probably in her mid-twenties.

"Where is your other friend?" she asked me. I told her that I had lost him in the city and that I needed to get to Wi-Fi soon so that I could see if he'd tried to e-mail me. She laughed with a worried face and hurried me up to her apartment—two bedrooms, brown carpet, and a balcony full of plants. She said her dad lived with her but was always traveling, so it was mostly just her. The place smelled of cigarettes and weed.

I thanked her profusely for welcoming strangers into her house. "I can tell from your Instagram," she said, "that you are not crazy. I like what you write and the journey you are on. I can tell you are a nice person. I wanted to make sure you saw a good Mexico City." I checked my e-mail, but no Weston yet. I was worried. Beatriz brought me a beer and she lit up a cigarette and we swapped stories. She didn't like her job and fantasized about travel. What Weston and I were doing was very inspiring to her. She had used Couch Surfer to see Europe on a budget, and had traveled quite a bit. I liked her. My phone beeped and I had a Facebook message from Weston. "I found an internet cafe. Oops. I got lost. What's the address? I only have 5 pesos so I can only afford 10 minutes. Maybe someone will give me a bit more."

When I sent him the address, he replied. "Ok I'll ask how to get there. See you soon. :)"

He showed up at the door two hours later, sun-kissed and grinning. I shouted with joy and hugged him. "You motherfucker, I thought you were dead!"

"I am not the dying type," he said through a charming smile. I was so happy to see him. But I also wanted to strangle him, to unleash a tirade against weed and his addiction to it.

Beatriz made us feel at home. We'd ordered in dinner and sat on the carpet telling stories. She rolled a joint with Weston. She took pride in the way she rolled a joint, a delicate precision, and Weston was thrilled by it. "Can you show me?" he said. "Of course! I learned in Europe." She told us about the museums and the cafés and the history of Mexico City. She tried to get us to properly pronounce the volcano to the south of the city. "Popocatépetl," she said. "Pocahantas-potato?" I said. We laughed and laughed as they got higher and higher.

With her expertise, we spent the next two weeks exploring Mexico City. We consumed every morsel of street food we could get our hands on. Tiny Buddha-shaped women, with dark skin and aristocratic noses, sat on the ground next to black round skillets, frying blue corn tortillas, then serving them up with white cheese and mystery meat soaked in an earthy brown sauce. The flavors were addicting. We waited in line for more, along with men in business suits, fashionable hipster girls, a few lucky tourists, and elderly couples.

Mexico City reminded me of Los Angeles in some ways, with beautiful old buildings situated next to hasty new construction and derelict buildings covered in old spray paint and new street art. The elevation makes its temperature entirely dependent on the sun. At 1:00 p.m., the city can feel as hot as the desert. But when the sun goes down, the temperature cools markedly. You'll be out exploring in your T-shirt during the day and end up shivering at sunset.

We researched the best coffee in the city. I wanted a taste of home: some bougie hipster coffee. This was not easy to find. Yelp is so overrun with tourist reviews that it is difficult to differentiate between popular places reviewed by cheesy tourists, and places that got the vibe right. We wanted third-wave coffee, the kind with pourovers and single-origin beans and baristas in denim aprons with thick leather straps and good hair. There had to be a coffee snob or two around Mexico City somewhere, right? Deep googling and horribly auto-translated blog articles helped us find a lead—a place called

El Tercer Lugar, claiming to be "craft coffee made with the precision of science and the care of an artist."

We hopped in a cab and headed straight there.

The cab whirled through the chaos of the Mexico City streets to bring us to the edge of the Zona Rosa, a part of town with European-looking buildings, old fancy mansions, and lush squares with mature trees and beautiful people reading on benches. Beatriz had said it was the "It" area, with the best restaurants and hip people and speakeasies. The place where rich kids open restaurants and bars with their parents' money.

We found the coffee shop on a side street with tall, thin brownstone houses and arching witch-fingered trees. We walked in and immediately felt at home. Exposed brick walls, antique chairs lining a communal table, fancy coffee gadgets behind the bar: all of it overseen by a barista who looked disinterested and intelligent. Absolute snobbery, and perfection. We started to pathetically order in broken Spanish, but the barista mercifully interrupted. "You can just order in English if you want. But thank you for trying."

"Oh, thank God," I said, laughing.

"This place is amazing," Weston said. "We haven't had good coffee since San Diego."

"Did you just get in today?" said the barista.

"Yesterday. It's been quite the journey."

"What brings you to Mexico City?" he asked.

"We're bicycling to Chile."

"You've got to be kidding me," the barista said with wide eyes and a wide grin. We had gotten used to people's surprise, but hadn't heard someone speak with an American accent in a while. It was funny.

"Wow! You speak English really well," I said.

"Because I went to college in Oregon."

"Are you from the U.S.?"

"No, I'm Mexican."

"Oh, you're the owner!? . . . How old are you?"

"Twenty-five. But there are other investors. I'm the majority owner."

"Whoa. Cool," I said.

He was handsome, with dark hair and small round glasses. He told us that he'd been living in Portland, which was where he'd fallen in love with coffee. And where he'd had an epiphany. "I noticed that the coffee-drinking countries weren't the coffee-producing countries," he said. "And that seemed to be a disservice to the places where the coffee comes from. I wanted the best coffee in the world to be roasted right where it grew. Grown, roasted, and enjoyed right here in Mexico. So I started this place."

His name was Diego, and the name of his shop, El Tercer Lugar, translated as the Third Place. "You know the saying? The three places. The first place is your home," Diego told us. "The second place is your work. The third place is where you go by choice. Where you meet friends. Hang out. We want this to be that third place."

As he talked, I realized Diego was the type of person I would be friends with. (I was tempted to write "in real life" to finish that sentence, as if this moment weren't real life.) Whenever I meet someone, even in the most passing way, my brain subconsciously analyzes their speech, their diction, their humor, their demeanor, looking for signals that fit into the preselected categories of "cool" and "like me." For the most part, my brain automatically discards the vast majority of people as forgettable. But sometimes my recognition software triggers a message. "We found one!" The brain then shoots waves of endorphins and energy and words to nudge me toward investigation. This was one of those moments.

Diego explained the finer things of coffee to us for an hour, then invited us to his roasting headquarters down the street. He made a phone call and a pretty young barista showed up to relieve him of duty so that he could spend more time with us.

OVER THE NEXT few days, we spent a lot of time with Diego. It was obvious that he enjoyed shaping our view of Mexico City. He would bring us to a new bar, a restaurant, an art installation, and watch us absorb it all. He was tasting his city through the eyes of a newcomer, seeing it fresh again, glowing with an ambassador's pride.

He took us to a wild and huge market, full of fruits we had never seen and fish and pigs split down the middle and displayed. The smell of ripe fruit, flowers, raw meat, spices, mushrooms... it was almost too much to handle. The smells combined to make a new aroma, unrecognizable to the brain, alien.

He took us to the National Museum of Anthropology, a giant building too big for one visit, overflowing with the most important artifacts of the Maya, Aztecs, and all the native peoples of Meso-america. I stumbled through the halls, slack-jaw gawking at statues and bones, trying to read the descriptions for every stone head, every hieroglyph, every carved column.

At the center of the museum's capacious main entry hall we came upon a stone circle twelve feet across and intricately carved. It was lit up and wanted to be noticed. In the middle was a face and then carved scenes radiating out. I knew it immediately. The Mayan cal-endar, I whispered to myself. I had seen it printed on countless Mexi-can shirts and flags and painted on walls. There it was, the real one. I walked up to it as if possessed by it and went straight to the plaque. No. It isn't a Mayan calendar. It isn't even Mayan. It's Aztec. That is a common mistake, it said. It's also not exactly a calendar. Anthropolo-gists disagree, but modern scholars now believe it was a battle floor, a ritualistic altar for gladiator sacrifices. It does seem to depict differ-ent eras, and it has the Sun God in its center. So its proper name is the Sun Stone, or the Stone of the Five Eras. It seems to have been carved in the early 1500s, and wasn't meant to be displayed upright on a wall, as it is now. It was on the ground, like a holy boxing ring, where warriors would wrestle or fight to the death. Or it was an altar for sacrifices. I stood there, imagining their blood flowing through the carved stone images as they died.

Pre-Columbian cultures have always been a keen interest of mine—the complexities of their cities and customs, all developing in the absence of the arch, the wheel, and for the most part, written language. The stories of their doomed resistance to European con-quest and disease. Their religions, their kings, their sacrifices. How the Spanish tricked them, wowed them with firepower, won their trust only to lie and steal from them, so rabid were those Christian warriors for gold and power. How the contagion of greed mixed with evangelism led Spain and Portugal to take over a landmass much larger than Europe, toppling empires that had been thousands of years in the making. All the while congratulating themselves for civilizing the savages.

As I walked through the museum, a familiar sense of guilt set in. My white skin, my European heritage. Europe had gotten rich off stolen gold. Stolen labor. Stolen land. The United States prides itself in being this great democratic experiment—a modern representative democracy of 300 million inhabitants that has a low corruption rate and the largest economy in the world. I love my country. I love reading the words of the Founding Fathers, the thoughts they tested while trying to build a nation on virtue, wisdom, and fairness. But the wealth, beauty, and privilege of the West parades on top of the bones of the defeated.

Mexicans tell their story in a different way than we do in the United States. They show patriotism, but less confidence. They cannot cover up what happened to their indigenous people. There were too many of them. Their native cultures were too large to erase or silence. In modern Mexico, and through most of Latin America, both the original cultures and the conquests of imperial Catholicism are still everywhere apparent. Maybe that's why I sensed in Mexico that people see their past more soberly. They seemed to hold pride and shame in the same hand.

Perhaps a Mexican can see the United States more clearly than we can, too. Maybe our neighbors can view our imperialism around the world, our bloodstained hands, with more understanding than I ever did as a kid. I was told that America won wars (besides the Vietnam War), and led the world in freedom and democracy, and gave its people the best lives possible. I never questioned that, until I traveled.

Mexico City is full of the ghosts of a brutal past. Of dead Mayan kings, Aztec kings, and the mystery pyramids of a time before the Aztecs, a mystery to them and a mystery to us. The footprints of these people, these tumultuous centuries, exist freshly. More like Europe, I would guess. But for me, markedly different than in the

United States. You can feel it in Mexico City all around you, in the cathedrals built by captured slaves. Built to demand worship by the sword. Built to ensure every last drop of gold made it back to Spain.

The giant complex city had seduced me. All it took was a couple good new friends as guides, and the surprise that comes from a place exceeding expectations, lazy biases, and half-thought thoughts. I'm sure my mom had said at some point, "Mexico City is the most dangerous city in the world." Maybe so, but I hadn't seen that. I saw incredible coffee and stylish people and the best museum ever. Mexico City was my dirty juggernaut of charm and creative energy.

The newness and surprise of the city messed with my sense of time. I was tasting the street food and learning the history and gawking at the architecture and time was slow and fast. Days flew by. But I felt like I'd been there for months. I was living in a vortex, an autonomous moment.

After a glorious week exploring the city, we had Thanksgiving with Diego and told stories of how it's done in the States. We Face-Timed our families. I spoke to my mom. And then my dad. Weston spoke to his mom and not his dad. I missed my family and missed the feeling of an American holiday. I thought about missing Christmas. Being on a beach in southern Mexico or El Salvador for Christmas was beautiful and romantic, but somehow it sounded so unappealing. I began to think about a visit home to catch my breath.

WE SPENT ONE more week in Mexico City. We weren't ready to leave it just yet. Weston sat at cafés and swiped his way through Tinder. He wanted to find a beautiful Latin girl, here and there, to have a romp with. But as he swiped over and over, and chatted with girls and more girls, he discovered that this was harder than he thought it would be. A friend had told him to match as many as he could, swipe right on all of them, and then sort through the matches. He included in his profile that he was "just passing through, cycling to Patagonia" to make clear that he wasn't looking for a relationship. He just wanted to have fun. Unfortunately for his libido, women didn't find much appeal in that. He'd chat with a lady, and make himself crystal clear, and they'd stop chatting back. "I'm finally a guy who's honest and not playing games, and they want none of it," he said.

Weston wanted me to cut loose and be freer, too. He kept asking me if I wanted to go to a gay bar. "We're in a big city now, there's got to be tons of gay guys here. Don't you want to kiss someone? Get a little drunk and have fun?" I wished I could be so free. I wished I could be flippant. But I couldn't.

He convinced me to download Tinder on my phone. I swiped through some cute boys, but couldn't take it seriously. I mostly laughed and showed him profiles that amused me. Guys without shirts, lying in their beds in only underwear, pushing their butts out in unnatural ways. Or grabbing a bulge. Wearing sunglasses. In bed.

I kept thinking about the last conversation I had with my mom about my sexuality. I could hear her in my ear.

It was two years ago, on the phone. She had called me after finding out that I'd started a gay Bible study group.

I was living in San Diego and stepping closer to accepting myself. A major reason I hadn't kissed a boy, or tried to date, or even examined the theology around homosexuality was that I had never seen a gay Christian man modeled for me. I didn't know any. And I deduced, if there wasn't one, maybe that's because something about being gay inherently corrupts the relationship with God. But a friend said to me, "Jed, there's always someone that goes first. Maybe God wants you to be that person in your community. Be the godly Christian gay man you wished you'd seen." I was shaken. I'd expected to be told and shown, not commissioned.

I started going to a gay-affirming church. I asked them if I could start a Bible study for young gay men, a support group to navigate the oddness of being a paradox: a believer in a religion that didn't believe in us. They said yes. I thought, Maybe if I start this, I can finally meet a godly gay man and find love. Maybe we can model a Christ-centered gay relationship. I wrote on Facebook about my decision to start the study. I said I wasn't convinced being gay was against God's plan. I said I was no longer running from my questions, but looking for answers.

My mom called me the moment she read it. "Jed, we need to discuss this," she said, her voice controlled and curt. It was different from any voice I'd ever heard her use.

"What's wrong, Mom?"

"I read what you wrote on Facebook."

My face got hot and my heart started pounding. I hadn't even thought about her reading it. Somehow I thought only my friends would see my post. I forgot my mom would be there, first in line.

"It breaks my heart, Jed."

"I don't know what to say, Mom. I didn't really mean for you to read tha—"

"The fact that you would say those words, it's very sad and not you. You just give up? You think you can't overcome that? Sexual sin is one of the darkest sins, because it springs from the deepest part of us."

I knew she believed these things. But we'd had years of avoiding the conversation. I'd been such a good Christian boy, never making any overt statements affirming homosexuality. I'd been all over the map, believing it was okay, not believing . . . flip-flopping back and forth. I guess the fact that I'd never come home with a boyfriend, or shown any outward sign that I was still gay, let her believe that I'd been in the process of healing, of reprogramming, of getting over my little "gay phase."

"Mom, it's not like I've walked away from my faith. I'm just being honest with my journey."

"I love you so much, and I just want you to be safe and I feel like you lean too heavily on your own understanding. You don't seem to respect the word of God. It has survived for thousands of years, through civilizations, and you think your one life knows more than it?"

"I am not saying that, Mom."

"I don't want you calling yourself gay. I don't believe that is the truth."

"Well, Mom, it's an honest observation. I am not attracted to girls." It was much easier for me to say "not attracted to girls" than to use the affirmative "I am attracted to boys."

"Well, I believe that you just haven't met the right girl yet. I am praying that a girl comes along and inflames your passions. I know

God will provide that. I've been praying about this since you were two years old."

"What do you mean, two years old?"

"Yes. Your father said that he thought you might be gay when you were two. Why on earth would any normal father say such things? It was like he spoke a curse over you, and I prayed to God many times to break the curse that your father spoke over you. It was like he was passing his sexual confusion on to you. He left a wake of sexual pain, adultery, more than you know. I believe that had an impact on your development. I've been praying for years. It makes me so frightened to hear you speak this way, Jed."

"Mom, I don't know what to tell you. I know you love me and want to protect me, but—"

"You need to look honestly at the cost of your father's choices, he hurt a lot of people. And he hurt you by not being a right example to you. I've worked for thirty years to forgive him, to process the pain and betrayal. But you haven't. You don't know the effects. You wanting to accept these things is not a sign of strength, it's confusion."

"Ugh. I just don't see it that way—"

"It is an abomination. It disgusts me."

I got quiet. I froze at that word. I had never heard my sweet mother use a word like *disgust*, much less direct it at me. It echoed in my head like a gong. I felt my jaw tighten and then my fear morphing into anger.

"Mom, don't say that. Don't talk about things you don't understand."

But she didn't miss a beat. "I know what God says about it, and what more do I need to know? It isn't ambiguous language. I love you dearly, and it is a mother's job to protect her child. I know you're an adult and I fear every day for you. To see you embrace a lifestyle that leads to disease and death? You will be childless. It is a sad life. I don't want that for you. God doesn't either. What kind of mother would I be if I encouraged you to walk down this path? Is that what you want, a mother who doesn't care about her son?"

Her words were frenzied and strange. As if something exploded from pressure. As if she had stored up thousands of words over decades for this exact conversation. Fearing I might be corrupted by the "mainstream media" and the ideas of the secular world. Fearing I would rebel. Fearing I would contract AIDS and die like so many gays on TV from the eighties.

"I'm heartbroken, Jed."

The conversation was terrible and trailed off and I said I needed to go. My thoughts were formless and hot and achy.

I hadn't spoken to her about it since then. For two years. We just ignored it.

I DELETED THE Tinder app. It didn't feel right. If I was going to be gay, it had to be monumental and honorable and moral. I couldn't meet my almighty Christian husband, the man that would impress everyone and change everyone's minds, on an app.

As the second week ended, what had been the wonders of the city settled into the stuff of everyday living. We knew our way around. Beatriz had work and things to do and let us alone. Even Diego had things to do. We started to feel like an imposition. I found myself ready to leave. No less in love with Mexico City, but busy in my head. The Tinder thing had shaken me up a little. Weston was so adamant about me kissing someone, having fun. I didn't want to know I could download Tinder again and look. I didn't want temptation. I wanted the road. My questions about life and God diminished when I was biking into new territory. My purpose became where to camp, where to find food, how to avoid angry dogs, on the collapsing distance between myself and Patagonia. There was no time for other confusions.

NICARAGUA

COSTA RICA

PANAMA

MANAGUA

SAN JUAN DEL SUR

TAMARINDO

LIBERIA

LAGUNA DE ARENAL

LIMÓN

PUERTO VIEJO DE TALAMANCA

BOCAS DEL TORO

MOUNTAINTOP SHACK HOSTEL

PANAMA CANAL

SAN BLAS ISLANDS

PANAMA CITY

DARIEN GAP

Chapter 9

WHAT HAPPENS IF I GO HOME?
(Oaxaca and Christmas)

10,441 miles to go

Weston and I said goodbyes to Beatriz and Diego. Weston gladly accepted a gift of weed from Diego and we prepared to head south. Diego had raved about Oaxaca, 280 miles southeast of us . . . famous for its mezcal and spirituality.

Before we left town, I FaceTimed my mom once more. She liked me to talk to her before we headed out into the backroads or camping. She liked "to know how hard to pray." She asked me to come home for Christmas to see my family and my new baby niece. She said, "This baby will only have her first Christmas once, and you're going to miss it?"

"Mom, I can't leave the road," I told her. "It's cheating."

"Cheating on who? Cheating what?"

"I feel like I have to stay on the bike and not leave. It's part of my rite of passage."

"Jed. I am sixty-six years old. When you're my age, things like that don't matter. What matters is time spent with those you love, and not missing moments that matter. Don't be stubborn. This is your trip. This is your life. Do what you want. No one that I've ever heard of has ridden a bicycle clear from Oregon to Mexico City. And you'll go right back down there. Just come home for a couple weeks and hold this baby and see your momma. I've prayed you wouldn't die every day in Mexico and here you are alive, and I think God owes me the chance to lay eyes on you."

I said I'd think about it.

We bused out of town far enough to clear all the chaos of city congestion, then started biking. Soon the terrain was hilly and green. Not wild or remote, but easy two-lane streets. I biked for a day and I thought on it. My mom's words rang in my ear. "Cheating who?" I remembered Andrew Morgan (the fellow whose trip inspired mine) and his words to me: "This trip belongs to you, no one else. Don't let anyone dictate your life to you." I walked out the idea in my mind. *If I do it, I'll just go and come right back. Maybe Weston will want to do that, too. We can ship our bikes or just leave them in Oaxaca and come back for them.* It felt good to think about. Felt calming and free. Felt like I was in control of my trip and my story. On a rest break, I brought it up.

"Weston?" I said. "I think I may go home for Christmas."

"Really!?" he said. His surprise embarrassed me. He thought a moment. "But you'll come back, right?"

"Of course I'll come back. Would you want to go home, too?"

"No. I don't have the money. And I wouldn't want to spend it on that anyway. I'm here to be here."

I felt like a fake. And maybe I was. But my heart desired to see my family and my baby niece, and even saying it out loud felt good. So good that my embarrassment at Weston's certainty in staying didn't deter me. I had decided. I had only been on the road three and a half months, but I was going home for Christmas. Because I wanted to.

Weston and I rode to Oaxaca in less than a week. We surprised ourselves at how quickly we readjusted to biking after such a long break. The road did get more remote, winding, mountainous. But the elevation changes weren't terrible, as we were already high and remained on the plateau. The nights were chilly and the days sharp and sunny. Trees and farms and cows kept us company along the way. We stayed mostly in cheap hotels in the towns that sprinkled the route.

We pulled into Oaxaca in the early evening and went straight into a mezcal bar. We got two shots and tried the famous drink. It tasted like tequila, but smoky and earthy. The bartender was proud of it and handed it to us over the bar like a magic potion. "Is not like other alcohol. Doesn't make you drunk. No crazy. It makes you awake. Alive," he said. We asked him about hostels and he told us of a good one just a block away.

Oaxaca is a famous escape for artists and weirdos. A place with magical energy. Close enough to Mexico City to be a weekend get-away. A place for second homes and retreats.

Diego had put us on e-mail with a local Oaxacan archaeologist. He had spent decades studying the nearby ruins of Monte Albán, one of the oldest archaeological sites in Mexico. The archaeologist, named Alfonso, responded with a short e-mail: "I have an extra room. You are welcome to be my guests." We met him in town the next day and he offered to take us to his work at the ruins. He was a small, soft-spoken man who wore loose clothes and a khaki bucket hat. We sat in the bed of his truck and he showed us worn-down pyramids and grass mounds that looked like nothing but were intact ancient pre-Columbian homes, temples, and pantries.

We stayed with Alfonso for five days. His quiet voice and knowl-edge of the pre-Columbian world made for lovely, gentle conversa-tion on the terrace of his home. The house was modest and modern, with big glass windows and books stacked high along every wall. We had our own room and bathroom, which was nice, especially as Weston found himself unable to keep food down. Something he'd eaten, we supposed. When Alfonso said that Oaxaca was famous for mushrooms and shamans and guided experiences, Weston's gray complexion perked up. He began talking to people he met in town, to backpackers with dreads and baggy pants, with bartenders. He was investigating. Finally, falling asleep on Alfonso's futon, side by side as we always were, he told me that he'd found a spot in the moun-tains that hosted mushroom ceremonies. "A place with real magi-cians. Indigenous wisdom. And travelers from all over." He told me he was going to go.

"Perfect," I said. "Why don't you do that, and I'll go home for a few weeks and meet you back here."

"I think a bunch of homies are doing New Year's in Nicaragua. I may try to get down there by then."

"Oh," I said. "Shit. Well, what would I do with my bike? And I'd be missing El Salvador and Guatemala." But truth be told, we were behind schedule, and if I was to track my timeline right, to follow the dry season all the way south and avoid bad weather, to reach Patagonia in the Southern Hemisphere's summer, I needed to be in Panama by January. That was 2,800 kilometers from Oaxaca, or 1,740 miles. We'd spent too much time in cities and towns and making memories with new friends and waiting out the cartel. But since my purity was already ruined by deciding to go home, I could go home, then jump to Nicaragua. Which is what I proposed to Weston.

"What if I mail my bike to wherever New Year's is gonna be, and then we meet there?' I said.

"Fine by me," he said.

So I made plans to bus back to Mexico City, mail my bike to Nicaragua, fly to Nashville, then fly to Nicaragua after Christmas. While I was booking flights, Weston organized his spirit quest and terrorized the bathroom with diarrhea.

"I'll wait for you to leave, then I'll go to the mountain," he said. "I don't want you tainting the vibe."

"What does that mean?" I laughed.

"It's spiritual. You don't like stuff like this."

"I'm spiritual!" I said.

"Yeah, but you're like churchy. This is witchy. Pagan. You wouldn't like it. And mushrooms make you sensitive to people's energy. You'll fuck it up," he said with a grin.

"Oh. Well, in that case, yeah, I wouldn't want to harsh your mellow."

We both chuckled and I felt good with our choices. The moment I made the decision to go, I felt a weight lift from me.

I LANDED IN Nashville with stinging wet eyes and a lump in my throat.

My mom picked me up in her shiny Nissan.

"Not a scratch on you," she said. "Prayer works!" She leaped from the car and hugged me.

"Or perhaps Mexico isn't as dangerous as you thought, Mom," I said with a smirk. I was playing it cool.

"Don't take this away from the Lord," she said.

I got in the car and we headed down the interstate at 70 miles per hour. It felt like flying. The roads seemed so freshly paved. I didn't have my bike stored underneath or in the trunk. I felt so light. Just my body and a little bag. It was a twenty-minute ride from the airport to my mom's house, and I was glued to the window. The houses had no fences, no walled-in courtyards, no security gates. The yards looked manicured and orderly.

The Nashville trees were without leaves, and everything felt crisp and organized. The twenty miles from the airport to my childhood home would've been almost a day's ride on the bike. I was staring at everything. My mom was talking about the holiday plans. I'd slipped right back into a previous life. The bike might have been a dream. We were home before I would've had time to tie my bags to the rack.

My sister and new baby niece were waiting at the house. I held the baby and thought about how life had moved on without me. I thought of my dad saying, "No one will change. Everyone will be the same when you get back." In this case, that was a lie. This baby was twice as big as when I saw her last. She had a different, fuller face. She had a personality. I had missed her becoming herself.

I was home for ten days. I saw old friends, and we went to Santa's, our favorite karaoke bar. We sang and drank cheap beer and they asked me all the standard questions. "Were you scared?" "How'd you charge your phone?" I had canned answers at this point.

I hated jokes like "Hey, you're home!? Did you quit? You can't just come back, cheater!" I'd give a snarky response. "Did you just bike to Mexico City? Or did I? I can do what I want. This is my trip." They'd laugh and say, "Good point."

I had Christmas with my mom and siblings and the new baby. We ate honey-baked ham and watched old home videos. We laughed a lot and did next to nothing. My brother said, "How's the trip so far?"

"Good . . . and hard," I said.

"Cool." And we didn't speak of it again.

My mom and I didn't talk about anything too serious. We'd never talked about my sexuality in person. Only over the phone. Like twice. And by e-mail, once. And she was so happy to see me, I knew she wouldn't taint it all with a confrontation. Neither would I. I wonder how many millions of relationships are alive because of this, avoiding conversations.

I told her stories about Weston, about how much he loved weed, about getting lost in Mexico City and buying drugs. I told her these things to punish her for forcing me to invite someone else. I'm not sure why I felt the need to challenge my mother with these stories. She had been right—I was grateful she'd made me bring a friend, and I indeed loved Weston. Yet some spiteful teenager inside me wanted to poke at her.

My mom would walk past me and put her hand on my shoulder and leave it a little too long. She would sit next to me at dinner and pat my knee and talk about her dogs or how the deer kept eating all her flowers. She kept touching me. She would ask me the same questions over and over with different words, as if the act of talking was the goal, not the exchange of information. And she would often launch into stories of walking across America. Some I'd never heard.

"You know why I want you to be so careful on those roads? I was walking in Texas, minding my own business, your father way on up ahead of me because he didn't like walking as slow as I needed to, and I got hit by a car going sixty miles an hour. This was before cell phones in the car, so I don't know why they didn't see me, it was broad daylight. But they hit me square in my backpack and I flew forty feet in the air. And I landed on my backpack, on the grass lawn of a mortuary. When I opened my eyes and realized I was alive, and saw that mortuary, can you believe it!? My pack saved my life. Well, the Lord saved my life, but used the backpack," she said with a laugh. "With you on a bike, I just worry so much, but I trust if the Lord could land me in a mortuary, and wink at me like that with a little joke, He'll do the same for you."

I was glad to have come home to see her, if for no other reason than to make her as happy as she was that Christmas.

"You know there's a lot of Scripture that talks about journeys, walking through the desert. Have you been reading the Bible I gave you?"

"Oh yes, I have," I said, lying. "It means a lot to me that you gave me your Bible from the walk, truly," I said, not lying. It hadn't dawned on me until that moment that I hadn't read the Bible once on my trip. I hadn't wanted to. But I had seen it in my bags. I had felt it on my bike, traveling with me. God with me.

After the holiday and good lazy days with my mom, it was time to drive down and see my dad. He had been spending most of his time in Mississippi with his girlfriend. I had met her once before. She was from there and was quick-witted and crass in a classy way. She had a refinement about her but would gossip with language like "horse-shit" and "a real backwoods racist asshole." I liked her right away.

She gave my dad shit. She didn't worship him or coddle him. She just liked him. And I had never seen him that way with anyone.

It was the flirtatiousness of twenty-year-olds. Strange and simultaneously inspiring.

Ever since my dad divorced my stepmom back in 2006, his romantic life was a minefield in the family. Especially for my sisters. He'd been married to my stepmom for seventeen years. My half sister came from that marriage, which I had thought would last. They seemed so in love. Then it ended. I was twenty-three years old. My sisters hated any new woman that came close. "This bitch can't just pretend like we're gonna play house with her," my older sister would say. My brother and I didn't hate anyone, we just didn't care to invest ourselves. I was off in California, far away from Tennessee. I wanted my dad to be happy, but I also wanted him to be with someone that wouldn't take advantage of him, or be terribly annoying. I had discovered my dad's humanity pretty early. He was never a god. Not like my mom. He was my friend.

When he called me to tell me he was divorcing my stepmom, I asked him why. He said he wasn't in love and he'd met someone else. I told him I was disappointed in him. He couldn't stay married. To me, it seemed like he married the way other people date.

"Dad, you think love is the feeling of being in love, and when the feeling fades, you think it's because you made a mistake. So you leave. That's not love, that's not commitment," I said, with the confidence of never-married, Christian arrogance.

"Jed, I remember my dad was a real asshole. I remember he took me out in a boat, when I was a teenager, and he had been real bad to my mother, and he said, you can hate me, or not, but that's up to you, I'm the only father you'll ever have. You can hate me, but I'm just doing my best. He took me out in that boat and gave me permission to hate him. Took the rage right out of me. So, I'm sorry. But I'm tired of being sorry. I took all the blame with the divorce from your mother. And that's fine. But I can't take it anymore. I'm not sorry anymore. Life is really complicated. I hope you won't hate me."

That took the rage right out of me. I felt his tiredness with himself. He was tired of guilt. Tired of mistakes. Tired of carrying it all. He wanted freedom. My sisters weren't ready to give it to him. I don't know if my brother was. I was.

That conversation had a big impact on me. Not just in humanizing my father, but in acquiescing to vice. I was in my twenties and fighting my vices, my sexuality, my manipulations . . . and here was my dad saying "I used to fight them. I quit that."

Maybe you'd think it was inspiring to hear that kind of freedom. It was terrifying. He had wrecked several families, and left daughters that wanted to strangle him. Ex-wives spoke of him like a hurricane they'd lived through. This was life? Quitting the fight and accepting yourself, flaws and all? I don't want to accept my flaws.

I was melancholy about it all for a while. Then, like God hand-delivered some hope into my hands, I was at a New Year's party a few months later and a guy I didn't know gave a toast. He was drunk but I think he said it right. "Be ever at peace with your neighbors, ever at war with your vices, and let every year find you a better man, that's ol' Benjy Franklin!" he said, and cheersed his beer, splashing it high.

In a moment, my thoughts were beyond the party, floating above us. "Ever at war with your vices." It didn't say "let each year have you conquering a new vice." No. It wasn't about winning. It was about fighting. Continuing the project of improvement. The intention and effort was what built character. Not success. That changed a lot of things for me. I think it kept me from kissing boys for another four years, thinking that was a vice I had to fight forever. I think it also kept me from nihilistic meltdown. It was a double-edged sword.

I never felt victimized by divorce. I never longed for some cohesive family unit. I can't explain why. I just didn't like the thick air that would form around my mom when she would complain about my dad. As for me, divorce was what normal families did. It's all I knew and all I remembered. Did my dad still love me? Yes. Did my mom still love me? Yes. Did my stepmom still love me? Sure. Then what's the big deal?

But my sisters felt the divorces differently. They hated the blonde my dad had dated for a while. Then he met Kelley. She was smart and financially independent and had a good family and didn't give two shits about my dad's writing fame or money. But she didn't stand a chance. My sisters didn't like Kelley. Not necessarily because of anything she did; they just didn't want anything to do with another woman. "Dad thinks we're just gonna invite her in, like she's part of the family?" my older sister would say. "I'm not doing this with every flavor of the month."

In the past, my dad would have fought for my sisters. He would have said, "Kelley is different, this one is real." He would have made time and tried to explain himself and sought out the girls over and over, bending over backward. He did try for about a year, but then something snapped. It dawned on him that he'd been apologizing his whole life. He'd been begging for forgiveness since the mid-eighties. He was older now. He grew tired of the theatrics and decided to retreat. Nowadays, he spent most of his time at Kelley's house in Mississippi. My dad was in love with Kelley, in a way I'd never seen before. There was a completeness, a brightness, an absence of guilt or escape. Seeing them together, it was strange. I wondered if they were each other's soul mate, and if that meant my mom and dad never were. And yet, here I am. It was all confusing.

The politics of family, my dad staying at the farm, my sisters avoiding him, my brother avoiding conflict and not taking sides, the expectations of Christmas and family harmony, the things unsaid and the hurt buried—I didn't like it. It was like a squirming thing under the covers on a bed. It made me remember why I liked living in California, free from the odd feelings of family obligation and love. Somewhere inside my relationship to my family was the root of fear, fear of my sexuality, the root of my faith in God. My friends in California and the life I'd built out there were all on top of this small group of people that made me. I wondered for a moment if I had gotten on my bicycle to escape my family. Then I thought, "No, I love these idiots. This mess is what made me. I just need to control my doses. It's easy to overdose and get sick."

So it was just me, my dad, and Kelley down on his farm for a night. We ordered in Indian food and Kelley was chatty.

My dad didn't say much. He was watching us talk. I thought he would ask me all kinds of questions about the trip, and slide into story mode about the first months of his great walk. But he didn't. The emotion of Christmas seemed to eat him alive. The decision not to beg my sisters to come down. I think he had asked my brother, but he hadn't come. The tension turned my dad into an introvert. I think he watched as Kelley and I laughed and hit it off, and was glad, but also sad that it was only me. I think he was quiet because his thoughts were loud. At the end of dinner, Dad, in a peacocky way, said to me in front of Kelley, "Maybe we come visit you in Paraguay? Or Peru? Or Patagonia? Maybe we go on a trip and treat your tired legs to a nice hotel room. I've never been to South America."

Kelley seemed thrilled. "Oh, yes! I've hardly ever been outside of Mississippi. I've barely ever seen a mountain. Let's go drink wine and see mountains!" Her thick southern accent was like music in the room.

No definitive plans were set, but the sweet intention was comforting. I loved the thought of adventuring with my dad. Of witnessing something foreign to both of us, together, for the first time.

At first arrival in Nashville, I'd thought my dad's advice was wrong. Home had changed, I had changed, and I was sad for it to flow by without me. I had a new niece. My sisters weren't talking to my dad's soon-to-be fiancée. Things felt like they'd been advancing quickly. But even a few days later, as Christmas wrapping paper was being thrown away and the post-holiday melancholy of monotony set in, I saw the truth of my father's words. The place went right back to normal, and that normalcy was what I was escaping. I had left my family for California, and now left California for the road. Not forever, but for this season. Only a year more. And it would be here when I got back. Perhaps tweaked and slightly changed, but not transformed. It would be the thing I stepped away from. It would be the routine I could return to.

WHEN THE TIME came to go back, I e-mailed Weston. He was already at the beachside hotel in Nicaragua with friends. He said my bike had arrived. He also said he had tracked down some San Pedro cactus and would be making a potion on New Year's Eve. I didn't ask follow-up questions.

I had seen and tasted home. It was still there. But I had dethroned it from my infatuated desire in Mexico. I could return to the bike, knowing that all the comforts of home would be waiting for me when I was ready. I was also reminded of what I was looking for. A shaking-off of that film over my body I feel at home. Of confusion. Of self-loathing. Of constriction. I had to peel it back and see myself clean of what I had been told.

I boarded my plane for Nicaragua, more excited than I had expected. From Managua, the capital city, I bused my way to the thatched-roof beachside haven of Maderas Village on the west coast. The stress of boxing up my bike and finding a service to mail it had paid off. There it was, the box beaten and crumpled, but all together. I felt affection for my bike, seeing it there waiting for me. Like a dog. I pictured it wagging its tail to see me.

A few of our friends from LA and New York were there. They had planned this group trip to Maderas Village and talked about the fun drugs and parties we'd enjoy for New Year's. Weston quickly said yes and had already been down here a week. I hadn't checked in on him much over the holiday. But I did miss him. Even ten days apart now felt like the loss of a limb.

Maderas Village is perched on a dusty cliff overlooking the Pacific coast of Nicaragua. The trees were crispy, and the dust from the dirt road kicked up into the air, coating every low leaf. It was the dry season. The world was browned, the air hot, the ocean cool and inviting. I walked up the property looking for friends, passing by a few cabins and a main house, and asked an overly tan man in short board shorts and Ray-Bans if he knew Weston. The guy was obviously American. "Oh yeah, he's making some magic potion up behind the last cabins. Just keep walking up the hill."

I found him in the woods, stirring a cauldron over a wood fire with people I didn't know. He was shirtless, shoeless, with tattered khaki shorts and a big stick stirring the brown milky substance in the pot. The strangers were sun-crispy and barefoot, too, staring intently into the mixture. "Jed!" Weston exclaimed, as happy to see me as I was to see him. "Come come! I got us some San Pedro cactus, and I'm making a potion. I have to boil it for twelve hours, then drain it with this cheesecloth. We're on hour two."

"You have to stir it for ten more hours!?" I asked.

"Yeah, or it will burn."

"What does San Pedro do to you?" I felt like a dad asking about his son's new toy.

"It's one of three cactuses with mescaline," Weston explained. "In the right doses, it makes you euphoric, gives you visions, exposes the parts of the brain that can only be reached by this. It's actually one of the safest natural ways to experience an altered spiritual state. Not like datura or angel's trumpet, which can kill you. You just don't want to drink a lot of this, because it tastes like worm snot."

"It's nasty? Yikes."

"Well, yeah. But it's magic that has to be respected. It's called the Grandfather in shaman lore. He is wise and guides you gently with love. But doesn't that make you ask questions? About God or the universe? Why would the universe make parts of our brains, parts of us, only accessible by these plants he placed around us in nature? Seems to me like we're supposed to access truth through them. Nature is reaching out to teach us right now, show us things, because our society is killing nature. Mescaline is one of the doors the universe wants us to walk through. And it's a bitch to prepare right. But I think it's worth it."

"Wow, sounds amazing," I said, no longer patronizing. Actually interested.

"Yeah, but it's better to be sober and have an empty stomach for six to twelve hours before, or you'll vomit. So I'm starving. But it's worth it. Makes it last longer. I've got to stir for a few more hours; go have a look around this place. It's beautiful. Go stake a hammock spot. Our homies are down at the beach."

"How was your Oaxacan mushroom thing?" I asked.

"Incredible. This house in the mountains with people from all over. Germans, Canadians. It wasn't one of those Mickey Mouse hostels for tourists. It's the real people. We did a full-moon hike, tripping, and I went off by myself and got lost in the woods and I was barefoot and I must've been out there for six hours and the sun came up and it was amazing. You wouldn't have liked the place, though, it was all psychedelics and crystals."

I laughed. "You know me so well."

I left Weston to his potion and explored the little coastal resort. Cabins made of bamboo and palapa roofs. A main open-air lounge attached to a communal kitchen. Hammocks everywhere. Weston and his salty buddies had their magic juice and the sun got low and the howler monkeys started screaming and I was back.

Weston stayed high most of the time at Maderas Village, smiling and lying in a hammock, or mixing potions and planting the sliced tops of his San Pedro cactuses around the property. He said he didn't want to kill the cactuses, just "borrow" them. He filled me in on his travels, what it was like to bus across Guatemala and El Salvador, lugging his bicycle and his dirty panniers. He had spent Christmas on a beach in El Salvador and visited Lake Atitlán in the Guatemalan highlands. "So many rich California hippies renting houses," he said. "It was too expensive for me."

I thought I would be sad, hearing him describe these places I had missed. But I wasn't. If anything, I was sad I couldn't brag about having been there.

We had six days on the coast in Nicaragua to party with our

friends, tell stories, and work on our sunburns. January 1, 2014, arrived with a bonfire on the beach. I felt wild. This was the year I would finish my trip, and I was already excited for it to be over. I'd learned what life on a bicycle was like. I'd escaped the office life and learned some shit. In many ways, I'd exchanged an old routine for a new one. No mind-reshaping epiphany had come, and I didn't feel like it was on its way. I hadn't read my Bible once on the trip. I hadn't kissed anyone. I hadn't tried any crazy drugs. I was excited to see Panama, Colombia, Peru, Patagonia. I was. But the damn bike. I wanted to take more buses. To skip the boring parts. But I also didn't want to. I felt the duty of the promise I made myself and the expectations of all my friends watching. This trip had become my job. Hourly, my thoughts transitioned from dread to duty to excitement to anxious in a cycle.

By then, Weston had developed a crush on a Swedish girl, and he wanted to follow her to a surf spot on the coast of Costa Rica. He needed sex, he said. I said that was fine, I'd meet him down in Costa Rica. I was rejuvenated from having spent ten days at home. If Weston needed more time to enjoy the beach, to make his potion, to have some sex, I was fine with that. He would ride with her in a surf van. I would bike alone down the rest of Nicaragua and into Costa Rica. It would be my first time biking alone.

On January 5, I packed up my bike. The task had become a ritual, robotic and easy. Tie my backpack onto the back. Tuck my sleeping bag next to it, resting them both on the rack between the panniers. Tie my boots by their shoelaces to my backpack. Take my rope, which by now was worn and fraying, and tie it back and forth across my things to secure them. Fill my water bottles. Done.

I said goodbye to the Nicaraguan beach, to Weston and our sunburned friends, and headed south.

BIKING TO THE Costa Rican border over a few days, I stayed at tiny hotels for cheap. I didn't talk to anyone except as a means to an end. I listened to *Radiolab* episodes in my headphones and biked. I passed farms, brown in the dry season. I rode around goats and emaciated horses in the road. I went through towns that looked much like the ones I'd seen in Mexico. At the border check, tourists swarmed off buses to get their passports stamped. I waited in line, and when I got to the front the border agent asked for proof of a departing flight.

"A departing flight? From Costa Rica? Oh, I don't have one," I said.

"Costa Rica requires that you have proof of a temporary stay. You will not be admitted without proof. You need proof of a purchased flight out," the border agent said, annoyed that I hadn't done my research.

"Well, I don't have that because I'm riding my bicycle. I'm going to Patagonia?"

"Patagonia? What is that?"

"Yes, the bottom of Chile."

"You're riding a bicycle to Chile? Where is this bicycle?"

I pointed through the glass window to the bike outside, leaning on a railing. My pointing and the agent's craning his neck caused the twenty or so people in line behind me to turn around and see what we were looking at. A crusty, dusty bike piled with bags.

"Look, I have passport stamps in Mexico, and Nicaragua, coming in and out, see, temporary," I said, flipping through my passport in his direction. "I am going to leave Costa Rica in about three weeks, I promise."

He pulled his lips into his teeth while he scrutinized my passport. Then he peered out at my bike again.

"Patagonia," he said to himself, as he loudly stamped my passport and handed it back. Only then did he offer a flat smile, proud of himself for letting me into his country.

Costa Rica was quickly greener and the hills steeper than Nicaragua. The pavement was fresh and the country felt different. Richer. I enjoyed the pace of being alone, stopping at a whim, taking an impromptu nap under a tree. I would have been frightened to cycle alone a few months ago, but this was my new life, and life on the road was my new normal.

Dry season was in full effect, even in the greenness of Costa Rica, and it was very hot. Sweat built up in my helmet and poured down my face and neck and back. By my fourth day alone, my bike shorts had turned into a science experiment of filth. I made it to the coastal town of Tamarindo, where Weston and I had decided to meet up. We had picked a decent-looking hostel online, and I hoped I'd find him lounging in a hammock when I pulled in.

Close. He was playing cards and smoking cigarettes with some overly tan white boys with beach-knotted hair. I walked in with my bike, and stood there with a big grin, excited for him to notice me. Our little separations were nice. We worked better in doses. He looked up from his cards to take a drag of a cigarette, saw me, threw his cards down, leaped up, and waltzed over.

"He biked alone!" he said for everyone's benefit. "*Castaway*, the sequel!" and grabbed me in a hug.

"How was the Swedish girl?" I asked immediately.

"Oh, oh," he said, smiling wildly, "she drained me right up. She's incredible. I am empty, if you know what I mean. Empty."

"Dude, you're gonna get someone pregnant," I said, thumping him on the back and laughing.

"I hope so," he said.

Tamarindo is a tourist trap of themed bars with names like Dragonfly and Sharky's Sports Bar with fifteen-dollar mai tais, and beaches with Jet Ski rentals and horrible souvenirs. We stayed a few days at a touristy hostel for eighteen dollars a night, the most expensive we'd seen yet. "How are you on money?" I asked Weston while we were lying in hammocks, waiting out the midday heat.

"I mean, I have none," he said with a chuckle.

"Dude, we have another year of this," I said.

"I know. But I'll be okay. I'm getting a little money from my mom soon, and I don't need much. This is an experiment. Do we need money really?"

"This hostel is like twenty bucks a night."

"Yeah, I'll need to leave soon. It's wasted money. I bet I can find a girl, on the beach or on Tinder, and stay for free for a few nights," he said, grinning.

His travel plan didn't include me, and didn't appeal to me anyway, so I tried to explain my concerns without starting a fight.

"I know. You have money. I don't. We'll be okay," he said. "Remember, we can split up and hang during the days, that's fine."

I didn't like this idea, but I didn't know what options we had. You know someone best by traveling with them. When someone is outside their comfort zone, when they are hungry or exhausted, and when money is involved, you see the sides of them that are often covered up in social niceties. Weston and I were slamming all of that together. And it wasn't easy.

Tamarindo was full of Israelis, Australians, and Americans, all of them loud. The Costa Rican locals we saw in the streets, the vendors and staff, seemed vacant, robotically offering us boat tours, zip line excursions, cocaine—exactly what I didn't want for this trip. And Weston didn't want to spend another dollar, so after a few days, we packed up.

The baked-out blonde who ran the front desk of the hostel told us that the east coast of Costa Rica was the real gem. It was Caribbean, with a totally different feel, way fewer tourists, and beautiful. I studied the map and saw that we could cross the country, pass Lake Arenal and the volcano, and drop down onto the Caribbean side. It would take only five days.

To GET THERE, Weston and I rode uphill for two days. Mile by mile, the dry season gave way to higher altitudes and wetter land. The golden grass turned to green ferns and tangled forest. When we reached the lake, it was foggy and dramatic and dark blue. We dropped our bikes, ran to the shore, and dove in. The winding road around the lake was littered with mansions and cabins ripe for Airbnb, with sweeping views, wildflowers, and waterfalls. Around one corner, we came upon a stopped car in the middle of the road, and a woman with her flashers on. She was out of the car and seemed to be covered in cats.

No, not cats. Dogs. Jumping on her. As we approached, the dogs looked very strange. Like monkeys. Wait, were they monkeys? What the hell?

The woman had crackers in her hands and she was laughing as they crawled on her legs. She was talking to them in German. Weston and I parked our bikes behind her car and called to her. "What the hell are those things?" I said.

"They are coatis! They want my crackers," she said with a cackle and a thick German accent. She was dropping crackers at her feet, where about twenty of the creatures were frantically eating them. They looked like a cross of a monkey, a dog, a raccoon, and a lemur. They walked on all fours but could stand on their hind legs and had useful little hands. Their snouts were very long, cartoonishly long. They were orangish brown and their tails had rings like a raccoon. They were taller and bigger than raccoons, though. About the size of a cocker spaniel.

I got closer. I wanted to touch one. I wanted to feel its fur. I wanted it to wrap its tail around my neck and be my sidekick.

Somehow, in all my Discovery Channel watching and deep Internet diving, I had never, not once, seen an animal like this. I didn't know this combination of features was an option on planet Earth. And yet here I was, ten feet away from a swarm of them. Alien life forms. In that moment, my fantasy of being an old world explorer felt real.

As soon as the woman got back into her car, the swarm of beasts turned to me, their tails pointed straight up like shark fins. I would've been scared if I hadn't seen how gentle they were with the German. I reached into my backpack and pulled out a granola bar. A brave one walked right up to me, reared up, put one little hand on my knee, and pointed his long snout at the bar. I held the bar closer, and when he opened his long mouth, I saw rows of sharp teeth. He snatched the bar, held it in both of his hands, and chomped with delight. I heard a rustle and spun around to see two of the creatures on my bike, opening my backpack to find more bars. When I jumped to zip up my bag, they hardly moved.

Weston had pulled over and was cracking up, but keeping his distance. I was cackling. When I petted them, they ignored me, possessed by hunger. Their small hands had long claws and one of them, on a quest for more granola bar, clawed my leg and drew blood. Once

I had gone through a few bars, I affectionately informed my audience that I had to leave. They cocked their heads in sadness, and we rode away.

We stayed at a little hostel at the far end of the lake and talked about the coatis and drank beers at a little bar. The next day, on our way down the mountain, now heading off the volcanic highlands and toward the Caribbean coast, incredibly strong headwinds nearly held us in place. I had to stand my full weight on each pedal, just to make a snail's pace. We pushed down the mountain and came upon miles and miles of banana plantations. We biked a good fifty miles and camped in a grove of trees between plantations, then rode another day after that through flat farmland. Sixty miles, easy. That felt good. One more night at a dank and dreary hotel, for six bucks a person, and finally, we were nearing the ocean.

Entering the port town of Limón, we began seeing lots of black people, and they weren't speaking Spanish. Instead, they were speaking some kind of Creole English. I could understand maybe 40 percent of what was being said. This side of Costa Rica felt old and unpolished. The buildings were cracked but beautiful, clearly built in more prosperous times. Trees loomed over the streets.

We biked through town and straight to the port. Weston struck up a conversation with three men who spoke more English than Creole. One of the guys had long dreads, the other two cropped hair and sunglasses. They all leaned against the wall like they owned the street. When I asked if I could take a photo, Dreads replied, "Hayll yes, you can, brothuh. You tell us where to stan' an' we will look all de badass."

I took their picture and showed it to them and they laughed with approval. One handed me a beer from a six-pack of Imperial at their feet, and said, "Dis man say you rode de bikes all de way from da otha coast?"

"Yeah, from Tamarindo. Took us about six days," I said.

They all found this fact hilarious. "Wow. True athletes. You are professional athletes!" they said, amazed and still laughing.

Weston didn't miss his chance. "Do you guys have any . . ." He pinched his fingers together and made a motion to his mouth like he was smoking something. They laughed, as if knowing the question was coming.

"For you, da athletes, yes," Dreads said. "Wait here." Somehow Weston always manifested ten or twenty dollars for weed. When Weston got his little bag, he was very happy.

We found a bench by the water, with a plaque in Spanish I couldn't read, facing the once busy port. I sat there, looking at the ocean, and felt accomplished. We had biked across an entire country, from the Pacific coast to the Caribbean coast. I felt athletic. Those big burly men said I was an athlete. Almost no one has ever said that about me in my life. It felt good.

I was embarrassed that it felt so good. It soothed an old wound. My thirteen-year-old brain had made a note, "You are not an athlete, and athletes are what you should be." I grew up and never threw out that note. I became funny and charming and accomplished, and I collected all kinds of notes. But beneath those piles of paper, the original note remained. "You are not an athlete, and an athlete is what you should be."

We spent just a day in Limón before heading south. Two days farther on, at Puerto Viejo de Talamanca, we met a woman who ran fishing trips in town. She and her husband had moved from Oregon to live the tropical dream in Costa Rica. She invited us to stay in her house and we became fast friends. We ate meals together and she showed us her beautiful little town. Puerto Viejo was touristy, but without the cheese or intensity of Tamarindo. I loved it there and didn't ever want to leave. We could walk to the beach and ride our bikes to town. But we needed to get to Panama.

Two more days' ride took us to the border.

We saw plenty of cars and pedestrians making the crossing, but no tourists. And no one else traveling by bicycle. An official gave my passport a strange sticker, which I assumed was the entry stamp, and said something to me, pointing out the door. I didn't know what the man said, but he seemed frustrated and hurried, so I left. Weston got his sticker and followed. As we walked out, he shouted out the door at us. But what? We yelled back, "Gracias!" and walked on.

FROM THE COSTA Rican border, Panama curves eastward in a giant "S" before turning down to South America. After a day's ride along the coast, we took a ferry to a small touristy town called Bocas del Toro, famous for snorkeling and Spring Break drunken fun. We arrived at sunset, and the ground was wet with recent rain and stray dogs trotted along the sidewalk. Palm trees lined the streets and the wooden houses were on stilts, built with steeply pitched roofs and painted bright colors. They gave the place a proper Caribbean Crayola look. It was filled with hostels and travelers and coffee and drunk twenty-somethings. We stayed there a few days, snorkeled, met some forgettable Americans, and then headed back to the mainland.

I want to write you scenes of people and places I saw as we left Bocas del Toro and recrossed the isthmus again to the Pacific Coast at Panama City. But this stretch of the trip went by in a blur. We were tourists and stayed at hostels and camped in the woods and pedaled over mountains, but it all seemed normal, and I mostly stayed in my head. Can you remember what you did two weeks ago? Two Tuesdays ago? Could you walk me through the day? Probably not, because it was a normal Tuesday and you were doing normal things, and your brain wasn't wide awake and paying attention. For five months now, I had been putting up my hammock, taking it down, packing my bike, looking for a place to sleep, fumbling through Spanish, replacing popped tubes, explaining my trip to curious strangers, and talking to Weston about the quality of various strands of weed and the injustices of our police state.

One scene stands out, though.

A mountain range divides the skinny nation of Panama down the middle like a spine, with jungle on the Caribbean side and golden grass and hot air on the southern side. Birds squawked and tree limbs shook from unseen animals jumping around as we made our way up. At the top of the divide, we found a little guest room in a wooden shack perched on stilts over a ravine and leaning toward the sunset. It had a "hostel" sign, though it really looked like a large outhouse.

"This is like a postcard," I shouted. "Let's see if they have room!"

A tiny woman met us at the door, visibly thrilled to have guests. She had deep wrinkles and jet-black hair. She ushered us in with a few words, showed us a room with bunk beds, and then sat us down on a dusty old couch. The place was crammed with knickknacks and piles of crusty *National Geographic*s. While our host went off to the kitchen to make us beans in an ancient metal pressure cooker, I flipped through a magazine.

I remembered holding *Nat Geo*s as a kid like some kind of port-hole to a life of discovery. Now I gazed upon the adventures with a different eye. One article featured an anthropologist in Indonesia, traveling into the mountains to document rare birds-of-paradise. A year ago, I would've lusted for his experience. Now I saw his bags, his cameras, his bug spray, his soggy clothes, and thought, *He must be miserable.*

I looked at Weston, sitting next to me, writing in his journal. "Are you having fun?" I asked.

"On this trip, or like, writing in my journal?" he asked.

"The trip. Is it what you thought? I've been struggling a bit. Not bored. Just . . . we have so much farther to go, and it's hard. And monotonous."

"You think that? I do, too," he said, "but I didn't say anything because I didn't think you did. You're always so amazed by everything and every bird, I thought you couldn't get bored."

"I can. Though I'm ashamed of it for some reason."

"My money experiment stresses me out. Mostly because it stresses you out."

"It doesn't stress me out," I said, lying.

"I know it does. You don't hide annoyance well. It's okay. I know it's annoying. But my experiment isn't just an experiment. I don't have access to money like you do."

"Access? I saved money up," I protested.

"Yeah, but if you run out, your parents can bail you out. You know that no matter what happens, you'll be okay. I don't have that. If I needed a hundred bucks, I wouldn't be able to get it from my family. I mean, they'd find it for me, but it would hurt them. That insecurity fucks with my mind. It's a different existence."

I looked down at the *National Geographic* in my hands while Weston continued.

"I wanted to go on this trip to prove that someone like me could. You're an upper-middle-class white guy—of course you can do this. I wanted to show that almost anyone could. And it's been hard. I know you get mad at me buying weed. But it helps my anxiety. You're on this trip to reach a destination. I'm on this trip following ideals."

I felt transparent. "Dude, I'm not a rich kid," I said.

"I didn't say you were. But you are, in the scheme of things. That's okay. I'm rich in the scheme of things, too. But that's the cycle I'm trying to get out of. There's lots of people richer than you. But if that's all you compare yourself to, then those left behind get lost. That's the problem with capitalism. I'm just saying I don't have it quite like you, and that's just how it is. Though I know I'm a straight white guy with all the privileges, I'm not going to be incarcerated by the U.S. government because of my skin color, or the gram of weed I have in my pocket. I know that. It's just something I think about, economic access and ability and the psychological burden of financial insecurity. And food insecurity."

"That's what you think about while biking?" I said with a smile, trying to lighten the conversation.

"Yes." Weston laughed.

"Do you think we'll get the excitement back? For biking?" I said.

"We have to choose it. It's like a marriage. The honeymoon's over, and we can jump ship or we can choose to love the one we've got, and make it fresh. I mean, dude, we have Colombia next! That's exciting. That's like, when you're married and then you have a kid."

"This metaphor is stretching," I said. "And don't you ditch girls after a few months? What do you know about marriage? You get bored with jobs and girls and philosophies faster than anyone I know."

"Easy, tiger," he said. "I outgrow them. I want this trip. I am testing my philosophies. I know what I'm doing."

"*Frijoles!*" the lady called from the kitchen. While we'd been talking, the shack had filled with the aromas of refried beans, rice, and fried eggs.

We went to the kitchen, where she had us sit at a small wooden table. She served us the meal and watched as we ate hungrily. Learning what he thought gave me a new sense of Weston's depth; it brought him closer. I thought I had him figured out, but I didn't.

We slept peacefully, with full bellies, in the woman's shack, and in the morning we headed down the mountain. I watched Weston load up his bike and ride off ahead. I thought about all he was thinking about. I thought about how he thought I was spoiled. Or lucky. Or just free from the burdens he carried.

Jungle gave way to golden grass and cows and a landscape that reminded me of California. Trees clumped in dark green patches, cleared fields, ponds, farmhouses and barns. We passed coffee farms, with signs for tourists to stop and buy beans or take a tour. For a whole day, we rode downhill, covering seventy miles without breaking a sweat. Then the land leveled off to a busy freeway along the coast toward Panama City.

We slept that night on the coast in a cheap motel and then started out for the city. The heat was so intense and the exhaust from trucks so terrible and the road so busy and ugly, we decided to hitchhike in.

"I'm not fucking riding in this congested shit after that full day downhill in paradise," Weston said.

When hitchhiking failed us, we tracked down a bus, threw our bikes underneath, and let it carry us into Panama City, its enormous white skyline of condo towers standing over the ocean.

The family of an old friend had offered to host us here. I was ready. I wanted to drink some nice beer and enjoy the city. I wanted to get a tattoo.

Chapter 10

HARRY DEVERT
(Panama)

8,514 miles to go

Our friend's house was located in a maze of suburban streets, with homes built for Americans back in the fifties and sixties. Strange but nice. A haunting of American influence, now proudly taken back by the Panamanians. Our friend's dad was a Panama Canal boat captain, which felt very cool and on the nose. We called him "Captain."

Suddenly, it was the end of February. I spent mornings reading the news and catching up with friends on Instagram and Facebook. One morning, I noticed that someone had left me a strange comment on my Instagram.

"Have u heard of Harry Devert?"

Harry Devert? No idea.

"#prayforHarry" they said.

I clicked through the hashtag. A bunch of photos of a handsome thirtyish guy on a motorcycle, smiling. It looked from the photos like he was in Mexico. Everyone was saying #prayforHarry. Why were we praying for him? Obviously, something had happened. I found his account. He had last posted on January 25, in Morelia, Michoacán, putting up a photo of the very cathedral I had marveled at a few months before. I found a news story from his hometown. Harry had been missing for a month. In cartel country.

Lots of people were worried. In the comments on his last post, I read, "I haven't seen a recent post from you. Hope you are ok, bro."

Then, "Harry, I read your mom's message on Facebook. Hope all is well! Stay safe."

Then, "Come on Harry post a photo of you enjoying a tequila shot on the beaches of Mexico already . . . I'm praying to all the higher powers, cosmos, energies and everything Alan Watts has mentioned . . . that you are safe and happy."

Then, "I will move earth and sky until you give some life signs. Maybe you'll laugh at this when u appear hahaha."

I learned that Harry Devert was thirty-two years old, a former stock trader who had given up his job to travel the world for the last five years. He was taking his Kawasaki motorcycle from the U.S. to Brazil for the World Cup.

I found his blog, called "A New Yorker Travels," and I started reading his posts. He reminded me of me. He had left his job to travel and see the world and celebrate it. He had a brightness, a bravado about him that felt bigger than me, more exaggerated. But even so, he felt like a kindred spirit. Like someone I'd enjoy swapping stories with.

"I've run with the bulls and broken 3 ribs because of it in Pamplona," he wrote in the "about me" section on his blog. "I've spent time in a small jail in Paraguay, swum in the highest waterfall in the world and almost died swimming in a hurricane. I've climbed the highest Tepui mountain in the world and almost got stuck at the top of a mountain in Brasil until I made a rope out of vines and got myself down . . ." The stories went on and on. "I've run 3 miles to try and save a bird's life, and I've sat and watched as someone was hacked to death with a machete only a few meters away from me. I choose my battles. I've been in the largest food fight in the world in Spain and eaten some of the world's best in France. I've been chased with a gun in Colombia, chipped my tooth on a gun that was shoved in my mouth in Venezuela . . . danced with a pirate on a beach in Peru . . .

"I think that life is a pilgrimage.

"My life is something like a small boat in the middle of an ocean driven by the weather and the tide. All I carry is faith.

"I dream, I search, I love, I live."

Sure, it was cheesy, but he seemed to really be living. He seemed rungs ahead of me. Less confused. So full of discovery that discovery itself had become a religion. I felt like I was sitting here, hunched over in a tangle of feathers, while he was flapping his wings over the world.

Harry Devert's Instagram posts and blog had one sustained theme: Human beings are lovely and kind. Each story testified to the kindness of strangers, the beauty of travel, the universal goodness of humanity, and the freedom of deciding to ignore fear and trust people. His first post in January read: "Feliz Año Nuevo from my new Mexican friends and I . . . wishing everyone all the best in 2014. . . . have a feeling this is going to be an amazing year!!"

He was so full of life that he made me feel shitty for being tired. I should be more joyful. I should be more grateful. I am on the trip of a lifetime. I am staying with a Panama Canal captain. I am amazing. This guy is doing it right.

Where the hell are you, Harry?

He was a year older than me and living in parallel lines, following almost the same route as I was at almost the same time. The only difference was that he was traveling alone, and by motorcycle. Wouldn't that be safer for its speed?

A young man goes missing in Mexico while chasing his wanderlust for travel. His last Instagram post floats indefinitely on the Internet, showing a beautiful cathedral in Mexico. And there I was, in Panama, waiting. Not sure what I was waiting for. Well, yes, I was. I was waiting for my mom to find this story and send it to me. I was waiting for Harry Devert to surface from one of Weston's spiritual sweat lodges with some vision to bring down capitalism, and to vindicate me.

I checked his Instagram every day for weeks, hoping he'd start posting again. I added his name to my Google alerts. I read everything he ever posted. He said that he was headed to Zihuatanejo, the beach from *The Shawshank Redemption*'s closing scene. He had always wanted to go there. I loved that movie. I had always wanted to go there, too. I began to care for him because he was like me and he was missing, and his poor mother, and his family, and all of it.

As I explored Panama City with my temporary family, and planned to cross into Colombia, the thought of Harry colored everything. The way someone waits for news about a job application or a doctor's call back about a biopsy. Everything I did carried with it the smell and shadow of the question: Where the hell are you, Harry? What will the news bring? When I'd forget about him, something would trigger the story, and the weight of it came right back.

Google alerts told me that his mother flew to Mexico. That there was a campaign throughout Michoacán to find him. That the Guerrero state police asked for tips on Harry's whereabouts.

Harry sat in my mind, whispering to me.

Chapter 11

A NEW CONTINENT
(Crossing to Cartagena)

8,430 miles to go

O ur week in Panama City gave us good food, craft beer, and a few dance clubs. The towering giant white condominiums of the city fascinated me. "They're all empty," the Captain told us. "They're built to launder drug money. They're just empty. No one lives in them."

The economy of the drug trade never felt real to me. Sure, I knew the cartels were big. I knew millions of people do drugs. But it always seemed like something in the movies. Not a real thing. Panama showed me that it wasn't just a Weston-like friendly handoff here or there. It was a multibillion-dollar industry. San Francisco had its skyscrapers built from tech money. Panama City had skyscrapers built by cocaine.

We had to plan our route to Colombia. There was just one problem: the Darién Gap. Panama and Colombia are separated by a stretch of roughly eighty miles (maybe a hundred miles, no one really knows) of absolute wilderness. There is no clear border between them. Just jungle and mountains and rivers. There is no road that connects. The impenetrable, untamed jungle is home to indigenous tribes, antigovernment rebels, and the drug trade.

The Panamanian side is mountainous and steep. The Colombian side is mostly the Atrato River delta: marsh, swamp, bugs, and mud. The Captain's stories about "The Gap" left our jaws on the floor.

The first crossing by vehicles—a Land Rover and a Jeep—occurred in 1960. It took the expedition 136 days to go 100 miles, and most of their forward progress happened by barge. That same year, a man named Danny Liska attempted to cross the gap with his motorcycle. He was traveling the entirety of the Pan-American Highway and refused to let the Darién Gap stop him. He ended up abandoning his motorcycle in the jungle and making it to Colombia on foot and by boat. In 1987, drivers in a CJ-5 Jeep completed the first all-land auto crossing. It took that Jeep 741 days to travel 125 miles.

"We are definitely doing this!" Weston said, looking to me for enthusiastic agreement. I thought about Harry Devert's disappearance, and wondered what would happen if we disappeared in the gap.

Then, just as I was ready to agree to it, the Captain said, "You can't. You have to have military permission to go now. You won't get it. It's too dangerous. You have to go by boat."

Weston looked crestfallen. "Should we still ask the military?"

"You will not get permission," the Captain said dismissively.

But I was already thinking about Plan B. "What's the boat situation?" I asked.

"Many backpackers and travelers do it," the Captain said. "It is a sailboat. It takes five days. You sail from the Caribbean side, through the San Blas Islands, which are very beautiful, to Cartagena, Colombia. Many tourists do it. It is very good."

I got on my computer that night and did some research. It was expensive, $600 a person. It was five days, meals included, and would take us through a Caribbean paradise to Colombia. Fifteen people per boat. Shoot. How would Weston afford this? I wondered if we'd have to split up. I mentioned the price. "I can't afford that," he said.

We sat quietly for a minute. I was thinking about how much money I had left. About five thousand dollars from the sale of my car. Weston had next to nothing. *I guess I could pay for him. That's twelve hundred bucks. Sheesh. But I can't do this trip without him. I'm not ready to be alone. I really rely on him. And once we get to Colombia, it's a straight shot down. I won't have to pay again. I guess it's just a cost of the trip.*

"I'll pay for you."

"You sure? I bet I can find my way onto a boat. Maybe a cargo ship," he said with a playful tone.

"I'd die without you. You know that."

"Yes, I do," he said. "See, the universe provides—just kidding, just kidding."

"I'll kill you."

"I guess that's the thing," Weston said, an aside to himself. "This experiment with money. The universe will provide, but it'll cost you your pride. Seriously, thank you, brother."

"Just fix my tires when they pop, okay?"

We took a taxi to a hostel downtown that brokered the boat trips. The girl told us we could choose among several skippers and services that could take us there. Weston, with his love of warm air and warm water and boats, was cheery. If he couldn't risk his life through the Darién Gap, why not work on his tan and hope to kiss a Swedish or Israeli girl on a boat?

We booked a trip on a sailboat called the *Wildcard*, and on the night before departure, decamped to the hostel. Jeeps would pick us up at six the next morning. We woke up at five and carried our things out to the sidewalk, where a cluster of sleepy backpackers awaited. A fit Asian man with a shiny bald head and nice clothes; an angel-faced blonde girl with a scowl and a predawn cigarette hanging from her mouth; two more blondes in their pajamas speaking Swedish; a handsome boy and his pretty girlfriend leaning on him, unhappy at being awake, speaking a European language I didn't recognize.

Weston studied the blonde girls, calculating possibilities and interest. We took the front wheels off our bikes and removed the panniers, while the crew looked on, seeming annoyed that they'd have to jigsaw these bulky sharp bikes into their vehicles.

The Jeeps climbed up the mountainous center of Panama and dropped into the jungles on the northern coast. Most of us slept along the way. I stared out the window, wanting to capture every mile of the road in my mind's eye, watching tree species and terrain change almost by the mile.

We were approaching the end of North America. The beginning of the great south.

At the coast, our drivers offloaded our things to small wooden boats that took us through a tangle of canals and mangroves out to a bay, where several large sailboats waited at anchor.

There she was. The *Wildcard.* Long and white and beautiful. We pulled up next to her, and a leather-skinned man with Oakley sunglasses and sun-bleached dreads called down to us. "Welcome to your chariot! I'm Wayne," he said. He had cracked, rough hands, and a cigarette bounced on his lips when he laughed.

We were assigned to bunks, got our bags organized and put away, and they handed us beers. Wayne tied our bikes to the railing on the foredeck. He said he'd never taken on cyclists as passengers before. Then he called out for passports. "I'll keep them in one place so that we can have them stamped out of Panama and then into Colombia." He took them below, only to reappear.

"Jedidiah and Weston?" he called to the group, not knowing who was who.

"Yeah, that's us," I said.

"You guys don't have a Panama entry stamp. How is that possible?"

"What? It's that little sticker they gave us," I said.

But Wayne shook his head. "That's not the stamp. That's some customs thing. You need the stamp. How did you get the sticker and not the stamp?"

"I have no idea. The border was weird. We did it on the Caribbean side."

"Well, you can't get stamped out of the country if you haven't been stamped in," Wayne said.

"Well, shit," Weston said.

The other passengers looked at us with curiosity and Wayne stroked his wiry beard. Finally, he said, "I know the guy who stamps us out. He's just on a dinghy making the rounds before we set sail. I'll see if he'll just overlook your stuff. He owes me a few favors. This is a tricky one. Worst-case scenario we might have to take you back to shore and you'll have to go back to the border and get the stamp."

"Oh my god," I said.

Weston and I paced anxiously on the boat for an hour while we waited for the border agent to show up and stamp everyone's passports. How the hell did this happen?

When the border agent came aboard, Wayne handed him the

passports and then pulled him aside, speaking to him quietly. Weston and I craned our necks to watch. The border agent began stamping the passports, they exchanged some words we couldn't hear, the agent handed them back without stamping ours, then climbed down to his dinghy. He rode away as Wayne began passing out the passports.

"Well," Wayne said, "he said he wouldn't stamp yours out because it would only raise more suspicion. So, hopefully, Colombia doesn't notice. But I have an idea. I know a woman in Colombia who is pretty high up. I think it'll be okay. Let's try it." He flashed an adventurous smile.

"What'll happen if they say no?" I asked.

Wayne shrugged. "I don't know," he said, and began prepping the boat for launch.

Within an hour, we set sail, and the bright blue water and the beautiful backpackers on our boat began to push away our anxiety. "Let's just believe it'll work out," Weston said. "Wayne's a salty dog, I like him."

"Yeah, I choose to believe," I said.

We drank our beers and soaked up the sun and ocean air, and quickly felt camaraderie with our fellow passengers. They all spoke English well. The crew on the boat were all white, and American. Wayne's age was hard to assess. He was either thirty-five or fifty-five. The sun had turned his skin to dark brown plastic. He wore torn khaki shorts. Two blonde girls and a tall younger man with brown hair crewed for him. The voyage would take five nights and six days, and our phones wouldn't work again until Colombia. For part of the trip, we would hop from one island to the next. One would be a tourist stop, seeing a native village and the chance to buy some souvenirs. The others would be empty white sand paradises, a chance to swim and play, and then two nights in the open sea as we crossed to Cartagena, Colombia.

Weston soon settled into a new level of Westonness on the boat— shirtless, shoeless, tan, and happy. The captain had either a cigarette or a spliff in his mouth at all times. Weston happily rolled him fresh spliffs.

Meanwhile, I synced my phone with the Bluetooth speaker to DJ the journey, then I cued up Michael Jackson and Beyoncé and hits from the nineties, going for commonality and nostalgia. The Dutch couple loved my music and bobbed their heads in affirmation.

"What is it like to have all music in your native language?" the boy asked me.

"What do you mean?"

"Katy Perry, Beyoncé, Michael Jackson, they all sing in English. You can understand every word, yes?"

"Well, yes, of course, I've never thought about it. You don't have Dutch music?"

"We do. But most of the radio music is American, or British. Pop music is almost always in English. We can understand a lot of it, but we miss a lot, too. When music is in Dutch, it is usually folk music, or holiday music. So, when we hear music in our language, it feels different. Special."

"Huh," I said. "I guess the closest I have to that is country music. I am from Tennessee, so it is nostalgic and feels down-home."

"Down-home? What does that mean?" his girlfriend asked.

"Like, from the country, where I'm from. Old-timey maybe. Feels like my childhood."

"Yes, that is how Dutch music feels. But you don't feel that with Katy Perry, even though it's in English?"

"No. I've never thought about it. It's just pop music. I've never thought about what language it was in."

On the second day we dropped anchor off an island the size of two football fields. The villagers had no natural water source, so big plastic containers held water on the roofs of their palm-frond houses. I asked our captain how they survived out here, and he said, "They used to live only by fishing. But now they survive from tourists." It felt a bit like visiting a zoo. The children ran up offering beads and brightly colored scarves and dolls made from folded palm fronds. It didn't feel like life in paradise. It felt like poverty tourism.

We camped that night on a nearby abandoned island. We cut down fresh coconuts with machetes and sliced them open. We passed around a rum bottle and poured rum into the coconuts, mixing it with the coconut milk for a refreshing cocktail. We collected fallen palm fronds and made a massive bonfire. We had the whole island to ourselves and danced on the beach into the night.

Two more days of island hopping and swimming and talking about our cultures and stories. Then two days out at sea. The waves got big and we stood on the bow to ride them like a roller coaster. The boat divided into the people who loved the thrill of the boat pitching up and down, and those who threw up for two days straight.

I thought about the symbolism of the crossing. From North America to South. The old route from Atlantic to Pacific had meant a perilous voyage around the tip of Patagonia. These warm Caribbean waters separated by a thin strip of land, Panama, and then the cold Pacific. The old route from Atlantic to Pacific was all the way around the tip of Patagonia. A hundred years ago the Panama Canal gave boats the ability to bypass an enormous landmass that ran half the length of Earth. We were sailing through the same Caribbean waters where pre-Columbian natives had witnessed the arrival of Spanish galleons. I remembered the stories of the ships showing up on these beaches for the first time, and the pre-Columbian natives seeing them, or not seeing them. I'd heard that the ships pulled up to the beaches, and many of the indigenous people were unable to see the ships at all. They were so strange, so alien to anything they'd seen before, that their brains didn't recognize them, or acknowledge them as real. They were invisible until the ships themselves were right up on the shore. The Spanish descended from the boats on horses. The indigenous people didn't know it was possible for a human to ride an animal. No similar animals existed in the Americas. They existed only in legends and myths. So they mistook men on horseback as centaur alien creatures with giant bodies and human parts coming out the top. Some were frightened. Others were fascinated and kind. They had little idea that these aliens carried with them guns and germs and the end of their way of life.

It is a trippy thing, to ride across the waters of first contact. To feel the air that the Spanish felt, bringing with them the future. Bringing with them death. On this stage of unimaginable paradise.

On the final day, the coast of Colombia came into view. The fabled southern universe. This continuous stretch of land would define the rest of my year. The Andes. The headwaters of the Amazon. Machu Picchu, Chile and Patagonia, and all their peoples and cultures. I had given it a power over me, an invitation to change me, to reveal me. As I watched the continent rise up on the horizon, I felt like a kid waiting for college, having bestowed it with answers to questions that he hasn't even asked yet.

I would live my entire thirty-first year in South America.

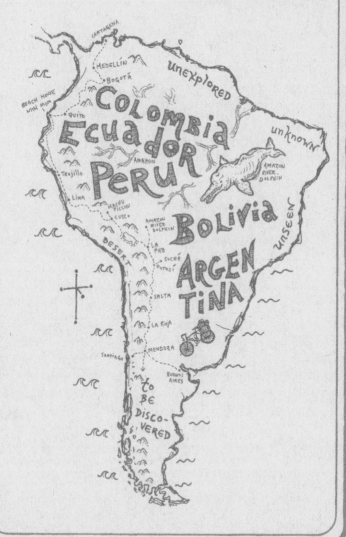

Chapter 12

COCAINE AND CUTE LITTLE MUSHROOMS
(Cartagena and Medellín)

S ailing around the jetty to enter the harbor of Cartagena, Colombia, the skyline seemed filled with cranes and high-rises. Weston was squinting, studying the city in the distance. "I've been thinking," he said. "What if everyone is an addict and everything is a drug?"

"Weston, do you ever turn your brain off?" I said.

"Some things that we all accept are actually addictions. The Internet, we're addicted to it. Our phones, are you kidding? The dopamine hit of checking your phone. We can't function without them. Notice how these five days on this boat . . . no phones, no access to the outside world. There was a withdrawal period. It was weird, right? Everything is a drug. Coffee. Caffeine. Sugar. Sugar is in everything. It's all drugs. What does addiction mean? Can we choose or help our addictions?"

I had gotten used to Weston tossing out deep thoughts in odd moments. He could have remarked on the skyline, the houses on the water, the beautiful yachts pulling in behind us, the new cultures and experiences we'd find in South America. Instead, Weston, a plume of smoke jetting from his lips, was staring past all these things and seeing addiction and unjust social expectations.

"Society thinks people are addicted to weed, which is medicine," he went on. "Mushrooms grow wild on cow shit. A gift from nature. But if you walk across your own land and collect them, growing all on their own, the government can arrest you."

"You don't think you're addicted to weed?" I interjected. "You smoke every day."

He turned to me with an earnest look on his face. "What's the difference between being addicted to something and wanting to do something because you love it?" he said.

"I'm not sure."

"*Addiction* is a term people use to label and categorize and dismiss. It stops you thinking about it. Addiction implies that the thing is bad. It's all made up. I just want to think critically."

The boat pulled into the dock and the staff hopped off and tied her down. We lined up and got off the boat and waited to be led to customs. I was nervous about our passports, but I also had confidence in our skipper. You don't get leathery skin and a swagger like that without knowing your shit.

He came around and collected all our passports again, taking special care of mine and Weston's, putting them in a separate pocket. Then he led us from the dock to a large marble-and-cement building a few blocks away. Inside, bored tourists sat waiting, some on their iPads, some reading, some dead asleep on the shoulders of their friends. But our eyes were on Wayne. He seemed to know an important woman who sat behind a glass wall at an old wooden table stacked high with manila folders. As he handed her the passports, he patted her shoulder and smiled at her and said something. She didn't smile back. She glanced at our group with deadpan consideration before disappearing back into an office. Wayne spun on his heels toward us, smiled wide, and shrugged.

We waited for about an hour. Wayne left to "grab something," he said. The rest of our group passed time by reminiscing about our boat trip, but Weston and I were growing more and more worried. Our fates were in the hands of grumpy Colombian government workers behind glass.

Then, all of a sudden, Wayne was back, holding what looked like a potato sack full of lumpy objects. As he strolled in, an older man waddled out of the back room where all the official business was happening. Wayne handed him the bag, and they shared a joke. The old man looked inside, grinned from ear to ear, shook Wayne's hand,

and walked back to the back. Two seconds later, he emerged with a stack of passports and handed them to Wayne. Were ours in there?

Wayne passed them out, winked at us, and handed ours to us. Sure enough, they had been stamped like everyone else's. Colombia. We were official, even though there was no proof we'd been in Panama.

"What was in that bag?" I asked.

"San Blas lobster," Wayne said, smiling big. "They love it down here."

WAYNE HAD DIRECTED a group of us to a hostel in the old town. "It's clean and cheap." I wondered if he got kickbacks or something for directing business to them. We wound our way through the narrow streets, with Spanish architecture and flowers on every balcony and terrace. Weston and I were so happy to be in Colombia with our passports. We were in South America. We'd made it to a new continent.

Cartagena reminded me of the French Quarter in New Orleans. Some of the buildings were falling apart, but their tall shuttered windows and ornate carvings gave testimony to a former glory. They looked haunted. The hostel turned out to be an ugly white box of a building, stained from humidity and rain and soot. But we could get a big bunk room that fit most of us for $11 a person per night. Not bad.

During the week we'd spent on the boat, Weston had bonded with Henry, the bald Asian man with good hats and a kind smile. A former military man, Henry was traveling the world solo, hoping to reignite his love for the world. He and Weston had a shared love of weed, but now that they were in Colombia, they wanted cocaine. "It comes from here, so we owe it to ourselves to have it from the source," said Weston.

I'd never done cocaine. People who "do drugs" do cocaine. Coke was the drug in the movies that gave people nosebleeds, funded the cartel wars and beheadings, and fueled the sloppiest of Hollywood parties. It didn't have the lazy harmless charm of weed, or the spiritual gospel of mushrooms. It seemed darker, dirtier to me. And now

Weston and Henry were heading to the streets to find some. "Y'all, just please don't go down any alleys or anything," I said. "It will be very annoying to try and bail you out of jail." I was feigning irritation, but I was actually nervous.

"Every gringo on the street down here is looking for coke," Henry said. "Don't stress. We'll be right back."

By the time I unpacked and took a shower, they were already back. I laughed and they laughed and the anxious kid inside me that doesn't like breaking rules twisted and turned. They had cocaine in their pockets.

Henry saw my laptop on my bed and asked, "Can I use that for a second?" Then he sat down next to it and poured a bit out—right on top of the Apple logo. White powder, just like in the movies. I thought about my laptop having cocaine on it. About drug-sniffing dogs in the airport detecting it. I just watched, frozen.

Henry took out his credit card and cut two lines. He leaned over and sucked one up. Then Weston bent down and did the same. Henry wiped the bit left with his fingers and rubbed his finger around his gums. Done and done.

"Uhm, please wipe my laptop clean," I said. Henry smiled an understanding if not patronizing smile and wiped the laptop with his T-shirt.

"Okay now," he said. "Let's go check out this town!"

We rounded up the other boaters—the Swedish girls and the Dutch couple—and headed to a bar.

Along the way, the streets were crawling with locals trying to sell us coke. As we walked by, men would mumble "coca," "coca-ee-na" under their breath. Some said it full volume with bravado. Some of the guys had bruises on their faces, tattered clothes, strung-out speech. It was dark. I kept watching Weston for a change in his behavior. I expected him to get glazed and spacey like he did on strong weed. He didn't. He was hilarious. His wit was sharp as we laughed and told stories.

"Are you feeling anything?" I asked him between beers at the bar.

"God, yes. I am alive."

"But you don't seem like you're on anything."

"Coke is an upper. It just gets you going."

I didn't know drugs could be like that. A thought crossed my mind: *Wow, I like Weston so much more on coke than weed. Maybe this is a good change.* Another thought crossed my mind: *I am glad my friend is on cocaine right now.* My new normal would have shocked my teenage self.

The next morning, we took our salty bikes to a local shop and got them cleaned and lubed. Then we said our goodbyes to our boat family with lots of hugs and Facebook friending and promises of trips to Europe, and we headed south out of town.

Our next goal: Medellín.

I had heard that it was a beautiful city located in a narrow valley between mountains. That it was at 8,000 feet elevation, and because of its proximity to the equator, this altitude gave it almost perfect weather year-round.

I was happy to be on the bike, though my legs felt heavy and my tailbone was sensitive again. The towns weren't so different from what we'd seen in Panama and Costa Rica. The small towns in Latin America were starting to look the same. And we were looked at the same—the smaller or more remote the town, the more Weston and I were stared at, the more kids would run alongside us to ask us where we were from and demand photos.

Colombia didn't feel so different, but I felt different. I could feel myself on a new continent. One giant landmass. Nothing separated me from Patagonia now except dirt and mountains and snow and people and llamas. Machu Picchu and Patagonia were just miles away now. Many miles, but connected. The road I was on, headed up the beginning of the Andes to Medellín, was connected to the roads in Patagonia by an unbroken chain of pavement.

But I also thought, *Jed, if you quit now, at least you can say you made it to South America. That's a big thing. So, if you get really over this, there's an out. You won't be too embarrassed to quit now. Just saying. There's an out.*

It is astonishing how ideas can change an experience. How we can be in a beautiful forest, on a hike through verdant beauty, but if someone told us that the forest was the site of a brutal massacre, the entire hike would be transformed. It would turn ominous and sad. Or if I was told the forest was where Walt Whitman had walked every morning before working on *Leaves of Grass*, the place would take on a holy majesty. Same forest. Same trail and trees. But the idea layered on top of it mutates it, glorifies or damns it. I had decided South America was the land of Indiana Jones adventure and sacred mountains and my spirit-quest revelations. I expected it, and so, now biking it, I felt it coming, I felt it promising me everything.

On the multiday journey uphill to Medellín, we fell in love with Colombian breakfasts. Beans and rice, eggs, arepas (fried pancakes made of maize dough), chorizo, chicharrón (grilled beef), some kind of delicious salty white cheese, and hot chocolate. It was pure fuel for the day, and we craved it. We'd camp and then wake desperate to find it again.

We biked for days across miles of rolling green hills and farms. We camped in thickets and forests. One night we camped in a woman's cowshed. As I was falling asleep in my hammock, dangling from beams in the shed, Weston spoke out of the darkness from his hammock.

"I didn't like that cocaine," he said.

"Dude, we're going to sleep, why are you thinking about cocaine?"

"It's a commercial drug. Henry ended up telling me how street coke is made. The first ingredient after the coca leaf is gasoline. That's not what I'm about. I'm not doing that again. It didn't teach me anything, it just made me want more cocaine. And I don't want to support that supply chain. Well, I guess it taught me what not to do." He was talking to me and to himself.

"That sounds wise," I said, drifting off.

I hadn't really tracked our elevation change, but we were going up. Day after day the land steadily turned from hot and humid to cool, damp, and green. One day in the mountains, we biked to what seemed like the end of the road, a cliff. The land disappeared, just fell away from the highway like it had been stolen. Far below we could see a coiled snake of pavement, dropping two thousand feet to the valley floor and the city of Medellín. At an overlook point, we saw bright colored triangles soaring in the sky. It was a hang-gliding center. People were lined up on a steep grassy slope, taking a few steps, and soaring over Medellín. Weston and I pulled over to watch them take off, then thread effortlessly between misty clouds in the valley.

The downhill ride was wild. Weston sped way ahead of me, going as fast as the cars, hugging the turns and loving the adrenaline. I watched him weave into the oncoming lane to pass a semitruck and squeeze in front of it just in time to miss a car. I was scared and took my time. Beautiful houses dotted the road. I paused at vista points from which I could see Medellín in the distance. Most of the city's houses appeared to be built of red brick; it looked like God had poured red clay cubes across the valley. Tall apartment towers crawled up the green slopes. After twenty full minutes of coasting downhill, we made it to the bottom and rode toward town.

I saw gondolas going up the hills. Big enclosed ones. But they were not for skiing. They were dangling commuter cars, taking people to their houses up the steep hills.

We tracked down a café with Wi-Fi. Weston was drawn to a specific hostel because it had mushroom murals in the photos. "This one is my style. I bet they'll take us to find mushrooms. At this altitude, they grow wild in the fields."

"Wild? Really? That seems dangerous."

"No, no, if you know what they look like. It's fine."

We biked to the mushroom hostel, and the moment we walked in, the people in the lobby knew they had a friend in Weston. They were all barefoot, wearing poofy cloth pants, and smoking weed. The hostel was an old house divided up by a hodgepodge of stucco walls to create bunk rooms. The creekside yard had hammocks strung between trees. Puffs of smoke came from the hammocks, heavy with some chill backpackers enjoying their weightlessness. The hippies who ran the place showed us to our own bunk room and offered us some weed. Weston obliged.

We spent the week in Medellín. We poked around the city and its suburbs, went to cafés and museums. We rode the gondolas. Walking in town, I kept seeing nuns. Tiny women, the size of middle schoolers, but mostly old. I walked beside one old nun for a few blocks. She had dark skin and her face was almost entirely wrinkled, as if her eyes and button nose had been poked into the wrinkles like chocolate chips into dough. I thought of her life, how at some point she had decided to give up sex and romance for the Christian God. She didn't show a trace of European blood. She looked older than conquest. If so, when the Spanish came, they had destroyed her own people's gods and their myths, tore down their temples, and built cathedrals to a new god over them. And this woman, centuries later, serves that same destroyer god. She had bound herself to the church that "civilized the savages." In that god's name, she quietly serves the poor and prays for the lost.

Of course, I was only walking near her and imagining her story, her life. Still, her small frame, her determined walk and body language, and the commitment she made, inspired me. Was I strong enough to commit to something the way she had? Believe so deeply? I wondered if she ever doubted, if she ever thought about walking away. She turned down a side street and disappeared, but I can still see her tiny, wizened face. I can see her walking with somewhere to go.

We were there long enough that I spent some time apart from Weston. Doing my own thing. Going on side trips. It was nice. A little breather. I came home from exploring one day to find Weston very excited. "We're going camping! They've never done a mushroom excursion, and I talked them into it. The guy who cleans up has an uncle in the mountains outside of town with a big cow field where he's seen them grow. We're going," he said.

Cut to two days later.

HERE WE GO. A mushroom adventure.

We are headed on a camping trip with ten people from the hostel. But really, we're on an excursion to find wild magic mushrooms.

After six months on the road, Weston has worn me down. I don't like weed. I'm scared of cocaine, no matter how much I prefer Weston on it. But mushrooms? I'm out of good excuses. Weston's evangelism has worked. The way he sells me on it is strategic, like he knows which things to say to get my guard down. "Mushrooms are natural. There is no hangover. It connects you to nature. You don't feel like someone else, not like being drunk or high. You're lucid. You're still fully yourself. You'll just see how everything is connected and meaningful more than you ever have before." With a sales pitch like that, I feel prudish to say no. He wants me to experience it with him. He wants to be my guru, my shaman. I say I'll do it.

Fernando, the buzzed-headed tattooed man in MC Hammer pants who runs the hostel, knows a farmer with a large mountaintop cattle farm, and the hostel has several big tents we can all stay in. Two of the people staying at the hostel are chefs from Argentina, so we all pitch in for them to buy a smorgasbord of food.

The journey takes two hours by bus, then a two-mile hike. It feels like we're ascending into a postcard. Steep mountains, neon green with healthy plants. Cattle roam the terraced fields, mists floating through like wispy cotton ghosts. The moisture in the air would be humid, were we not 8,500 feet up. But the air is perfect. Crisp and beautiful.

At the top of our climb, we walk down a dirt road, hop a fence, cut around some barking dogs, hop another fence, and end up in a field that covers the entire hilltop. It's probably thirty acres, naturally terraced, with dotted clots of trees and a few giant boulders sticking out. We walk to an overlook and begin setting up our tents in the midafternoon.

Once our little oasis is ready, Fernando calls us all to attention. Everyone is grinning and giddy. I seem to be the only one who has never eaten a mushroom.

"Who has never found wild magic mushrooms before?" Fernando asks, his Colombian accent handsome and raspy.

About half of us raise our hands. I raise mine.

"Okay, great. It is special to find them in nature. They grow here all on their own. They are a gift from nature. So it is simple." He holds up a mushroom in his hands. He had either found it as we walked or brought it. But it looks very much plump and alive. It seems very fresh. It's about three inches tall, the umbrella top about the size of a Lay's potato chip. "It looks like this. And the thing that sets these apart is the little collar. Underneath the fan is this, like a turtleneck." He holds it up for us to see. Underneath the typical mushroom fan, there's a small fold around the stalk, just as if it's wearing a little turtleneck sweater. The outside of the turtleneck is white like the stalk, but inside the fold is dark brown. "These also bruise purple. The other mushrooms you find, if they don't have this turtleneck, or bruise like this, they are not for eating. But the collar is clear to see. Do you see?"

We all say yes like a first-grade class.

"They grow on cow poop, mostly. So find the poop." He laughs.

We break huddle and spread out across the mountaintop. The field is so large, we hardly see one another as we search. The mushrooms are hard to find at first. Empty cow patty after empty cow patty, the whole thing feels like a scam. Then, twenty minutes in, I find one. Does it have a collar? Yep. Then another. Then another. I curl up my T-shirt like a kangaroo pouch and collect a mountain of them over the next hour. I zone in for my Easter egg hunt, and time begins to pass imperceptibly. By the time I fill my pouch, I've wandered far, to the tip of the brow of the hilltop. The light is beautiful and the valley below is blue with haze. Mountains layer away into the distance, turning levels of blue-green and then just blue. I can't believe the scale of it all. It feels like the scene in *The Sound of Music* with Julie Andrews running through the field. Except I have magic mushrooms in my shirt.

We return to camp and dump our hauls onto a blue tarp. I'm proud to learn I found the most. Weston found a good amount, too. Some people find only one or two. But all together, there's plenty to go around.

Even though these are mushrooms, and they grew out of poop, I am enchanted by it all. It feels clean and pure. So different from the cocaine vibes in Cartagena. I had grown up on a farm surrounded by cow patties, and cow poop had a cleanness about it. It's just grass, really. And these sweet little mushrooms had dressed up, put a turtleneck on for us. Everyone here is so calm, so collected, not fiending for a high, but rather pleasantly waiting to commune with nature.

"Fernando, how many should I eat?" I ask. "This is my first time. And I'm generally very sensitive to stuff."

"Just eat three little ones for now."

Weston, proud and protective of me, chimes in. "You'll be fine. We'll be all right here. This is the best place in the world to do this. The best. Eat them soon, while the light is still out. You'll want to look around and enjoy the view."

I eat them. Chomp. All at once.

"They'll taste pretty disgusting," Weston says after I've stuffed them into my mouth.

But they don't. They are gummy, the normal texture of a mushroom. And they don't have much taste at all. I wash them down with some water.

I wait. I drink some more water. I sit in the grass and chat with the others. I have a few false starts: "Ooh, I'm feeling it . . . just kidding, no, I'm not." "Okay, now I am! No, that's an ant on my ankle."

Weston floats up to me, maybe feeling it and smiling. "Do you hear the world yet?" He seems cartoonish to me.

"Listen to Weston, trying to make everything so mystical," I say, mockingly. I get a laugh out of a couple of the other campers. Weston doesn't laugh.

"But everything is mystical," he says emphatically. He looks at me like I have hurt him. He slinks away. I don't really register it. I'm laughing about something with my new friends.

I pull out my journal because I think it would be fun to write down what I'm feeling as it's happening.

Then—I feel it.

A widening. A tingly slowdown of color and light.

I hear sounds, as if I were a wolf. Sounds are isolated, far-off sounds, and feel very close. I don't feel drunk or high, this is different. I don't feel dumb or slow. I feel like myself, just . . . heightened.

I feel what Weston had told me about: that nature would take on special holiness. I feel an intense love of it all.

I pull out my pen and start to write.

I want to push my face into the mountain.

Not the one I'm on.

The one far across the paradise valley

that I could never reach.

But the birds see it, and every
mountaintop is just another stone
poking out of the stream, hopping
across.
The birds have so much to say . . .

I put my journal down and look around. The ten of us are sitting around in the grass, near one another. Everything is hilarious. My cheeks hurt from laughter.

Twenty feet away, I hear a ladybug land on a blade of grass. I squint to see. I see it. I think I see it. I hear her wings flap and then stop and the mechanics of her red-and-black shell close over her wings. I hear everything.

In the calmness of one phase of my mushroom trip, I sit and watch Weston from afar. He looks so happy, grinning like the Cheshire cat, inaudibly chatting and using his hands to tell a grand story. I think about his quest for answers, his fluctuations from atheism to Christianity to humanism to nihilism to animism. I think about how badly he wants the world to make sense. How it tears him up, so he tears through ideologies, testing them with all his might. As the mushroom magic courses through my brain, I suddenly understand why he loves experiences like these. For a few hours, the world makes sense. Everything has meaning. Everything is alive, in perfect friendship with everything else. I want, in this moment, for Weston to have peace in his heart. I want him to feel what I feel all the time: total conviction that it all means something, and it all is meant for good. I hear another bug land on a leaf, and my mind goes elsewhere.

The sun goes down, and the Argentines start cooking. The food is an assortment of sausages and purple potatoes and onions and other things. Our headlamps create a little microworld of light in the darkness.

At one point, during a rare lull in the giggling, someone sits up, spooked. "Did you hear that? Something is over there."

We turn our lights to the field and see a semicircle of eyes. No—a full circle, all the way around us. Fifteen pairs of eyes glowing back from the darkness.

Dogs. Wild dogs have surrounded our camp, waiting for us to make a mistake. Fernando is calm.

"It's just dogs. We'll just need to be careful to pack up our food and put it in the tent with us."

We go back to our food and our laughing. Every few minutes I turn my headlamp behind me, and the eyes are there. Waiting. Weston gets up and scares some away. We find it all very funny. But I have waves of dread, looking behind me at the patient beasts.

We eat, pack up, and go to bed. We are careful to wrap up all the leftover meat and put it in bags and bring it inside the ten-person tent. We make pallets and get in our sleeping bags. One of the guys does a last run-about-screaming session, to get the dogs away. They run into the dark. We zip up and fall asleep.

I WOKE UP to bright morning light and the front door being un-zipped. Then a gasp. "They got the meat!"

I sat up. We'd left the meat outside??

No. We'd brought it in with us. But where the meat had been, there was now nothing. In the corner of the tent, a perfect hole. Somehow, the dogs had pulled an *Ocean's 11* heist, chewing through the tent, stealing the meat, and eating every last morsel without one of us waking up. Outside the tent, plastic was strewn all over the hillside. We were so amazed . . . cleaning up the plastic wasn't even annoying. We were too impressed.

I expected a hangover or something, but felt nothing. In fact, I felt excellent. Weston was so proud. "You see. There's no hangover. It's natural. It's a gift from nature. You enjoyed it?"

"I really did."

Chapter 13

GOD ON THE TRAIL
(Medellín to Salento)

7,689 miles to go

n the morning, we packed up, joking about scary dogs, and headed back to Medellín and the hostel. I kept thinking, *I did mushrooms in Colombia. Who am I?*

The next day, we said our goodbyes, and biked into the green mountains beyond Medellín toward a town called La Dorada, 150 miles away, and beyond that, Bogotá. One night we camped in a dark thicket of vines and trees, so thick that it wasn't until morning that we noticed we'd camped only meters away from a house. The next night we camped under the highway below a bridge. We wanted to be under the bridge itself, but no trees grew under the bridge, so we hung our hammocks on trees that lunged over the river. Unfortunately the plan was more picturesque than practical. It turned out to be very difficult to get into our hammocks and impossible to get out during the night to pee. It rained harder than any rain I've seen in my life that night. The humidity that enveloped us felt so thick that I thought I could bite the air. The rain broke my rain cover and filled my hammock with water. Sleep never came. The next night, tired and hot as hell, we slept in a forest on the side of a hill.

After that, the highway dropped from the jungle into a long agricultural valley that cooked us at temperatures over 100. And not the dry heat of Baja. Crushing humidity, black clouds of smoke from trucks passing by, and beating sun. By 11 a.m., Weston had run out of water. He pulled over on the side of the road.

"I'm light-headed."

"You want some of my water?" I said.

"This is scary. I'm sweating too much. I'm dizzy," he said, the seriousness in his voice unsettling. I was hot as well but not dizzy.

"I have water," I said. "We can stop at the next gas station, hopefully one comes up soon."

"I don't know if I can bike in this heat. I may need to hitchhike or bus."

I stood there, cooking in the sun, and checked the map on my phone. "La Dorada is coming up in twenty miles. Let's make it there, spend the night, and we can find a bus to Bogotá."

"I just don't want to pass out. Dang, this is freaky. It sneaks up on you," he said.

A miserable hour later, we rolled into La Dorada, a midsize town built along a river and bustling with motorbike taxis. We found a janky little motel with air-conditioning and sat in our cold room for the rest of the afternoon. I found a bus that would take us to Bogotá in the morning. I got on Warm Showers, the app that connects cyclists with free places to stay, and found a guy who'd host us in Bogotá. We messaged and he said he'd meet us at the bus station and take us to his house. Weston was shaken by how dehydrated and hot he had become.

The next day, we bused up more mountains and through thick forest to enter the giant metropolis of Bogotá. Like Medellín, Bogotá is another ocean of red brick, but instead of being wedged into a narrow valley, Bogotá stretches out across a high plain. A steep mountain rises next to the downtown area, with a gondola to the top. The air is thick with smog; cars and people are everywhere. Houses are jammed together like town homes covered in red brick and stucco and chipped paint. Power lines tangle above the streets like black knots of hair. Every intersection is a sea of mopeds and bicycles. The city sits at 8,600 feet, and the thin air and proximity to the equator make for sharp, piercing heat in the afternoons, and nights as cold as ice.

At the bus station, we waited by the entrance for our Warm Showers host. A teenager walked his bicycle up to the door and introduced himself. "Hi, I'm Luis." He was probably sixteen. Weston and I smiled at each other and hopped on our bikes and he led us through the city for an hour to his house—a brick sliver of a house behind heavy metal gates. He unlocked what must have been ten different locks to get us in. Inside the humble house we met his mother, who looked very surprised to see us. Clearly, Luis hadn't told his mom that two large gringos would be invading her home. She seemed pretty uncomfortable the whole night, and as she cooked us dinner, she was ready at any moment for us to rob or attack her. Weston sat on his phone, flicking his thumb across the screen. He found a girl on Tinder that said she would host us for a night.

"Your Tinder girl is going to accept two guys?" I asked.

"Yeah, she seems amazing. She wants to show us around."

"I thought Tinder was for sex?" I said.

"It's also a way for great people to meet each other. This is going to be great. And maybe she'll be into me," he said with a wink.

Mariana showed up the next morning with a small red car and a Bernese mountain dog named Copernico. She was tall, with long straight brown hair. She had a severe but pretty face, and spoke perfect English. She was talkative right off the bat, and addressed us like old friends. No niceties. "Get in, I have several places to show you before we do dinner." Mariana seemed able to answer every question. Even if she didn't know the exact answer, she could say something that felt like an answer. As we drove around, and her dog licked my face and slobbered everywhere, she answered my questions about the Colombian economy, the government, the history, the treatment of natives.

She told us she was from a well-to-do family and had studied political science. "Sometimes my grandmother says I look native," she said, "which is her trying to insult me. To look native is bad. Dark skin. Short. That is her generation, they are very racist."

"See all these nice cars?" she said at one point. "All these big trucks? Colombia is trying to be America. They want new and nice things, and they buy it on credit. It's all on credit. No one can afford this stuff. It's all going to crash."

We stayed at her apartment that night. Weston slept with her in her bed and I slept in a hammock hanging in the corner. While they made out, I fell asleep thinking about how smart she was and how glad I was to meet her.

Her place was pretty small, so she suggested a hostel for us to move into the next morning. But she made it known that she would like to show us more of Bogotá while we were there.

The hostel was a lovely old house with a big gate and a blood-hound living in the courtyard. The cheapest room had fifteen bunks, but Bogotá was expensive, so it was our only option. That or miraculously find more Tinder girls. I found out that a bunk room full of backpackers will punish you all night with snoring of incredible volume. No doubt the altitude and the smog weren't helping, but some of these backpackers must have developed brain damage from the choke-snoring they were doing. I lay awake for two nights, waiting for one or two to die.

We hung out with Mariana all week. She would tell us exactly when she would pick us up and where we were going. She was always in control. She took us to breweries, steak houses, coffee shops, museums, and even a cathedral in a salt mine. Weston thought she was only sticking around because of me.

"She doesn't even really talk to me," he said.

"She's my Colombian girlfriend," I said with pride.

Weston clocked the beautiful girl working the front desk of our hostel. She was short, with a Salma Hayek vibe and long beautiful dark hair. Her accent was Colombian raspy perfection. He turned on the charm and they went to dinner. He reported that they had raucous sex at a cheesy sex hotel. "Apparently these hotels exist because people live with their families till they're married, so they need places to bang." He said the television was on and it was *The Simpsons* turned up really loud. He said she was equally loud. He said she might have "broken his dick." He said she had changed him. "She did this ball-slapping thing. I am a changed man."

During a FaceTime with my mom, she tried out an idea. "Jed, what do you think about me coming down for Easter? I have a lot of airline points from my Costco credit card. What if your brother and Anna and I come down for Easter? I'll rent a house. Where could we meet you?"

The thought of seeing family again was a welcome thing. But at her offer, I noticed that my homesickness had lessened. I wasn't desperate to escape the road anymore. My dad was right, the road had become my life now. *I am a nomad,* I thought. *I am comfortable in this homelessness. This at-homeness on the road.*

A plan occurred to me. I told my mom, "Well, if we time it right, we'll be in Quito, Ecuador, by Easter. That's in two weeks. Why don't you check tickets and rent a little Airbnb down there and we can do Easter there."

"Ooh, Ecuador," my mom said with a playful Spanish accent, "that sounds beautiful. I'll do some research and let you know. This will be an adventure!"

Twenty minutes later, I got an e-mail from her with her Airbnb receipt and flight itinerary. She had rented an apartment in Quito for a few nights around Easter Sunday and then a house on the beach. My brother and sister-in-law would come, too. I was excited, though stressed about making it to Quito in time.

To be in Quito by Easter we would need to travel 1,100 kilometers in just a few weeks. Uh-oh. That would be a race.

We said goodbyes to Mariana and Copernico and cycled out of the city. It took us a whole day just to get out of Bogotá.

Camping at such elevations was cold and difficult, and we tried to stay in hostels and hotels when we could. The two-lane mountain roads were crowded with semitrucks and massive buses. Several people had told us we had to stop in Salento, a coffee-growing village in the mountains famous for its attractive buildings and surroundings. We didn't really have time to stop, but I got mad at having a schedule and racing to Quito, so we rerouted our course for Salento. After several days of biking, we arrived at the beautiful little town, loved it immediately, and ended up staying there for four days. Green mountains surrounded the town, and a picturesque river wound through the valley below. It is how I would imagine Switzerland if it had been near the equator. The high elevation and the weather—a mix of chilly and warm—made the region perfect for coffee.

Our hostel was tucked into an old Spanish building with high-ceilinged rooms. The owner was an American, a geologist with gray hair and turquoise beads around her neck. She had come down to study the volcano near Salento years ago, and fallen in love with the place. A messy breakup and perhaps a midlife crisis had brought her back. She said that the volcano nearby was due to blow at any time. She said the last time it blew, more than a thousand people died. She said this with the indignation of scientists in sci-fi movies, when they warn of the asteroid or alien invasion, and the world doesn't take them seriously. Weston and I liked her right away.

She recommended a hike in the Cocora Valley. "The scenery is stunning. Waterfalls and cliffs and a café at the end where you can get a beer." The valley, part of Los Nevados National Natural Park, also features the national tree, the Quindío wax palm. She pointed one out down the road, and Weston and I recognized it. We'd seen a bunch of them on the roads. It looks like a typical palm tree, but taller, as if Dr. Seuss had given it a cartoonish stretch.

In the morning we enjoyed our free coffee and pastry, then caught a shuttle bus to the trailhead, where the valley closed off into a box canyon and the river came cascading out of thick forest. Our trail crisscrossed the river with exotic-looking wooden rope bridges. I don't know if this valley had a special spirit about it, or if Weston and I hadn't had a real check-in in a while, but we got to talking about more than our usual surface observations.

"Jed, I have a question," he said.

"Yes?"

"Do you believe in Jesus? Like, for real?"

I laughed at the bigness of the question. He smiled in the asking, knowing it was almost absurd to ask something like that outright.

"Do I believe he existed? Yes," I said.

"Do you believe he is the son of God, the actual son of God, to wipe away the sins of humanity?"

I was quiet for a beat, thinking harder now. "I don't know." I had never been asked that point-blank, and my once intact certainty had been eroding for several years. I tried to convey what I thought now. "Yes. In a way," I said. "I mean, I believe in His teachings and His life and His message saving us from our sins."

"You do? Do you actually believe He rose from the dead? Like for real, did He miraculously rise from the dead?"

Weston's pointedness rattled me. I had spent so many years in church not actually being asked. He was like a reverse Inquisitor, demanding statements of unfaith.

"Well, I think so," I said.

"You think so? Doesn't it all come down to that? Like, all of Christianity rides on this miracle? If He died for your sins, and didn't rise, then was He really God, and what does it all mean?"

His questions weren't antagonistic or charged. He was just looking down, hiking, stepping over rocks, thinking out loud and asking me questions. You know, the masculine way of having vulnerable conversations: a shared journey, no eye contact, both looking ahead, seemingly uninterested in the answers.

"I don't know," I said.

"Do you believe in sin?"

"Yeah, yes."

"Okay, what is sin?"

"It's doing things that separate you from God. Like choosing yourself over God. Thinking you know better than He does."

"And how can anything separate us from God? He made everything, right? What's not His? Isn't He everywhere?"

"Yeah, but He gave us free will. Or some version of it."

"You really believe in free will?"

"Yeah," I said, without hesitation. "I know it's a weird concept, but how else would we be in relationship with God? Without a choice, we'd be robots."

"So sin is what again?"

"When we choose to do things our way, and not God's way, I guess."

"But wouldn't an all-knowing God forgive us those things? Like correct us? Show us a better way?"

"I guess that's what Jesus did, isn't it?"

"Yeah, but do you really believe He had to be tortured and murdered and sacrificed to make up for a game that His 'father' invented? One that He knew all the players would lose?"

I couldn't tell if Weston was on a quest to understand himself, or simply to challenge me. But he was thinking about something other than his body, his steps and his breathing. He had slowed his pace. I had, too, walking just a few steps behind. We kept on like that for a while—him peppering me with questions; me regurgitating what I'd heard and read over years of church and Bible studies, at once agreeing with what I was saying, wondering if I really believed it, and hearing how ridiculous it sounded when I said it out loud. Weston's mind was moving fast, his words starting and stopping, unfinished thoughts leapfrogging their way to other thoughts.

All the while, though we barely noticed, we were climbing higher, along and over the cascading creek.

"So you're telling me you really think this was the best idea God had for us ... to build the universe in such a way that we show up with a deadly handicap that will doom us, hundred percent, unless we learn a story about His son, and say His name, and understand the story of how it happened? That was God's best idea? That was the thing I could finally not overcome, and why I walked away. It didn't make sense." Weston was beside me now, looking at me when he talked. We had crossed the creek several times, and almost ignored the beauty of it all, our heads swimming in the meaning of life.

"God is so much bigger than us, it doesn't always have to make sense," I said, falling back on the time-worn justification.

"Jed, you're a smart guy," Weston said. "But I don't think you're supposed to be a Christian." I recoiled with a surprised laugh.

"I think you're really just a kind guy, trapped in a tradition," he continued. "You're gay and you're out and free but you were raised a certain way and you won't let go of it. You don't want to spin through space without a tether. I remember when I was a Jesus freak, I was preaching from park benches and screaming the Gospel. Salvation of souls was an emergency. I don't see that in your eyes. I see a guy who likes the idea of God, of love, of defending a faith system that is the norm and the majority, but pretends it's a victim and the underdog. If you really thought about it all, you would realize that the Jesus story is too small for God, if God exists."

I remember reading somewhere that when people argue, their

brains seize up and lose the ability to take in new information. But this wasn't exactly an argument. Yes, I was recalling defenses and thoughts, but I was also listening.

"Well," I said, "I don't pretend to have all the answers. I just know that God, if you zoom out a bit, doesn't have to be so small. I agree with you on a lot of this, Weston. I'm just not ready to throw the baby out with the bathwater. It feels untrue to do that. It feels like you're trying to convince me not to be a Christian. I don't need you to do that."

Here we were, walking through one of the most beautiful places on the planet, with giant mountains surrounding us—and the two of us were looking at the ground, our minds somewhere else, lost in our histories and cosmologies.

"You say the universe is patient with us," I said after a brief silence. "That the universe put magic in mushrooms and whatever. But aren't you just talking about God, with another name? Aren't you just personifying it the same way Christians do?"

"Well, sure, yeah, I guess that's right. But I don't think that the universe loves me, and calling it the universe leaves it open to mystery and implies how big and unknowable it is."

"You think we're the same as animals?" I said, trying to cover all angles.

"Yes. Why wouldn't we be?"

"Because we have consciousness, we have a soul. God made us in His image."

"Jed, what does that mean?"

We'd hiked a long way. I could see the café in the distance, surrounded by trees and steep cliffs high above. I looked up for a minute, and felt the strange juxtaposition of incredible beauty, and the fact that Weston and I had hardly acknowledged it. I broke the flow for a minute. "Weston, look around. Holy shit, we're so deep in our dismantling of the patriarchy and religion that we're missing this."

He laughed and brought it back. "Are you kidding? I've been seeing it all. What better place to destroy God than surrounded by His best handiwork? Or what better place to replace the white man's God with the god of nature?" He capped off his pronouncement with a few fist pumps in the air.

But we jumped right back in. "Paul says that the Gospel is a mystery," I said. "Look at Job. At Ecclesiastes. I think the Bible is teaching us how to think about God. It's a journey of understanding. It starts with a very humanlike God, because we were so primitive in the beginning, and as we advanced, so did our understanding of God, which reached its high point in Jesus. That's why God sent His son there, because then we could understand Him."

"Maybe so, but that was two thousand years ago. Why would our understanding of God have frozen two thousand years ago? All these pastors talking about what the Bible really means. They're trying to make this ancient document relevant. It's retarded—"

"Don't say retarded—"

"—sorry. It's ridiculous. As we learn about the universe, and 'God,' we have realized that He isn't a he, or human at all, but the universe itself. It isn't humanlike at all. This is the next step. Religious people are just stuck in a feedback loop of old information."

"You think I'm stupid for still calling myself a Christian?" I asked.

"No."

"You think I don't—"

"I think you're a coward."

"Whoa . . ." I said.

Weston realized how intense and heavy it sounded. "Okay, okay, listen, you want me to tell you what I really think?"

"And here I was, thinking you were just high all the time," I said jokingly. "Yes, go ahead."

"What I mean by coward is that, Jed, I think you know that your beliefs are old and archaic and meaningless in the modern world. I think you think that you know that, and have reasoned and rationalized faith so you don't have to be controversial, don't have to upset your family, or your mom, or whatever. I think your sexuality caused you to go extra on your faith, to be a good boy. You'd be a super Christian in order to overcompensate. You'd prove that being gay wasn't perverted. You'd prove it was reasonable and something good

boys do. I think you are wearing the costume, hiding from something you know is true. I think that you're scared, and that's bullshit.
I just want you to be free."

I realized then, after traveling down half the globe with him, that
he had been analyzing me as much as I had him. Perhaps seeking
safety, I tried to pivot. "Free, like you? Chasing one high to the next?"
I asked, surprised by my response.

"I don't expect you to understand. I have been where you are,
dude. Well, I'm not gay, but in every other way I know. I know what
it's like to want to be good, to want to be a good boy and a good son
and think that God loves me because my teachers love me, and my
friends' parents trust me. You don't love God, man. You love feeling
like you belong to something. That warm feeling of order in the universe. Of having the universe on your side, but really, having people
on your side. I just want you to be free from all that shit."

"I hear you. I hear you. I know you do. And I love you for that.
I'm just figuring it all out. I feel like some days I'm arguing for God,
and another day I'm arguing against Him. I wish I liked weed and it
didn't make me puke in my underwear."

We both laughed. Weston was visibly relieved to see me playful
and not offended. My mind was busily weighing all that had been
said, wondering what scaffolding inside me had been knocked away.
I thought about Weston's worldliness, his rugged edges, his impurity.
He carried a cloak of wisdom, covered in dirt.

We reached the base of the stairs to the café above. It was a wooden
cabin with a large wraparound porch and several hikers enjoying
coffee, looking back at the trail. Something buzzed past my head. We
both got wide-eyed and looked around us. We were surrounded by
hummingbirds. Fifty. Maybe a hundred. A species I'd never seen in
my life, with long hooked and split tails, like two opposite facing "J"s
hanging behind them. They were everywhere. Shining purple and
black and blue like an oil spot in a heavenly parking lot.

We came out of our spiritual stupor, our high-octane conversation, surrounded by fairies swirling around us.

The forest had taken on that other layer. It was beautiful, the air
was clean, the light angled just right. I was wondering what it meant

to be Christian. I wondered if I was going to heaven, if Weston was. I saw the other hikers, sipping coffee and speaking various languages. I saw them as eternal souls. Each one destined for something. For relationship with God or rejection of God. Or nothing at all. Just death and worms and eternal sleep.

We got coffee and I talked about the hummingbirds to think about something else. My mind turned them into a sign from the Holy Spirit, that God was with me. I didn't say that to Weston.

Chapter 14

SEX HOTELS AND HERE COMES MOM
(Cali to Quito)

Our conversation rattled me, though I didn't show it. Instead, in a move perfected by most men, Weston and I moved right into joking around and didn't speak about God or sin again, outside of the occasional "the universe made you do that, huh?" joke. On the hike back to the bus, I barely said anything. My mind felt twisted like a wrung-out washcloth, my theology bludgeoned and embarrassed.

We stayed one more night in Salento before heading south to Cali. Nicely paved highways and medium-sized towns and a comfortable ride. Farms and fruit stands and stray dogs. We arrived in Cali as the sun was setting on the second day. En route, I hadn't been able to find Wi-Fi, so we hadn't lined up lodging. We approached a cab driver, who was leaning on his cab smoking a cigarette, and asked for advice. He lit up and told us we could walk our bikes to a hostel nearby. The Hollywood Hotel was adorned with a painting of Marilyn Monroe on the wall. That should have been a clue, because it ended up being a sex hotel. Weston and I shared a queen bed with a mirror above it and the wall rattled with the sounds of people having sex in the next room, or perhaps in all the rooms. We laughed ourselves to sleep.

We didn't like the feel of Cali, probably because of the grime of the hotel, so we didn't hang around. Besides, we needed to get to Quito to meet up with my family. Over the next few days, we pressed on to the border of Ecuador and Colombia, to a town called Ipiales. By then, the Andes had begun. The mountains were still green but showed snow in the distance. Deciduous forests gave way to green grass and shrubs and evergreen trees in the narrow places where mountains met.

Ipiales was small and pretty clearly built for tourism. People came from all over to see the nearby basilica of Las Lajas Sanctuary, jutting out into a narrow canyon over the Guáitara River. It hangs in the sky like something out of *Lord of the Rings*—white, comically ornate, and built on top of giant stone arches over the canyon and river below. The jagged white spires made it look like the lower jaw of a dragon, or a dangerous wedding cake. We walked to an overlook spot, where I gave Weston my camera to take my photo. As he stood back, a group of thirty Colombian teenagers walked up behind us. They were giggling and it was clear they were talking about us. One of the braver ones interrupted and asked, "Gringo, are you from America?"

"Yes," Weston said.

"Can we photo? With you?"

"Oh, sure!" Weston said.

Suddenly the teenagers lined up, and their chaperone began taking photos of them with us. I thought it would be a group photo. But each kid wanted their own. And then each kid wanted their own and one with their two best friends. For thirty minutes, we were celebrities.

"What was that?" Weston said, laughing, once they'd left. "It keeps happening."

"I've been thinking about it."

"I bet you have a theory."

"Of course I do," I said. "They watch a lot of American television and movies, right? Full of white people."

"Yes, definitely."

"But there aren't a ton of white people around here. On the backroads we're on, I mean."

"That's probably true," he said.

"So they've seen white Americans in all these movies, and all these TV shows, and so the concept of a white person is, like, famous to them. They've been staring at people like us their whole lives, and only seen a handful up close. Like, think about a Masai warrior. Have you ever met one?"

"No." He laughed.

"But you know who they are, and what they look like."

"Of course, they're famous."

"And if you saw one at your local mall, you'd look at your friend and say, 'Oh my god, a Masai warrior in our mall!' and then maybe ask for a photo."

Weston gave me a head nod. "It's not the worst theory I've heard," he said.

Back in Ipiales, we walked uphill by the cathedral and past a row of touristy trinkets and guinea pigs on rotisserie spinners. They looked like skinned rats glistening with glaze over a fire. I had heard that guinea pigs—*cuy*, pronounced "coo-ee"—were native to the Andes and had been a major source of protein before the Spanish brought over chickens, cows, pigs, and goats. Now they were eaten at special occasions, for sacred holidays, and so on. They'd been domesticated thousands of years ago, so long ago in fact that there's now no such thing as a wild guinea pig. But this was the first time I'd seen these cute pets roasting on the sidewalk.

Little furry sacred creatures—for sale to tourists. Speaking of sacred, it was April, almost Easter. That meant Mom time was almost here!

MY MOM, BROTHER, and sister-in-law were due in Quito in two days. We had to get there, quick. It was 155 miles away. That would have been doable on flat land. But from Cali we had crawled up to 9,000 feet elevation, and with these winding mountain roads, we didn't think we could make more than 40 miles a day. We walked our bikes across the border, got our stamp out of Colombia and into Ecuador. From there, we decided to bike for a day, then bus or hitchhike the last bit.

As we entered Ecuador, the land felt different. For the first time we were truly in the Andes. The trees grew only in clumps of dark green evergreens on the mountainsides. The light was sharp, the air thin. We'd grown accustomed to wide swings in temperature, but up here, it was worse. If the sun was out, we'd bake. By midnight, the puddles had frozen. And the people we passed looked very poor and almost exclusively indigenous—worlds apart from the urban populations of Colombia. The Quechua people of this region date to the Inca empire. They are short, stocky, darker-skinned, often with sloped noses. They live in small clay houses in the treeless world of high-altitude mountains where they keep sheep. As Weston and I biked past, people would stare at us with sullen expressions. If I stared back, they showed no sign of relenting, or caring.

Rural Ecuadorian women wear felt bowler hats. The ones you've seen in old photos of British businessmen, or that famous painting of the guy in the bowler hat with a green apple in front of his face. Those hats. They love them. I kept asking people why, and they didn't know. I found that curious. You live in a country peopled with this interesting culture, and you don't know why they wear their very distinct costume?

Then I thought, why do some Native Americans wear suede coats with frills, or headdresses, or why do some black people wear picks in their hair or do-rags? Why do businesspeople wear ties? I have no idea. I've never asked.

Eventually, though, I got to the bottom of this bowler hat situation. When British companies were connecting South America through a vast railway system in the early twentieth century, the railmen wore them, and the Quechua-speaking people liked them, especially the women, so they adopted them. It was that simple.

As is to be expected, after I'd met a few Quechua-speaking people and heard a few locals explain how they live in the Andes, I drew firm and sweeping conclusions. My lazy brain saw the same patterns everywhere. Travel can do that to you.

Oh, I've been to Italy. The Italian people are so relaxed. So welcoming.

Really? How long were you in Italy?

Oh, for forty-eight wonderful hours.

The two-lane highway coiled around the switchbacks where buses geared down to puff enormous clouds of black smoke into our faces. Up a mountain. Down into a valley. We made it to the sweet little town of San Gabriel, slept there for a night in a small hotel, woke up early, propped our bikes up and put our thumbs out, hitch-hiked to the larger town of Ibarra with a proper bus stop, and took a bus from there to Quito.

As the bus crested the final summit, we saw the bowl of human civilization in the valley below: Quito. This was becoming a South American norm, cities at high elevations built in mountain valleys. It looked much like Bogotá and Medellín. Red brick buildings. A few tall condominium and office buildings. The spires of massive cathedrals piercing the sky. Wispy, low clouds hugging the cold mountains. Quito had one main mountain standing right over the city, just like Bogotá, and, just like Bogotá, a gondola rising to the top, leading to an overlook and visitors' center.

From the bus station, we tracked down a hostel, where we showered, and had beers with some Israelis and Germans. The next day, my mom, my brother Luke, and his wife, Anna, arrived.

The Quito airport was new—all glass, giant TV screens, shiny coffee shops, and polished floors. My mom appeared in the crowd at baggage claim glowing, seeing me from across the room, shooting her hands in the air with a little jig, and then struggling to get her rollie bag to go in a straight line. She was feeling international. Even as her bag was rebelling, she danced and wiggled her hips and made a duck face, all representative of how cool she was, flying to Ecuador. Amid a flurry of hugs, my mom couldn't stop talking about how clean the airport was. We picked up our rental cars—two tiny red ones—and drove to our Airbnb back in the city.

"Oh, this is a huge metropolitan city!" she exclaimed. "So cosmopolitan! Much more advanced than I thought!" But she got a headache from the altitude almost immediately and needed to relax on the couch. Meanwhile, we planned out our time in Quito. To begin, we would walk around the old town, and take in a nice dinner spot with opera singers in the city center. She was thrilled about the prospect of that.

It felt wonderful to be around family.

The next day we set out on foot and my mom was mesmerized by everything. By the old Spanish buildings. By the high-rise condominiums. Inside the gold-leafed cathedrals, she took a thousand photos.

"The Catholics really know how to build. This looks like Europe!" she'd say.

Quito seemed glutted with churches and cathedrals. They seemed to be on every block. The largest, the Basílica del Voto, was visible from almost any point in the city, its dark gray and menacing gothic spires pointing heavenward. We made our way to it, and Weston and I got to the top of the imposing steps first. As we walked into the basilica, two girls greeted us from a table under a massive gilded doorway. "*Dos dólares,*" one of them said to us.

"*Perdón?*" Weston said.

"*Dos dólares por persona, por favor.*"

"We have to pay to enter a church?" he said.

"*Sí,*" she said.

Weston spun on his heels to walk away. "This perfectly sums it up," he fumed. "Jesus is spinning in the grave He never rose from. A place meant for God, for a moment with God, charges money to enter. If that isn't moral bankruptcy, I don't know what is."

Back outside, I said to Luke and Anna as they walked up, "We're not going in there, they charge." My mom was taking a photo from the sidewalk. I just said, "It's closed, Mom."

"Oh, okay. I didn't want to walk up all those stairs," she said.

On Good Friday, we positioned ourselves for the parade through the center of town. We figured out the right streets, and drove our little rental cars to park and post up. All around us, people had brought chairs and coolers, claiming prime spots. My mom's camera hung around her neck, her fanny pack bursting full of God-knows-what.

As the parade began, so did the wonders winding through the narrow stone streets. Here came dozens of people in purple gowns and purple pointed hoods standing up from their heads.

"Is this a KKK march?" my brother asked in shock. I had no idea, but a woman standing near us on the crowded street chimed in.

"These are Catholic. Not like America. It is different," she said, smiling meekly as if to apologize for eavesdropping.

"Oh, thank you. We were so concerned," Mom said. I had come to learn that all over Latin America, I couldn't assume that the people around me didn't speak English. I couldn't gossip or giggle with

Weston, because someone, in any café, no matter how rural, spoke English.

I later researched the pointed hats and robes and learned that criminals were forced to wear the cones in humiliation as they were marched through town and pummeled with rotten fruit and mud. The Spanish Catholics adopted the pointed hat and cloak as a sign of guilt and humility during Easter week and marched through the cities as penance for their sins. The Ku Klux Klan co-opted the hood, for reasons unclear. Maybe in reference to holiness. Maybe to look like scary ghosts to intimidate blacks. It's fitting that those hoods were meant for dunces and sinners.

Some of the purple people paraded past with no shirts on, just the coned hoods. Some carried giant wooden crosses, so heavy that they had to put them down every few paces. The cross carriers were barefoot, and the pavement was scalding in the sun. A few of the crosses had green plants tied all around them. Other marchers, without crosses, had bundles of the green plants tied with string into a whip, and as they walked, they whipped their bare backs. My mom, worried, wondered out loud what the plant was.

"It is a plant that stings and cuts. It burns, it is very painful," our woman explained. "It is a way for the people to repent of their sin. To feel the pain of sin." As they walked by, I could see their backs were bright red and scratched. The plant looked like the stinging nettle that grows in North America that stings the legs with the slightest contact, like thousands of fire-ant bites.

Weston couldn't help himself. "Religion is so absurd. These people are cutting themselves for something imaginary, made up by Spain, their oppressors."

Along came a large group carrying a litter (one of those boxes that a king or queen or Oprah would sit on while people carried them on their shoulders), with a life-size Virgin Mary seated on it. The parade went on a full three hours, and by the time we made our way back to the apartment, our sunburns were setting in. But my mom had been affected more deeply.

"This is so much more powerful than America. It shames us," she said. "We are so complacent in our faith, in our abundance. These people have nothing and they show their commitment to the Lord like this. They take salvation seriously. We Americans are so comfortable, we think giving up chocolate for Lent is a sacrifice. These poor people are barefoot and bleeding and actually picking up their crosses for Jesus."

"Mom, you once told me you didn't think Catholics are saved," I said.

"No, I didn't."

"Yes, you did."

"Well, you must have misunderstood. God is mysterious. True, we Protestants don't believe in a pope and we may disagree on Scripture here and there and have different styles of worship, but they are so committed to Christ and salvation, how could God not reward them? Who are we to decide? Besides, the Bible says 'whosoever believes' will be saved."

"Mom. You have told me that Scripture is not a buffet, I can't pick and choose what is true."

"It isn't!"

"Well, wouldn't that mean that some Christianity is right and some is wrong?"

"Yes, but God judges the heart. And maybe Protestants get some things wrong, I'm sure we do, and Catholics get some things wrong, I know they do, but how can you look at the devotion we just saw and doubt their commitment to Christ?"

"I'm just pointing out inconsistency, Momma."

"Don't, it's annoying," she said with a grin.

MY CONVERSATIONS WITH Weston had me looking at my mom differently. My childhood. My upbringing. Taking it all apart. Figuring out what was real and what was not.

I remember lying in bed, maybe I was twelve years old, waiting for my mom to come sit beside me and say prayers over me, and hearing my sister scream at her from the kitchen, "I hate you! No wonder you can't stay married! Everyone hates you!" and then the familiar slam of my sister's door, and my mom coming in, her eyes red from tears she'd wiped away.

"Okay, cutie. Ready for bed?" She shut off all but the night-light so I wouldn't be able to see her face.

"Dear Lord, watch over Jed as he dreams. Thank you for all our blessings, for our family, for this house and the beauty of each day."

I lay there, eyes open, watching her talk. Watching for a tear, maybe. Wondering if God could really hear her. Her eyes were perfectly, effortlessly closed.

"Thank you for the hardships that make us strong, and make us rely on you, Lord. Amen. Sweet dreams, Jed. What do you want for breakfast tomorrow?"

"French toast."

"Okay. You got it. Good night."

I remember we went to church every Sunday morning, every Sunday night, and every Wednesday night. I would moan and beg not to go. "Mom, it's so boring. I hate it. You're making me hate God!"

"Well, as long as you live under my roof, you're going to church. Train up a child in the way that he should go, and he will not depart from it. That's what I'm doing."

I thought, *Oh I'll depart from it! Watch me!* I resented church and I resented my mom for making me go. Years later she told me in passing, "I was a single mother of three kids, no money, no help, no time to myself. Church was the only safe place we could go where I knew you'd be looked after and taken care of. It was the only place I felt less alone in all of this."

As a kid, it never dawned on me that my mother was overwhelmed or frightened or worried about the job she was doing. It never occurred to me that she had complex motives.

QUITO HAD MY MOTHER spritely and full of the joy of discovery. She took photos of every stone and doorway. That night we had booked a fancy dinner at an Italian restaurant on one of the city's picturesque squares. The restaurant, which famously served up an opera performance mid-meal, could've been a palace, with gold chandeliers, enormous paintings and tapestries adorning the walls, marble floor. Waiters in red tux jackets and black pants. The place was packed with older people, tourists, and families.

We ordered two bottles of wine. Weston and I had put on our best clothes—denim shirts, buttoned up, and blue jeans. My mom wore new jewelry she'd bought from a street vendor. She put on nice lipstick and seemed to glow with self-awareness that she was in another country, with her family, eating an expensive meal. I could feel her taking in the scene to tell her friends back home.

As we had wine and talked about the parade, Luke and Anna were canoodling and being cute. They were always like that—one of those married couples who actually like each other, and continue to. She would lean back and giggle at anything he said. He had his hand on her knee, a steady presence. My mom, historically, didn't drink much. I actually had no memory of her drinking when I was a kid. When I had asked her why, in my early twenties, she said she didn't like the taste. And that she didn't like drunks, having seen enough of them growing up in the Ozarks. But as her children became adults, she began having wine with us on holidays, and margaritas on hot summer nights. I discovered that she was a lightweight. Sitting here dressed in her Sunday best at 8,000 feet elevation in Quito, Ecuador, she was loving her life. She was drinking her wine and laughing deeply.

As she drank wine, she got gigglier. I made fun of all her rings and jewelry and the fact that soon she'd be weighed down, dragging her arms like a cartoon caveman. She flashed her many rings. "I look amazing!" she said. They were rings of different stones, mostly turquoise and tiger's eye. I told her she was beginning to look like a woman from Sedona.

Then the opera started. We were all a bit buzzed and therefore loud, encouraging, and jubilant, clapping and hooting. The song was by a man in a mask and a woman in a big poofy dress. They sang between the tables, and were playful with the guests. The man would sing at women eating and flip men's ties and mess up kids' hair. Each table thought it was hilarious and wonderful. And their voices were loud and excellent.

My mom was turned around in her chair and clapping along and just a bit fluid from her wine. Her movements were softer and her smile wider. The man came over and knew she spoke English, just from looking at her.

"Look at this goddess!"

"Who, me!?" my mom said. She looked at us around the table and her eyes were so bright.

"This is a woman. A beautiful woman," he sang and came up behind her, rubbing her shoulders. She raised her shoulders in affirmation and closed her tipsy eyes and smiled ear to ear and cooed.

"How can beauty like this be? How is your meal?"

"Woooooonderful!" she exclaimed. He told Anna she looked like an angel and made fun of my brother's shirt. Everyone was laughing, but I was looking at my mom. She was watching the opera singer, staring at him like a crushing teenager, hoping he'd come back.

I saw her young and beautiful. It crossed my mind that she had maybe not been kissed in fifteen years. Or longer. Since my stepdad divorced her for the secretary. I didn't know. She looked so beautiful. So regal in her womanliness, and yet childlike in her innocence. In that moment, I wanted her to fall in love again. I wanted her to feel as beautiful as she was.

The opera singer sauntered to another table. I saw my mom turn back into herself, close her inner doors with a smile. She returned to her wine. And turned to me. "Ha! Wasn't that cute! Oh, I just loved him."

"He liked you, Mom! He lit up," I said.

"Do you think?" she said. She looked over her shoulder at him, watched him move from table to table, lady to lady, and I hope she thought, "Yeah, but we had something special."

We finished our meal and headed back to our Airbnb. Quito and Easter and purple hoods and Christ on a cross and my mom were on my mind. What was I supposed to do with all of that? The faith of these Catholics, stinging and whipping themselves. Weeping in the streets for their sins. The faith of my mother. Her sweet humanity. The contradictions. I was comforted by her celebration of the Catholic Easter parade. She had definitely told me before that Catholics weren't saved. She had spoken about them as pagans in the abstract. But here, on the streets of Quito, she was shaken by their devotion. Exposure to them seemed to expand what she found acceptable. It reaffirmed my belief that exposure creates empathy. But it also shook me up. My mom's brand of evangelicalism was what kept me celibate, what kept me from kissing boys, because Scripture said it wasn't okay. Plain and simple. I can't "interpret" my way out of that.

I didn't know what I was holding on to. I had wrapped my life in the fear of messing up. Of disappointing God, which really meant disappointing my mom and friends. I was finding that so much of my life had been about avoiding the feeling of being in trouble.

MY FAMILY STAYED for ten days. We went to the coast for the weekend, where my mom had rented a beach house for a couple nights in Montañita, which looked like a Spring Break–style wild town. The drive was supposed to take eight hours from Quito, but took us fifteen. Google Maps wasn't exactly accurate when it came to side roads in Ecuador. Roads it said were there, weren't. Roads that weren't on the map suddenly appeared. We ended up driving down a sandy creekbed in the pitch black, certain that we were going to run out of gas and die.

Along the way, my mom's unshakable optimism was the only thing that kept me from bursting into flames. She took photos of every goat and cow she saw. She took photos of kids in the street. I told her she shouldn't. "How would you like it if foreigners drove around Nashville and took photos of your young kids without asking?" I asked her.

She replied, "That's ridiculous. But they're just so beautiful." She kept remarking about how happy everyone looked. How pleased in their poverty they must be, free from the clutter of materialism.

"I bet these people would love to have more money," I said. "They'd be materialistic like us if they could."

She did not agree. "No, I don't think so. I think they know what life is really about down here. And even so, they're lucky to be spared from all that."

We arrived at the beach house at 1 a.m., exhausted but thrilled to be alive. In the morning we went grocery shopping and Mom bought fresh fruit and was just thrilled by the exoticness of it all. "Have you ever seen anything like this!" she shouted, holding up a *guanábana*, a big melon-shaped green fruit covered in soft spines.

The Wi-Fi at the beach house gave my mom the opportunity to get off a mass e-mail. She loved writing long updates to her girl-friends back in Nashville.

I was cc'd to the e-mail, Mom making sure I saw her recap.

Being in a "third world country" with breathtaking beauty of the Andes, jungles, and Pacific shoreline, it makes me ponder matters of the world when I see severe poverty in all directions. Nature's beauty and poverty, they co-exist here.

Ah—Americans. We are materially blessed beyond what we deserve and the USA remains the land of promise regardless of messy politics (on both sides) or overreaching governmental controls.

Look at the typical rural or suburban home in Ecuador. Without infrastructure, a stable or growing economy, bank loans, higher education, or decent jobs, the people have little opportunity. Most homes take a lifetime to build because there is no money for materials. It's one cinder block at a time. The sale of fruits, vegetables, fish, and jewelry seems to be the main source of income.

Ecuadorians are physically beautiful, very short and highly creative people. Children play everywhere without fear of being attacked or stolen. They are gentle spirited and speak softly. Men take motor scooters and turn them into mini taxis to carry passengers on dirt and pot hole filled roads in small towns.

Our beach house sits high on a hill, and it took the owners 20 years to build. It is very comfortable, spacious, can sleep 10 and is far, far above the living standard of most. Anna has been sunbathing in the front yard when not on the beach.

Jed and Weston walk down the narrow road to the ocean to surf.

A typical lazy meal in the beach house. We have cooked beans, rice, enjoyed fresh tomatoes, onions, avocados, eggs, potatoes, bananas, strawberries, Ecuadorian coffee, wine, and more—we are really experiencing what it means for food to go from the farm to the table!!

A meal in town. We gave the waiter a generous tip and he couldn't stop thanking us.

Path to the beach. Usually obstructed by a donkey or horse. Or trash.

Although the most strenuous thing we do is walk to the beach, the days are passing quickly and soon, we will part ways. Jed and Weston will head into Peru while we return to Nashville.

Tuesday, we begin the long drive back to Quito. We pray for paved roads and to make it in 8–10 hours. Not the 15 hours it took us to get here through rutted roads and jungles in the middle of the night.

Today, we plan to visit a small cathedral on a bluff overlooking the ocean. It's not far from here. I'll say a prayer of thanks to the Lord, from whom all blessings flow.

Jed and Luke wait for big waves,
His blessings on you,
Barb

I enjoyed making memories with my family, cooking meals and lying in hammocks and going for walks on the beach. It was a dirty beach, but mostly empty and beautiful in its humility. We played gin rummy and watched Pixar movies and laughed as my mom tried to pronounce words in Spanish. One thing stood out: after scraping our pennies together and living cheaply for thousands of miles, Weston and I enjoyed my mom paying for everything. All the meals. The places we stayed. The rental car. We slid right back into the joy of adolescent, worry-free existence.

On Tuesday we found the proper roads and made it back to Quito in eight hours flat. Since the family was flying back to Nashville the next day, we stayed at a hotel near the airport. My mom felt empowered by her successful visit, and promised to join me in Patagonia at the end of my trip. "Now that I'm so accustomed to travel in South America, it'll be easy. And by December, I'll be in need of new photos to brag to my Bible study ladies about. These Ecuador photos will last me about six months."

At the airport the next day, my mom slipped me a hundred-dollar bill. "Buy a bottle of wine and a get a good shower when you need it." I knew a hundred dollars was a lot to her. That's how much she would give us for Christmas. I was sad to see her go. Through the cunning work of avoidance and humor, we'd had almost no hard conversations. My mom did say "your future wife" a few times to me while talking about the future. That was always a dig. But we had successfully avoided a blowup about Christianity or sexuality or politics.

WESTON AND I went back to our hostel and began planning our next steps. Our journey into Peru. It was almost May. We had nearly two thousand kilometers to go to Lima. Then another thousand to get up to Cusco, to see Machu Picchu. It felt daunting. And according to the map, once we left Ecuador, coastal Peru would become a sandy nightmare of endless desert. Oh no, another desert. Fuck the desert. I was trying to figure out where we would bike, where we would hitchhike, how far we could go, if there were stretches with no towns, and how much food to pack onto our bikes.

We sat drinking cheap beers at a table in the lobby of our hostel. I was looking at the map on my phone. Weston was journaling. He said almost in passing, "I'll need to camp more. I don't have money for hostels."

"Oh, okay," I said. "But our routine is camp and then hostel, camp and hostel, or host home, so we can shower sometimes. Where will we shower?"

"We'll need to find more hosts. I just can't spend money anymore."

"Like, you're out?"

"Yeah. I have like ten bucks."

"Right now?"

"Yeah. I'm supposed to get another fifty put in my account, but it's taking forever."

"Okay, wow," I said, bewildered. Why hadn't he told me before? I never really knew how much money he ever had. But wow. "Well, I can pay for you sometimes, for a hostel or whatever, so we can shower. We both need to shower."

"Okay," he said, not looking at me, drawing something in his journal. "That's up to you. I'm happy to stay on my own if you want to pay and I'll find a camping spot and we can meet up."

"Weston, you're not camping alone. We'll find cheap places or make it work," I said. I was annoyed. Sure, I wanted to be rugged and camp. But this deep into the trip, the novelty of "roughing it" had worn off. I had fallen in love with hot showers and actual beds like never before. I always thought I didn't need comfort, but the trip had taught me that that's something comfortable people say. I had enough money for ten-dollar hostels most of every week. But for two people, for nine months? No.

I thought about the hundred dollars my mom had given me. I could spend it on him. Or I could spend it on myself, because I wanted to punish him. For what? Sometimes pettiness feels good.

In frustration, I took to my journal. Writing it out helped me loosen the coils. I wrote, *I wonder if my friendship with Weston is like a marriage. We're in this together, headed somewhere. Our finances are bound together. I get annoyed at him. He gets annoyed at me. But we have somewhere to go. And I want to kill him. But I think I'd be helpless and sad without him. When the honeymoon phase is over, what's left is the continuous choosing of the other person. If I had done this trip with a boyfriend, we'd certainly have broken up by now.*

I looked up from my writing at Weston. We had Peru ahead of us. And then Chile. Another horrible desert. Ugh. And finally Patagonia.

Getting there together struck me as impossible.

Chapter 15

THE COLDEST NIGHT
(Quito to Cusco)

6,661 miles to go

After Quito, we biked through high country for three hundred miles, approximately paralleling the ranges of the Andes, camping along the way. Cuenca, a small city with its own beautiful cathedral, rolled out another full-day parade, I still don't know what for. We blissed in its postcard-quality streets and drank craft beer. From there, we descended out of the Andes on splendid, winding long downhill rides toward the coast. As we lost altitude, vegetation thinned and temperatures climbed. As we crossed into Peru, the vegetation dwindled to almost nothing, and the desert began.

Along the coast, the twisted, burnt bushes spreading between sand dunes reminded us of Baja. We rode by rusted trucks and wild dogs and clay houses cracking in the heat. Still, the sun felt less oppressive here because mists from the ocean hung over the coastal road in the mornings.

Days passed. We slept under the sky and saved money and ate simply. Stray dogs chased us and teenage boys gathered around to ask the usual questions. "Where are you from?" "How much does your bicycle cost?" "Are you married?"

I was proud of my bicycle, my Surly Long Haul Trucker. It was scratched up now, but the chain hadn't broken. I'd changed a lot of tubes but never had a tire mishap. The leather straps on my handles had turned darker—from the color of cappuccino foam to roasted coffee bean. My bike had become a part of me, and I'd hardly noticed. Weston's $300 "experiment" was still here, too. It was rickety and made weird noises, but it had made it to Peru.

We aimed for Trujillo, a touristy coastal town with nice beaches and hostels that promised young people and creature comforts. After a week of riding from Cuenca, we made it there dusty and gross.

Weston suggested we stop at a café and see if we could find free hosts on Warm Showers or Couch Surfer. But I didn't want the hassle. I needed the comfort of a place without the need to be sociable. When we found rooms at a hostel for fourteen bucks per person, I offered to pay for both of us.

The hostel was swarming with Israelis, tan and muscular guys with aviator sunglasses and cocktails in hand all around the pool. Attractive girls with dark hair and big laughs. They spoke English. Weston bought some weed off of one of the Israelis in our bunk room. While they smoked in the courtyard by the hammocks, I sat in the room and boiled. I had paid for the room, and he paid for weed.

"Oh, I see you found some weed? Did you buy it?" I said with an attempted softening laugh.

"I told you I wanted to camp. If you want to stay in places like this, I'm happy to, but you'll need to pay for it."

"Weston, I thought you were out of money."

"I am out of hostel money. I budgeted enough to smoke, because I want to, but I don't need a bunk bed and a shower, I can swim in the ocean and sleep on the beach for free. These are my priorities."

I dropped it. You don't have much bargaining power when you're all alone on a foreign continent and your travel partner is driving you crazy. I didn't want to bike up the Andes alone. I didn't want a blowout. And to be honest, I didn't want to damage the perception among those following our progress that Weston and I were on this perfect fantasy trip through South America. I didn't want to explain to my friends and our friends and his friends that we were at each other's throats. Which we weren't. It was just accrued tension and frustration making the air thick and every conversation feel like a negotiation.

We spent two nights in Trujillo, lying by the pool and chatting up loud Israelis. Weston wore his short shorts and walked around the pool barefoot and shirtless, attracting the eyes of girls and guys. His body, supernaturally fit, was always a spectacle. His tiny waist and abs and shoulders were perfectly constructed, as if made on a computer by some horny teen. He hardly worked out. He ate whatever he wanted. He looked like that for no good reason. Most days I didn't think about it. Normally I didn't compare his particular gifts to mine.

But watching him walk around that pool, attracting attention, I burned. Not with lust, but with jealousy. I thought about my vastly celibate life. How asexual I had always been. How late I bloomed. I wished in that moment that my body, my beauty, had made decisions for me. That someone had tried to seduce me years ago, and the chemicals of attraction had overtaken my prudent good-boy life. If I had been beautiful, would I have thrown off these Christian rules long ago? Would I have loved and been in love, and allowed the abandon of love to overrule my churchy world? I began to doubt that my choices had been a result of my incredible willpower, that to honor God and Scripture I had rejected the advances of cute boys. Because no boys had advanced. In my twenties I had been proud of how pure I'd been, but now, watching Weston, I realized that my goodness was closely tied to my plainness.

But by the pool in Trujillo, I wished to be hot and shallow and desired. I wanted to be heckled. I wanted hormones to make decisions for me. Not all this philosophy. Not all this prayer.

Weston, enjoying the stares of the girls, and the boys, kept circling the pool, smoking his joint in plain sight. And I wished God had trusted me with a body like that, that He had thought I could have the willpower to overcome it. I wished I had been given that calling, and failed, and had sinister sex, and felt guilt at how attractive I was, and how weak.

And finally, I wanted to get back on the road, away from the beach and the pool and all the jocks on vacation. I wanted to feel special again, intriguing and adventurous on my bicycle, not like I felt here, invisible.

ON THE THIRD MORNING, I paid for our rooms, and we packed up and headed south. Always headed south. I didn't like the desolate coast of Peru and hoped Lima would save us, but it was still hundreds of miles away. Weston complained about the desert, too. Yes, he liked the sun. He liked being shirtless. But he remembered overheating in Colombia. He remembered being dehydrated and scared. By the time we had biked a few more days down the coast, the landscape had become completely barren. For long stretches, we saw no leaf or sign of a growing thing. The only trees we saw had been planted in the little towns, leaving the stretches between human settlements rocky and lifeless. The traffic, though, was thick. Massive trucks assaulted us with trails of black smoke. Stray dogs scrambled from behind rocks and falling-down shacks to give chase and nip at our tires. Weston's tubes blew twice and mine blew once. When we were out of spares, we sat on a dune baking and worrying about running out of water until a truck stopped to give us a lift to the next town.

Casma offered a few trees, a few stores, some spots offering tours to archaeological sites in the area (common in coastal Peru), but no bike shop with the tubes we needed. We were fucked. Lima, our best hope, was still three days' ride away. Too far for hitchhiking. But with our shoddy Spanish and a bit of begging, we found a bus to Lima that begrudgingly let us shove our bikes in the luggage hold.

Lima is another giant South American metropolis, but unlike Bogotá, Quito, and others we'd seen, this one wasn't at high altitude, on some verdant mesa in the Andes. The Peruvian capital lies at sea level, and springs from the barren land like a mirage. Ten million people on a cliff next to the ocean. The dark desert was lit by street-lights on the outskirts of town, warm yellow beams cascading onto walls through the coastal fog.

Our bus approached the city at night, passing through a seemingly endless expanse of clay and cement houses. Were they gray, yellow, tan? I couldn't quite tell in the glow of the orange streetlights. I saw people and stray dogs walking in the shadows, appearing in the pools of light, then vanishing. Trash piled high in the ditches. As we neared the center of town, glass buildings rose up tall and clean. Then, just inland from the newer developments, we entered the old city of stately Spanish buildings, some preserved and beautiful, others derelict or crumbling. I knew Lima was famous for its food, and we wanted to stay for a few days. But it was expensive. We couldn't find a hostel for less than twenty dollars a night. We tried to find a host home, but hadn't had Wi-Fi in so long we couldn't lock one in. So we decided to stay a night or two in a hostel anyway to figure out our situation. It was hard on us. I was so worried about Weston's money that I couldn't enjoy spending a dime.

At a café the next morning, Weston informed me he was going to Hawaii.

"When?" I asked.

"In May. I can't miss my friend's wedding. They sent me an e-mail and I can't miss it."

"Okay, I get it. And you haven't been home yet at all."

"No, and I'm in the wedding. And it's all-expense-paid. I'm gonna go."

This was a new side of Weston. This air of certainty. The Weston I knew was a reed bending in the wind, smiling and squinting his stoner eyes at the flow of the universe. But here was a man with a firm plan. Telling me instead of asking me.

Truth is, a separation was already happening. We kept the same schedule, but were no longer in a common battle. We were like the couple who had long ago bought the fixer-upper, excited by the dream, but now just felt stuck in the mess of all they had asked for. We'd been through Oregon to Mexico to Peru now. And for me, Patagonia was still too far off to feel. We were in that part of the valley where neither the mountain we came from nor the mountain we sought was visible, and the river fog made us feel like the valley is all there is, forever. I was annoyed at worrying about money in a circumstance I had created. I felt indulgent and dumb. Lima was dirty and annoying. Weston was dirty and annoying. He'd found an escape. I needed one, too. I needed to get out of there.

Before Weston flew out for the wedding, he wanted to see Cusco, the legendary capital of the Inca empire. So did I. We'd seen enough desert. We both wanted trees and mountains and beauty again. But Cusco was at least a two-week bike ride away, plus the climb of getting from sea level to 12,000 feet. Fortunately, tons of buses ran up to Cusco from Lima because most tourists coming to Peru were headed there. We settled on traveling by bus up into the mountains, then riding to Cusco from there.

Before we left, I invited a group of friends from LA to come hike Machu Picchu with us. I wanted to do a popular five-day hike through the mountains, and I thought I could lure them to join me. *Once in a lifetime adventure! The chance to see some of the most famous ruins on earth.* And I would get to see some old faces and get some new conversations. A little break from one-on-one time with Weston.

As soon as I sent the e-mail, I got responses. "Looking at flights now!" "We're coming!" That felt good.

Weston and I took an overnight bus the 350 miles to Ayacucho, a humble little town of unpainted gray cinder blocks crammed in the narrow hollow between two mountains. We arrived in late morning to scenes of stray dogs, sheep, and vacant-looking people. Famished, we tried for an early lunch in a cement doorway that displayed a sign with images of food on it. We wanted fuel before we hit the road. Inside were two plastic tables, with tablecloths and lawn chairs. In a corner, a World Cup qualifying game played on TV. A little girl stood in the kitchen doorway, watching us. When a woman appeared, I asked for a menu. She cocked her head in confusion. "Do you have a menu?" I repeated, this time in Spanish.

"No menu. Only lunch."

"So is there a lunch menu?"

"No menu. Only lunch. You want lunch?"

"Yes," I said.

She walked into the kitchen through a floral-patterned sheet hanging in the doorway, and only then did I realize that she obviously lived at the restaurant. Or better said, the restaurant was her house. We had walked into her living room.

Weston and I watched the soccer game. I found something comforting about the game. Somewhere, thousands of people had enough free time to sit in the stands and scream for a team. They probably drove there. They probably all had beds to sleep in. Woke up in them and went back to them at night. Not like our life on the road, where we seemed caught in a cycle of repeating concerns: where to sleep, what to eat, are we safe, will we get rained on, will we be cold, am I saying this in Spanish correctly, are we imposing, does this family resent rich Americans, regret letting us into their home?

The woman reappeared with two bowls of soup, a whitish yellow thin broth in which floated one dark gray potato and a chicken foot. The foot protruded out of the bowl like a scrunched hand trying to fit through a tight bracelet. The sight devastated me. Hungry as I was, how was I supposed to gnaw on this lizard-like foot?

When she left, I whispered to Weston, "The food in Peru is so famous." We chuckled and I ate some of the potato. When we paid, the woman seemed sad that we hadn't eaten more. In mangled Spanish, we tried to assure her she was wonderful, then walked next door and bought potato chips, Oreos, and cokes.

As soon as we stepped on our bikes, we were hit hard by the 9,000 feet of altitude. We hadn't acclimated like we would have had we biked from Lima. We had stepped on the bus at sea level, and stepped off into mountain air. And per usual, the temperature fluctuated quickly. Clouds would roll over and chill us to the bone as we rode, then they would pass, and the sun burned like a laser. Just about the time we'd strip off our jackets or flannels and tuck them into our mounds of cargo, we'd cycle into the shade of a mountain and have to pull them back out.

We biked for the day and into the evening and as the sun set there was nowhere to camp. The road was carved into the side of the mountain with no shoulder and no thickets or forest. Finally, we found one small hotel in a woman's house and slept on cots. We froze all night. The next day we aimed for a town fifty miles away but we only made it thirty. The steep hills and the altitude combined to slow our progress to a crawl. When we asked a woman at a roadside market if there was a hotel anywhere nearby, she said of course not. We stood there feeling dejected and began trying to recollect if we'd seen any ditches or bridges where we might sleep. But the woman was listening. She walked over and said, "There is a barn behind the market. You can camp there." We enthusiastically accepted.

The barn was dark and cold inside but we were grateful to be out of the elements. We hung our hammocks from the rafters and settled in. I read *Time* magazine on my iPad. Weston used the light on his phone to read his book, *Siddhartha*. He was rereading it now. He kept saying "I hate this cold," as if to himself, or God, but I drifted off and slept well.

We woke up and cycled on. Up and up. We were making terrible time. The hills were too steep, and the altitude had done something to my head. There was a sharp, relentless headache deep in the middle of my head, and sometimes moving right behind my eyes. I'm not a hypochondriac, but all day I wondered if it was a tumor.

By that evening, we were still nowhere near a town. On my Google Maps, what showed as a town turned out to be an empty barn or an intersection with a dirt road. With no stores, we survived on salami and cheese and crackers.

Finally we saw a few trees beyond a field, tucked between two hills. We pulled our bikes off the road and slogged through the mud to get there. But when we got to the trees, we realized they were too close to each other. Maybe we could get one hammock up, but not two. Weston walked farther into the gulley, looking for a better option. Meanwhile, I was troubleshooting in my mind. Okay, we can lay our rain tarp on the ground. We can huddle together for warmth. What if it rains? God, I hope it doesn't rain. Maybe we could string the rain tarp over one hammock and the other person could sleep underneath. Hmm.

When I looked up I saw Weston walking back in defeat. Then he jerked to attention, looking behind me. He gestured with his head and eyebrows to turn around and look. I did. Coming around the corner from the road was a man on horseback, coming right for us. Shit. We're on his land. His horse wasn't trotting, but slowly approaching, as if the man was studying us, angry and choosing which words to use. He's gonna kick us off his land and it's twilight and we're fucked. It was in moments like this that my mind would zoom out, and I would remember that no one knew where we were. If something bad happened, no one would find us.

As the man on horseback got closer, though, he became a she, and the horse became a mule. The woman wore the standard-issue bowler hat. Two long black braids hung over a dark brown poncho. Her skin was very dark. As she came close, I could see that she was missing one of her front teeth, and she was scowling. I jumped into damage-control mode with a torrent of horrendous Spanish. "Hi, sorry! We are on bicycle to Cusco, from the United States, and looking to camp. Sorry. Is this okay?"

She replied with a few short words that didn't sound Spanish— Quechua, I assumed—and made a quick scooping gesture, indicating for us to follow her. We stood there, confused. She smiled this time, and scooped again. At that, we jumped to gather our things.

We walked our bikes behind her mule up a switchback dirt trail, to a crest. We could see the whole valley below, a green heaven with the last rays of sunlight turning it purple, pink, and lavender. She pointed us to a patch of grass where we could set up. No trees for hammocks, but the ground was flat and the grass looked inviting. It would be perfect for putting our tarp on the ground and sleeping under the stars.

Our braided Lady of Mercy gazed down at us with a sun-wrinkled dark face and wise eyes. She looked to me as much a part of this place as the trees themselves. Like she grew out of the ground. I surveyed the place and decided it would be easiest to just sleep under the stars. I asked, *"Lluvia? Esta noche?"* I hoped I said the right word for "rain."

She stepped off her mule and thought. She looked at the sky. Looked at the horizon. Looked at the sky again. She said, *"No, no lloverá."* I was certain she could feel the weather, and knew its ways like a prophet. When she offered water, we dropped our bikes on the little mesa and followed her to the next hill. There was her home, a disheveled pile of tin, wood, and clay, like a hobbit hole mixed with a child's fort. She lived alone. A thin plume of smoke rose from the chimney. It was weirdly beautiful. She tied her mule to a thin tree by her house. Next to her home was a black plastic tube stuck in the side of the hill. Out of the tube poured water. Crystal-clear water. She took a cup and filled it with water and gestured for us to do the same. A moment's hesitation. Can I drink water straight out of the ground? Then we filled our water bottles and drank. It was sweet and cold.

She asked, in simple fractured Spanish, "You from United States?"

"Yes."

"My son lives in United States."

"Really? Where?"

"United States is a big city. I do not know."

Weston and I made eye contact, and we loved her. She lived here with a few chickens and a goat and a mule. Her son is in the U.S., she thinks, she does not know where. Was he thriving or dead? For news, did she ride her mule to some distant post office? Was the son's father in the picture somewhere?

How different our lives were. She did not live in the world of the Internet, of push notifications and endless crises, of social media and texting and passive-aggressive e-mails and life in the modern age. She lived in a shanty on the side of a mountain, all alone with her few animals. I wondered if she was happy. I wondered if she thought about happiness and how to get it, the way Americans do.

Meeting her and drinking that sweet water made my headache go away. We put our big blue tarp down and lay on top with our sleeping bags. We didn't chain up our bikes. Who would take them? I used my jacket as a pillow. The temperature was dropping quickly.

"She just lives out here, all alone," Weston said.

"There are so many different ways to be human."

"I like her."

"Can you believe, we would have been ruined if she had been a mean rancher shooing us away."

"The universe," he said.

A moment of silence later we were asleep.

SOMETIME IN THE NIGHT, I was awakened by cold. My face was inside my sleeping bag, but my butt and legs felt odd. Damp. I pulled my face out. It was raining. And our tarp had collected the rain into a pool of ice water around us. Weston and I were in our sleeping bags, half underwater, in a pool. I leaped up. My sleeping bag was soaked. My backpack was soaked. I quickly moved my phone into my pannier and rolled it tight and waterproof. Weston stirred and sat up and realized he was soaked. He moaned a sad and dejected moan. No outrage. Just total defeat. We crawled around in the dark, trying to help our situation. We had been lying on two tarps, one Weston's and one mine. So we drained the pool from the center of our ground tarp, wrung out our sleeping bags, then spread the second tarp as a cover and crawled back in. We were shivering and my piercing headache had returned.

"This is horrible," Weston said.

"I know," I said.

"I've never been this cold before," he said.

The rain continued for hours. And hours. It never stopped. The pool returned but we were too cold to move. We didn't sleep again. At least I didn't. An eternity passed.

Finally, at first light, we wadded up our soggy clothes and sleeping bags and tied them on our bikes.

"That was the worst night of my life. I can't do this. I can't believe I ever left the beach," Weston said, to himself more than to me. I thought of his trip to Hawaii. I thought, "He won't come back to this."

We pushed our sad bodies and sad bikes to the road and tried to ride. The road wound up and farther up, as if never intending to level off or turn into downhill again. Before long, the freezing cold and the wet made riding unbearable. Weston stopped and got off his bike and began walking it. I did, too. "Let's just hitchhike," I said. Weston nodded.

We stood by the side of the road and thumbed as a few trucks drove by. We were willing to wait all day. The rain stopped, then the sun came out but we were too tired to celebrate. Just exhale. After an hour or two, a police SUV stopped. When I asked if they would take us to town, they said yes. We had to take the wheels off our bikes to fit them in the back. The policemen must've known we were too tired to talk. They just drove in silence, listening to the radio, and dropped us in town.

"Wow," Weston said, walking his bike. "I trusted that native woman with the weather, just because of how she looked. I thought she was a gift from God, like He brought her to us. I was lazy and just assumed she knew everything. And I had the worst night of my life. And we were rescued by cops. Cops!" He shook his head. "God's favorite lesson is humility."

We got a cheap little hotel room to warm up. We took hot showers and laid our clothes out. We ate some soup in the tiny hotel restaurant. An older couple walked in suited up in elaborate motorcycle gear—expensive jackets and helmets, and special rip-proof pants and boots. The woman had blond hair and the man had spiky gray hair. They were probably in their fifties. After a few minutes of overhearing Weston and me speak English, they introduced themselves. They lived in Malibu and were on a motorcycle adventure across Peru. I impressed them with all my knowledge of Malibu and the fact that I knew exactly where their house was on the coast. But the familiarity and shared knowledge and laughter made me terribly homesick. To meet strangers and just speak with them. Effortlessly. To not worry about misunderstanding or cultural difference or otherness. To be the same. I'd wanted to run from it. And now I wanted to run to it.

The couple ate their soup and hopped on their fast motorcycles and disappeared down the road in seconds. I looked at our bicycles chained up outside. Those slow metal idiots.

Along the final eighty miles into Cusco, Quechua people crowded the road, or stared at us from beside their sheep and mud-clay homes. The children ran out to gawk. Trees were rare up here, except for planted groves of eucalyptus. Mostly we biked through grassland and steep mountains and over streams of snowmelt.

Weston and I barely spoke as we rode. I thought about his trip to Hawaii. I felt an anger that I couldn't place. Just a knot in my chest. Just a feeling of "I want to get away from you." I assumed it was simply too much time together and too many hard circumstances. When I wasn't looking at him ahead of me on his shitty bike, I was thinking about Jesus. About what Weston had asked me. How he had forced me to say things out loud and made me sound foolish. How he'd called me a coward. He had such the upper hand on the other side of faith. But I scoffed at him in my head. Drug addict. Nihilist. Always skipping from one thing to the next. Running from the truth. Running from himself. Assuming the answer is hidden in some chemical or lifestyle.

As I rode I made the case for faith. If God exists, He'd want a relationship with His creation. Right? And if so, He'd have to anthropomorphize Himself, or else He would be completely unknowable. He'd have to stoop to our level, express Himself in a way that we could understand. Okay? So if He did that, anything He did would look too small for Him. Indeed, it might look made up. And the story of Jesus is the story of life, sacrifice, death, and rebirth. This story is told in nature. The seed falls to the earth and goes into the ground to be born again as a tree. The caterpillar dies to become a butterfly. Every day the sun must submit to death and night before morning can come. Maybe the Christ story is God's humble way of reaching out to us, saying things a little too plainly, even brutishly, in order to have a relationship with us. And then there's the beautiful community of the church. The friendships. The sense of purpose. The upside-down priorities of Jesus. He was a revolutionary. Putting the poor first. The meek. The weak. The left behind.

Making the case to myself helped me feel better. Whatever was good in me, my culture, my mom, my friends, and my mentors was tied into this story of Jesus. Jesus had kept me from kissing a boy for twenty-eight years. Jesus had kept me from myself. I had thrown myself upon Him so that He might fulfill me. If He unraveled before me, or worse, vanished, what would I make of my youth?

The thoughts and feelings came in waves. In heat in my chest. In dizziness. In staring at Weston with a knot in my stomach and a desire to run away.

WE HAD ARRANGED to stay in Cusco with a friend of a friend from back home who had lived there as a kid. Her host family was excited to have us, and I was excited to have a home base for a few days. A free place to stay. I just hoped the family would be chill and let us come and go. But I was excited to pick their brains and learn from them. They were tour guides to Machu Picchu. I'd dreamed of it since sixth grade. It was the ultimate Indiana Jones fantasy to me. These people knew all the history. I was excited to ask all the questions.

The farms and sheep gave way to gas stations and markets and suburbs and brown-brick apartment buildings. The traffic got congested. We were approaching Cusco. I found a café with Internet, e-mailed our host, got my Google Maps working, and then navigated us to their house. It was a town house lined up with dozens of identical ones in a grid. The mom opened the door and welcomed us with a big hug and excellent English. They gave us one of their kids' bedrooms and hot showers and home-cooked meals. They showed how well versed they were in American culture by giving us Smart TV control, their Netflix password, and beers in the fridge. They were also devout Christians, and we held hands to pray before each meal. Weston was polite with the praying, but when everyone else's eyes were closed, he would be wide-eyed, looking at their faces, looking around the room. I'd peek through squinted eyes, and quickly shut them before he saw me looking. I don't know why I felt embarrassed for him to see me looking.

Checking my e-mail at the house, I found that my friends had booked tickets and organized the whole hike to Machu Picchu while I was out of contact. The idea that they had committed to coming, and organized it all, felt comforting. I had feared that my friends weren't thinking of me, weren't wondering where I was, weren't impressed. But they had booked the tickets. They had booked a guided hike. They had found hostels and restaurant recommendations. When I told Weston about it with excitement, he just said he couldn't afford to pay for a guided hike to Machu Picchu.

"Oh," I said. I sat for a minute. "I'll pay for you. You can't come to Machu Picchu and not see it."

He said, "Okay, thank you," as if I'd just passed him the salt.

The city of Cusco floats in the sky. It sits in a bowl of hills at an elevation of 12,000 feet, looking as if it had been poured out of a giant wheelbarrow—bricks and stone dumped into the valley to create a vista the same color as Medellín and most of Bogotá, a reddish brown. Ancient, narrow streets of cobblestone lead through a town that shows Inca architecture everywhere. Walls built during the Inca empire, so massive that the Spanish couldn't destroy them. Giant stones fitted together as if by laser. As if a crane lifted them into place.

We stayed for a week. Weston bought a little weed from kids at a hostel. We were online most days, reading articles and Facebook and talking with friends. I was figuring out when my friends would arrive, what we needed before the five-day trek, where they'd stay. We walked the town, even did a guided tour of ruins inside the city. I bought a beanie and a two-person tent. I thought we'd need a tent now, because the high Andes were often treeless and too cold for a hammock.

Then it was time for Weston to leave for the beaches of Hawaii. He'd be gone for about a week, he said. Then he'd come back, and everyone would descend on Cusco and the hike of our lives would begin.

I was relieved to see him go for a spell. I didn't like how I had grown frustrated with him. But damn. The money thing. The endless conspiracies and questioning of society. And questioning of me. How can you enjoy the day if you're dismantling the world and the people around you piece by corrupted piece? I remembered the joke "love minus distance plus time equals hate." I just needed a minute of distance, so I could appreciate Weston for who he was. I was excited to think less and enjoy more, even for a week.

After he flew out, I spent time with our host family and read at cafés. I wandered around town and spoke very little. I liked the autonomy. My mind settled, and I quickly forgot everything about Weston that annoyed me. I pictured him happy, out of the cold, barefoot on a Hawaiian beach, free of this trip and of me. He wasn't shivering anymore. Did I already miss him?

I found an old book in our host family's house: *The Conquest of the Incas,* by John Hemming. I read it every day, swept up in the wild tragic sadness of the Spanish invasion, the Incan empire in civil war, the European diseases racing out ahead of the conquistadors, doing most of their bloody work for them. I found the best cafés and stores in town, excited to show my friends. I was excited for the new energy of new friends. I was excited to love adventuring again. And the repose was nice.

Weston Instagrammed every day, something he never did on the road. Photos of him shirtless on the beach. Of wedding festivities. Of warm sunsets, coconuts, surfers. The day before everyone was going to fly into Cusco and he was set to return, he texted.

"Hey, man, I missed my flight. Trying to see if they'll change the flight for free."

"Oh, no. Well, we head out on the Machu Picchu hike in two days. Think you can make it before then?"

No response for a few hours. Then he texted, "Looks like they'll charge me over two hundred bucks to change my flight. I don't have that. Looks like I'll be in Hawaii for a while. Just following the signs, you know? If one door closes, maybe that's how it's supposed to be."

"Oh. Okay," I wrote back. I had already spent hundreds of dollars to pay for his Machu Picchu hike. He missed his flight. I didn't ask him why he'd missed it. I was simply not surprised.

"Do you think you'll be able to get back down here? Is your return flight just gone?" I asked.

"I'm not sure. Not trying to force anything. I'll call them later and figure it out."

"Didn't they buy you a round-trip flight?"

"Yeah," he said.

His short replies sent a clear message. He was not desperate to get back to the Andes. My mind went straight to: *Well, it's just me now. He's gone. Bummer. He's always following the damn universe. Is anything ever his fault? Did I scare him away? Is my bad attitude to blame?*

Chapter 16

EMPIRE FALLS TO EMPIRE
(Machu Picchu)

When I said goodbye to my host family, we hugged for a long time, and it was then that I realized how restful my time with them had been. How safe and nourishing. It felt nice to have a family and a mom again. Heading to the airport I felt giddy to meet my incoming friends.

The six of them filed off the plane and into the lobby, bringing with them a happy barrage of energy.

"Wow! This altitude!"

"I already have a headache."

"I have an entire CVS in my fanny pack."

"I need to exchange money."

"I need a poncho, stat!"

"I took four years of Spanish. I remember nothing."

Seeing them was a reminder of my father's advice: Your friends still love you. They haven't forgotten about you. When you see them again, it'll feel like nothing has changed. We were laughing and telling old inside jokes and talking about politics and gossiping about friends who can't ever seem to get their shit together. Even at 12,000 feet in the Andes, being with them was home. A few of them were best friends, some were newer friends in their "year of yes." Me? I was excited for any taste of home, so even relative acquaintances who asked if they could come along got a hearty "Yes!" All of them were exactly what I needed.

Two of them, Annabelle and Jordan, were among my closest friends from Los Angeles. We'd processed relationships, family drama, philosophy, and life together for years. I was excited to talk with them again, and in this holy place, too. I had Weston's words, his challenges, my own inner debates, swirling. But also the pain of the ride and the fatigue of it all. Seeing them lit the spark of curiosity again. Of wanting to understand. With Annabelle and Jordan, I had a safe place to test and examine what Weston had wrought upon me. The room of my mind felt torn up and turned over.

We all spent a day in Cusco acclimating and exploring. Jackie wanted to go to Starbucks. She had never left the United States before and was a bit shaken by the foreignness of it all. We acquiesced, and with a grande passionfruit iced tea in hand, she cheered up, and we explored the town.

For our five-day trek to Machu Picchu, the tour company would drive us through rural villages and river valleys to the base of Salkantay peak. There, we'd unpack and load up the mules, then hike over a 15,000-foot-pass and down to Machu Picchu, which sits at 8,000 feet. My friends had convinced the trek company to do the whole thing in three days. I asked how you could hike five days' worth in three, but they assured me that our guide was confident we could. "The trek was made so that older people can do it. You're all young. We can push it," he had told them. Besides, we would have mules to carry our gear and porters to cook and help set up the tents. It all sounded so opulent, and it was. But Machu Picchu and Patagonia were the two main draws for me in South America. I had camped and kept it cheap for thousands of miles. For this experience, I was ready to go big.

The night before we left, we picked a seafood restaurant and enjoyed a big dinner together. Jordan, ever the experience creator, had asked us each to bring a Hafiz poem to read aloud. We drank our wine and prepped ourselves for the hike of our lives with poetry from the Persian mystic.

I read one of my favorites.

> *Even after all this time,*
> *The Sun never says to the Earth,*
> *you owe me,*

> *look what happens with a love like that,*
> *it lights the whole world.*

My friends said, "Read it again!" I did, delighting in its simplicity. Everyone had it memorized by the time the second reading was over. The poem felt so true, it came into the mind and sat down in a chair that had always been there, empty and waiting.

Then we headed to our respective beds to get ready and deal with our headaches. All the hostels and hotels served coca tea in the lobby. This was tea made from coca leaves, the same plant from which cocaine is made. Inca royalty, though not the common folk, chewed coca often because it helped with headaches and gives you energy. When the Incan empire fell, the rest of the Andean world took up the habit.

As I went to bed, the thought of seeing the famous Inca holy city with my own eyes seized me like electricity. Here in the highlands, the evidence of an astonishing convergence of culture and religion was all around—the Spanish architecture beautifully folded into the Inca architecture, the Quechua people in the same breath talking earnestly about Pachamama (the earth mother goddess of the Inca) and Mother Mary. A bizarre unity of conquered and conquerors.

I kept drifting back to what I'd read in *The Conquest of the Incas*. How Pope Alexander VI granted rights to the king of Spain to conquer this part of the Americas and take all the gold he could on the condition that the Indians were given a chance to convert to Christianity.

About November 16, 1532, the Inca king first heard the name of Jesus. On that same day, the conquistadors put his kingdom to the sword. Jesus saves. But you gotta accept Him real quick or He kills.

AS USUAL, I had repacked the night before, then in the morning double-checked each pocket. This is how it always goes. My absent-mindedness causes me to second-guess everything. The trekking company had given us duffel bags for our belongings, which our porters would load onto mules. My bag was full of jackets and shirts for layers. We'd carry just day packs. The nights at Cusco's elevation were already cold, but we would be hiking up another 4,000 feet to our first camping spot, where snow was said to be common. Oh my. Weston would've hated that.

The van came just before sunrise. We waited for it in the lobby and drank coca tea. The earthy taste had grown on me. Or maybe it was the cocaine in it. I refilled freely, and it really did help my headaches.

We came out lugging our stuff. Valentin introduced himself as our guide. He had a handsome Andean face, chiseled out of brown leather. We were all bundled up for the cold. When we moved, our limbs made that distinctive *swoosh* sound that comes from puffy down jackets. Valentin knew it was his job to set the tone for all the grumpy gringos. As we climbed in, he said, "We have a two-hour drive. Napping now is allowed." As if on cue, Jordan, Cyrus, and I fell asleep leaning on each other.

We woke up high on a mountain road with Valentin staring back at us from the front passenger seat. "Good morning, sunshines!" he said. "We are almost there!" His accent was thick, but he had obviously spent a lot of time around English-speakers.

The van drove into a wide valley, white-capped mountains high above us, green grass spreading away from the road and turning gold at the higher, rockier elevations. We saw boulders piled together as if on purpose, but this was the work of glaciers. A clear stream divided the treeless valley, looking like a snake on a golf course. By now everyone in the van was awake and chatting.

At the road's end—where the stream was born from the snowline and the trail began—porters and mules awaited, and breakfast was ready. The whole arrangement felt very nineteenth-century colonialist. Hiring local people to carry my bags, cook for me, set up my tent. I had even broached this topic with my Christian host family the week before, but they assured me that trekking with porters provided excellent jobs for these men. One of the best in the region. And while the hike would be a challenge for a typical Westerner, it was more of a stroll for a Quechua man.

Valentin introduced us to the porters, and their wide smiling faces and squinting eyes were kind but seemed otherworldly. How can I describe this? There is a light that we recognize in the eyes of someone with whom we would say we "connect." This means we have life experience in common. Or culture perhaps. Subtle movements of their eyes, the way they glance around the room, the way they furrow their brow, you can tell so much about a person. We are unaware that our culture teaches us ways to hold our face. But these Quechua men, tanned, with deep wrinkles carved by the sun, circular bone structure and short stature, they looked at me with a smile and smiling eyes, but no connection beyond that. I know they had a deep communication among one another, and over the next few days I watched them joke and laugh among themselves, but with the language in our eyes, our cheeks, our eyebrows, we said very little to each other. It made me feel strange.

Valentin seemed to sense what we were thinking and feeling. He told us again that working as porters on these treks was an excellent job for them. And right in line with their heritage. "In the time of the Inca, all messages were transmitted orally by messengers," he said. "Meaning men would run from Cusco to Quito, Ecuador, in relay fashion, to communicate between the kings. Through the most treacherous stretches of the Andean mountains, a thousand miles. These are their descendants. They are at home in these mountains, at these altitudes. Where you will be sweating and needing oxygen, they won't think of it at all."

It still felt weird, even with all this assurance. As our porters set out breakfast, I resolved to be the most thankful, outwardly grateful hiker they'd ever met. I probably insulted them with my groveling and white guilt, but I didn't want them thinking I was some conquistador.

Hemming's book on the conquest had told me what that looked like, and left me shaken. The whole bloody history felt much more recent down here than I'd imagined. I had written down my own summary, to process it, I guess. To feel it.

The Spanish conquistador Fernando Pizarro had heard rumors in Panama of a vast kingdom somewhere in the mountains of the southern continent. He wanted to become as famous and wealthy as Cortés, who had conquered the Aztecs in Mexico ten years earlier. After two failed attempts to find the fabled kingdom, Pizarro would not let his destiny evade him. He tried one more time, traveling south from the coast of present-day Ecuador with a band of just 168 men—62 horsemen and 106 foot soldiers. (He would lose a few on the journey.) Plus a priest, as required by the Pope.

Along the way, Pizarro captured locals as translators and guides, and a story began to develop. There was, indeed, a massive civilization ahead. With hundreds of thousands of people, maybe millions. With a king, Atahualpa, a god on earth who was descended straight from the sun, and who had just defeated his brother in a brutal war of succession. Their father had died of a mysterious disease that was now sweeping through the empire, killing thousands.

After weeks of marching south and west, up into the uncharted mountains, Pizarro had reached Atahualpa. He set up a base in an Incan stone fort at Cajamarca, near where the king was said to be camped. From there, Pizarro sent a messenger on horseback to ask the Incan god to meet.

Pizarro had a problem. Atahualpa traveled with an army of 80,000 soldiers. The Spaniard had no chance of overpowering the king, with his 150 men. Ha!

But he had a plan. He would do what Cortés had done in Mexico. Use the natives' ignorance against them. They'd likely accept a meeting. The strangeness of Spanish skin and horses and technology would lure the king in. And there, Pizarro would kidnap him. Then he would use Atahualpa's followers' religious devotion to bring the empire to its knees.

After a simple and delicious breakfast, Valentin called us into a circle. "I want to welcome you all to the holy Salkantay trek," he said. "This is a trail used by the Inca hundreds of years ago, and it was a sacred walk. I will explain to you many things about this trail. Before we leave, let us say a prayer to God. Please hold hands."

I was surprised. If this request had come from an American

guide, some of our group might have respectfully declined. But coming from a Quechua man, in such a mystical place, no one hesitated.

"Holy Father, we ask that you keep us safe. This trek can be difficult, and we ask for safety, for guidance, for protection. Give these tourists a good experience, and bless them. Let the spirit of Pachamama shine into us as we walk. And let them know that even though it's hard, it's not that hard. They are not babies. In Jesus' name I pray, Amen."

Valentin smiled. We were happier for the prayer. I wasn't exactly sure who Pachamama was, but I was going to ask. We set off up the mountain. It was not yet 8 a.m.

Atahualpa was traveling with his army to Cusco to sit on his newly won throne. As he went, he drank from the skull of one of his brother's generals. Well, the whole head. They had dried the severed head, with skin and hair intact, and fastened a golden bowl to the crown of the skull. They put a spigot through the top and out the mouth. From this, he drank. This was his favorite chalice.

He received the invitation from Pizarro. He did not fear the newcomers; how could he? He was a god. He was curious, so he sent spies to investigate the pale-skinned aliens.

The spies reported that the aliens rode on strange, giant creatures. Some thought they were half man, half beast.

But these Christians posed no real threat. They were too few. Too weak. Atahualpa accepted the meeting.

Our porters charged up the mountain and out of sight before the rest of us had ascended a hundred feet. Jordan was visibly troubled by the social divide.

"I think using porters is economic slavery," he said, hiking beside me.

"Why? Valentin said it was a good job for them."

"They don't have an option. You or I wouldn't do that job. They see white tourists as other than them, as magical aliens with money and leisure. As superior. It's slavery."

"You're so punk rock," I said.

"The world is messed up. But I'm not gonna let it ruin me. We just have to be respectful."

The Peruvian Andes were all around us now. They were the most dramatic mountains I'd ever seen. The absence of trees gave them a naked beauty. The quality of light in the thin air brought out a saturated richness to the green of the grass, to the yellow of the flowers, to the gray of the rocks. Salkantay stood high above the trail, completely, brilliantly white. As we climbed, the grassy meadow gave way to piles of rocks. The stream below became water tumbling over boulders. We crawled up and up, reaching for rocks that looked like giant steps for gods. Jackie already had her can of oxygen up to her mouth. It looked like a Febreze can, but with a mouth cup on it. The visual made me laugh, even though I hardly had enough breath for the next step.

Meanwhile, Valentin took side trips among the boulders, collecting purple and yellow flowers into a thick bouquet.

After three hours of almost vertical gain, we reached the pass, Incachiriasca. The plants had all but disappeared now, and we walked over dark gray stones, sharp from falling off the mountain peaks high above. Patches of snow lurked in the sunless places beside boulders. Salkantay was directly above us like a white tidal wave. At the pass, Valentin knelt in a space protected by giant stones and carefully laid his flowers on the ground in the shape of a heart. Then he asked us to gather in a circle. This was a ceremony of gratitude, he said. He told us that we should give thanks to Pachamama. We should thank our parents for bringing us into the world. Thank the oxygen in our lungs. Thank the journey of our life, no matter how hard.

We tried to follow his advice, but the air was so thin, we were so tired, the scenery so ridiculous, that some of us were in tears.

Meanwhile, he told us about Pachamama. For the Quechua, she is the goddess of the mountain, of the earth. She brings fertility and prosperity. She is nature, and she gets upset when people abuse the earth. "The Quechua people pray to her often," he said, then added, "She is the Virgin Mary, also."

From there, we began our descent, dropping into a mossy green valley with snow-covered mountains on either side. As we walked, Valentin kept up his narration.

"Salkantay Mountain is over twenty thousand feet high, or over six thousand meters. Its name comes from Quechua, meaning 'savage and wild.' This mountain was very important to the Inca. This trail we are on as well as the Inca Trail were used as a route of travel to Machu Picchu from Cusco. You are very smart people for choosing Salkantay over the Inca Trail. That one is too crowded. Like big-city traffic. Like in America. This is much nicer. And better views."

I asked Valentin to tell us about the worst group he'd ever led, but he demurred. "Oh, I don't like to say worst. I did have a group of Russians who hired five extra porters just to carry their vodka and cigarettes. And they made it! Coughing and cussing all day. I had a couple in their mid-seventies last year come, they were from Alaska, and they were faster than me. I found out they were mountain climbers. They amazed me. Last week we had some newlyweds. This was their honeymoon. Some people should not marry. They fought the whole hike. By the third day, they stopped talking to each other."

We hiked from sunrise to sundown that day, taking breaks for coca tea and for lunch. We saw wild chinchillas in the rocks. We saw a local man, older than time, sitting in a stone hut, smoking something, and selling handmade beaded tassels. We each bought one. How do you say no to an old man in a stone shack selling crafts?

When we arrived at camp, our tents were already up and dinner was ready. We ate and cheersed, proud of ourselves, then we slept like happy babies.

Each day of hiking felt like a little life all its own. The first day was the pass, snow all around, transitioning into a beautiful valley of tiny wild flowers.

The second was following a snowmelt creek down to scattered trees and more humans. We passed a few stone homes, built into the ground. Smoke came from a chimney. I asked Valentin how people lived out here when there were no roads.

"This community is about thirty people," he explained. "The children walk two hours each morning to school, and two hours back.

The government is trying to build roads and a bus. But for these children, it will be a long time."

The third was a descent into forest. As the air gained oxygen, plant life flourished and the temperature soared. We stripped off our coats and wore tank tops.

That was the day one of the girls got diarrhea and started throwing up. Then it hit Jordan. They walked like zombies, sneaking behind trees and boulders to erupt from both ends. Remarkably, they somehow stayed in good spirits, unwilling to let sickness taint a once-in-a-lifetime experience.

We played the "actor game" for miles and miles. This is where you say a movie, then I say an actor in that movie, then you say another movie that actor was in, then you say another actor in the new movie, and the chain continues until someone is stumped. Annabelle's movie knowledge made her impossible to beat.

At the crest of a hill, we broke out of the trees and saw the landscape in its grandeur for the first time. The Urubamba River had cut through these mountains in an absurd zigzag, leaving the ridges with dozens of spires like crocodile teeth. On this crest we came upon our first real Inca ruins—a roofless maze of stone rooms, the stones giant and perfectly cut. We sat in one of the rooms while Valentin taught us how to braid grass into a curiously strong rope. Then he pointed through the doorway to a distant ridge. "This is our first glimpse of Machu Picchu."

There, on top of a green ridge in the blue-green haze of distance, we could see a gray discoloration. The famous city on a hill. My stomach jumped with delight. We all whooped and hollered.

The next stretch of trail descended in a series of muddy switchbacks, dropping through coffee farms and huts down to the river below. Soon, the terrain was all jungle. Splashing streams of snow-melt had become cascading waterfalls. Roots of trees that protruded into the zigzagging trail served as handholds. We stopped at a little coffee farm, really just a woman's house with coffee plants all around it, and had some coffee in her kitchen. We stood around like white invaders, sipping her delicious earthy brew and watching the guinea pigs that roamed around her feet, eating random pieces of lettuce.

Servants carried their god Atahualpa into the courtyard of the Spaniard's fort on a litter—one of those lifted thrones—carried by eighty men. The litter was adorned with parrot feathers, gold, and silver. Behind it came two other litters and two hammocks. In them were other high-ranking members of Atahualpa's inner circle. Around and behind them walked many more men in ornate parrot-feather headdresses. Some six thousand soldiers crammed into the courtyard and those who couldn't fit stood guard outside.

The Christians hid behind the stone walls, peering out and shaking. Some of the Spaniards peed themselves from fright.

Atahualpa had decided to bring only 6,000 or so of his 80,000-strong army to the meeting, thinking it plenty enough to make the right impression. And at the last minute, he instructed his men to leave their weapons behind. Atahualpa would show his power through sheer numbers. With reporting from his spies, he had deduced that the strange giant beasts didn't eat men.

Pizarro, remaining inside his chamber, sent his priest and a translator to speak to Atahualpa. Under Spanish and Catholic law, any foreign leader of conquest must be given the chance to convert to Christianity before violence.

The priest walked up to Atahualpa, who sat high in his hand-carried throne, greeted him, and invited him into the chamber with Pizarro. The goal was to separate the king from his men. Atahualpa declined. The priest then began performing his duty and recited the Christian message. He said he had been sent by the king to reveal the one true religion to Atahualpa and the Inca people. He then handed him a special book of Christian tenets designed for moments such as this.

Atahualpa looked at the strange object in his hands. He had never seen a book, or writing. He turned it in his hands, and had trouble opening it. When the priest tried to help him, Atahualpa swatted his hand away. The book flopped open, and he saw thousands of scratchings all over it. Writing. He was amazed. Then, confused, he grew angry and threw the book to the ground in disgust.

At this, the priest turned from Atahualpa and ran, crying out in fury to the hidden soldiers, "Come out! Come out, Christians! Come at these enemy dogs who reject the things of God. That chief has thrown my book of holy law to the ground! Do you not see what happened? Why remain polite and servile toward this overproud dog when the plains are full of Indians? March out against him, for I absolve you!"

Hearing this, Pizarro gave the signal to attack. Cannons fired at close range into the hordes, while armored soldiers on horseback galloped into the courtyard. They had tied rattles to their horses to frighten the Incas even more. The terrified Incas turned to flee but were trapped in the courtyard and began trampling one another. In their panic, men piled on top of one another, suffocating and crushing those underneath.

The Spanish soldiers descended into the chaos and began hacking and killing and dismembering. The unarmed Incas were no match. Flesh and organs and blood soon covered the courtyard. The steel weapons made game of soft muscle and tissue. Meanwhile, the holy king was still held aloft by his personal guard of 80 men. When Pizarro's men sliced one man down, another would move into place. As the Incas' arms were cut off, they would continue to hold up the litter with their shoulders until their legs were cut or their heads lopped off. This awful cycle of sacrifice continued until the Christians reached the litter and tipped it over. At that moment, they leaped on Atahualpa and hauled him off to Pizarro's chamber.

In two hours that day, five or six thousand unarmed men were murdered. Not one Christian was killed. Of the massacre at Cajamarca, a proud Spaniard later wrote, "Truly, it was not accomplished by our own forces for there were so few of us. It was by the grace of God, which is great."

We had a long walk to the bottom of the mountain, and when our stock of games was exhausted, we turned to one another's spiritual histories for entertainment. For a stretch of trail, Annabelle, Cyrus, and I were hiking together. Only I had known Cyrus before the trip, and not well at that. He was fast talking and cartoonishly handsome, as if created in Photoshop. But he'd won everyone over with his helpfulness and tender heart. Annabelle wanted to know where Cyrus had grown up.

"Texas," he told her, sounding embarrassed.

"Oh, so super-religious conservative?"

"No, no, no. Not at all. My dad's Vietnamese. We didn't really go to church. But in Dallas, you kind of have to be Christian."

"Are you saying you are or aren't Christian?" she asked. Annabelle's curiosity was disarming. Her questions seemed to come without judgment. She could ask you when was the last time you masturbated and you'd be likely to answer without hesitation.

"No, I'm not Christian," Cyrus said.

"Wow, that must've been isolating."

"Yeah, I went to church with my friends, or with girlfriends because they wanted me to, but it never made sense to me. I'm not against the idea of God, but the whole Jesus thing didn't make sense."

"You know, if I'm being honest, I agree," she said.

"My whole life girls have liked me and then asked me if I was saved, if I had a personal relationship with Jesus," he said. "When I told them no, they'd be so upset. It's like they were nice to me, and then they'd change, like I became an alien."

"It was sort of like that for me in high school," Annabelle said, grimacing.

Cyrus was confessing now. "I've had girls walk up to me at Starbucks and ask me if I loved Jesus. Just walk up and say, 'Do you love Jesus?' And I'm like, no."

Annabelle understood what he was talking about. "I remember wanting to date hot guys but thinking it's not okay because they weren't Christian," she said. "I was like, how can I date someone if they don't care about what I care about?"

We were holding on to roots as we slipped and tripped down the trail. Leaves and branches reached out to whip us in the face. Across the canyon, we caught views of Macchu Picchu. To its right on a closer peak, a waterfall pumped an incredible amount of water into the canyon. The flow was so fierce, the mountain looked like it was purging itself.

Annabelle brought us back. "Jed, you grew up super Christian, yeah?"

"Yes. Well, I was agnostic in early high school, soon as I learned what that word was. I hated church. And I loved the Discovery Channel. Church teachings seemed to be at war with the Discovery Channel. But I was never atheist. Cyrus, are you an atheist?"

"I don't know."

"I think not knowing means you're not an atheist. The whole definition of atheism is deciding that God isn't real."

Ahead of us, Jordan had looked back to see us clumped together in conversation. He pulled aside to wait until we caught up. Valentin hiked close behind us, listening, not saying a word.

"I have to be honest, guys," Annabelle said. "This year, I've really lost it. Like I don't call myself a Christian anymore. Which feels crazy. I used to be involved with Young Life. It was huge in my life. And now I don't recognize that feeling." Annabelle said she had struggled with how the Church makes the label "Christian" mean everything. Say these words or burn in hell. Believe this specific story or burn in hell. "One day I was like, I don't think the universe is set up like that. It doesn't make sense," she said.

"But Christians say God's ways are not our ways," I said. "He is so much bigger than our understanding."

"Yeah, but they're starting with a premise that doesn't make sense. You're making sure everything makes sense according to a book written by men, instead of making sure the book makes sense according to reality. It's backwards."

"How do you know the Bible was written by men?" I asked. "Why can't it be inspired by God, intended by God, and written by men's hands?"

"Of course. Even Christians say that. They say it was inspired by God. But I just kind of got free from the assumption that life has to be reconciled to this book. That is only a reality because people say it is. I want my reality to be reality, and then test things against it."

"That's what I believe, I think," Cyrus said.

Annabelle's line of reasoning sent me into turmoil. Annabelle doesn't call herself a Christian. How terrifying. How alienating. I am a Christian, but how many beliefs can I strip away before I am not anymore? Do I believe the world is six thousand years old? No. Do I believe the Bible is the infallible word of God? Hmm, I think it's inspired, but open to interpretation. And maybe I think it's simply man's search for God, documented. The Jewish people's record of their understanding of God. That would explain how God seemed changed over time, from a wrathful angry God to Jesus.

And then I found myself going down the list in my head.

Do I believe Jesus was crucified? Yes, I do.

Do I believe He rose from the dead on the third day? I think so.

Do I believe in sin? Ugh. I don't know. Sin doesn't make sense to me.

From there, things crumbled. It seems the main belief of Christianity is "Jesus is the son of God and He died for our sins." Okay. Well . . . if I don't understand sin, then how can I understand God sacrificing His son for my sins?

Uh-oh.

I felt that an invisible census taker was standing over me with a clipboard, ready to check next to my name, "approved Christian" or "backslider" or "deceived heretic." I felt my mother crying for my lost soul. I felt her blaming California and liberals and the media and relativism. I felt her worrying about AIDS. It all depended on this one word: *Christian*.

Atahualpa, once in custody, buried his fear in regal stoicism. He was frightened of being killed at first, but he quickly regained his composure. He demanded his wives and servants and concubines and was appeased. His women fed him by hand in his cell. They collected the bones and scraps and anything he touched and put them in leather chests. Anything the king touched must be saved and burned. Returned to the sun.

The Christians asked Atahualpa why he had come unarmed. He told them he had been told by his spies that the Christians were so few that they could be easily overtaken. What he wanted was the horses. He was very impressed by the mighty beasts and wanted to take them and breed them. His plan was to capture

the Christians, sacrifice some of them to the sun, and castrate
the others and use them as slaves. He never guessed that they
would attack first.

About now, Jordan fell back on the hike and joined the conversation. He said a friend of his had quit calling himself Christian when he couldn't believe in heaven and hell, and that the only way to get to heaven was by accepting "the sacrifice for sin of one dude two thousand years ago." Jordan said his friend had decided if he did find himself at the gates of heaven, and wasn't let in, he'd say, "Well, what did you expect? I did what I could with the information I had. And the story I was told wasn't convincing. Isn't it up to y'all to convince me?"

Jordan's story reminded me of the James Baldwin quote: "It was really a matter between me and God. I would have to live the life he had made me to live. I told him quite a long, long time ago there would be two of us at the Mercy Seat. He would not be asking all the questions."

When I offered my trail paraphrase of Baldwin, Annabelle exclaimed, "Oh my God, yes, that's *it*! We're doing the best with what we have. But being out here in nature . . . honestly, last night, looking at the stars, I felt God. I felt that feeling again I had back in high school, singing worship with my hands up. I felt the bigness of it. That is God."

"Yeah, I feel God in that way, too," I said.

"Jed, do you call yourself a Christian?" she asked, turning her spotlight on me next.

"Uhm, yes, yes, I do. It's how I was raised. And the idea of selflessness seems to be most real in Christianity. Like believing we're God is such a lie, so submitting to God, and the idea that God would sacrifice Himself for what He loves as an example to His followers, that just feels truer to me than other religions."

"That surprises me. We've been friends a long time, and you've never, like, talked about Jesus or any of that."

"Yeah, well, maybe that's embarrassing." I laughed. "I'm not sure it's the truth. I just think it may be."

"I've never really heard people talk like this before," Cyrus said.

"Like what?" Annabelle asked.

"Like, talking openly about faith and belief without already knowing what the right answer is. No one I know talks like this."

Annabelle said that it was pretty special to be in this place, surrounded by mountains, all together, talking about life and what it means. To meet one another in this way. "These are my favorite conversations," she said. And we all agreed.

"I am changing," I said. "I can feel it." And I could feel it. Annabelle's comfort with unbranding herself challenged me. I was envious, but also cautious. I wasn't ready for the finality of saying "I am not a Christian." It felt too certain. Maybe that's what I was rejecting now. Certainty. But that's what faith is—believing without certainty. Yet I had been raised to assume otherwise. In my version of Christianity, certainty seemed propped up by a scaffolding of fear. Jesus doesn't want you lukewarm, preachers said. Be all in or all out. Stay away from the middle place, the gray.

"The heart is deceitful above all else." A.k.a., don't trust your feelings. The heart will trick you to get what it wants.

"Lean not on your own understanding." Don't think for yourself.

The scripture says, "Come let us reason together," but this is code for "yes, you can share your thoughts with us, by all means, but if they don't fit what we believe Scripture says, then those thoughts will have to go."

If you don't believe, sadly, you'll spend eternity in hell. So you'd better believe that Jesus loves you. He loves you so much, or else.

Annabelle was talking it out, trying to bring the threads together. "Saying I am Christian doesn't make sense for me anymore. But saying that something else is right or that there is nothing doesn't make sense either. I have found more comfort and have felt a greater faith in something bigger than me, I have felt a bigger hug from the universe by rejecting the obsession to call it something. To name it. Maybe there is life after. Maybe there isn't. Maybe it's Jesus. Maybe it's a giant oak tree. Maybe it's energy. Maybe it's stardust. Maybe we just shut off. But not calling it something certain has opened my heart more than when I was Christian, feeling like I was the lucky one who got to hear Jesus's name and thus be accepted into the club. And quitting that limited idea, that the truth is so small, has given me deeper curiosity in the universe, my world, and the people around me. I love them more. I love everything more. Because I don't see anyone else as right or wrong, we all just are. The not knowing feels so much bigger and more exciting and mystical and grand and beautiful than whatever words humans strung together to describe It, God, and how you attain It."

"There's something there that feels true," I said.

"Same," Jordan said.

"I've never said it all like that before," said Annabelle. "I guess I'm just really finding it."

"That's called mysticism, I think," I offered.

"It is?"

"Yeah, mysticism is when you don't have intellectual certainty about stuff, but experientially you do believe in things, like beauty and mystery and the universe as a force for good. You move beyond the dualism of good and evil to a more unified whole, a sense that everything belongs."

"Oh my gosh, yes, I believe that!" Annabelle said.

"Yeah, I've kind of been calling myself a mystic-Christian," I said. "That's what I've heard Thomas Merton was, and I think I'm down with that."

Even as I said it, I felt suspicious of the wishy-washy language we were embracing. Energy. Stars. Universe. It felt man-made, self-absorbed. But I was also thrilled. Walking in the wilderness of the lost Inca civilization, discussing God and what it means to be alive. I realized Valentin was still walking behind us. What did this Quechua man make of our odd American conversation?

"We're MYSTICS!" Annabelle yelled.

"Myyysticcss!" we all yelled together into the mountains. The birds in the jungle around us trilled and squawked. Valentin laughed.

In the early days of his custody, Atahualpa observed the Christians' obsession with precious metals, specifically gold, and proposed a plan. If he could fill a large room with gold and silver, could he buy his freedom?

Pizarro said yes.

Atahualpa sent word throughout the kingdom to collect gold and silver from the temples and have it brought to him. Over several months, a steady flow of ornate platters and chalices and statues came to the Christians at Cajamarca. The designated room filled with more than six tons of gold. The Christians had it melted down. Their eyes were feverish with excitement. So feverish that one of Pizarro's soldiers got his arm lopped off in a quarrel with another one over gold. It was the only serious injury to a Christian during the Inca conquest.

Once the room was full, piled eight feet high with gold from wall to wall, Atahualpa asked for his release. He was denied.

Instead, the Spaniards tied Atahualpa to a chair. The priest offered him the chance to repent of his sins and accept Christ. Atahualpa agreed. He asked to be baptized. The priest baptized him. He denounced his belief in the sun god and repented of his sins and accepted the Jesus that had led his enemies to victory.

The priest rechristened him Francisco, Pizarro's middle name. Then, acting quickly for fear Atahualpa would change his mind, they strangled him to death.

We'd reached the river. It was time to head into the little town of Aguas Calientes, where we would sleep at a hotel, wake up just before sunrise, and be driven up the winding ascent to Machu Picchu.

I wanted to save all I had seen and heard, all we had said. I knew it was monumental somehow. Appropriate to Machu Picchu. A spiritual vortex.

The next morning we woke before sunrise and piled into a rickety bus that took us up a zigzag dirt road with no guardrail. It felt like we were driving straight up the mountain. The driver, with half-closed eyes and a scowl, whipped the bus around the turns, terrifying all of us. We could watch gravel kicked up by the tires bouncing hundreds of feet down to the river. But I couldn't look. I closed my eyes and clung to the thought that the driver had done this fifteen times a day for decades.

At the top, we got out of the bus and kissed the ground. We were finally there. Machu Picchu. The place I'd seen in a history book in sixth grade. The real-life Indiana Jones adventure I'd always wanted to experience.

We walked through a maze of stone walls until we came upon an opening. We saw now that we had arrived above the town proper. There it was, laid out beneath us. Every bit of hilltop space had been used. A labyrinth of walls, meticulously made with stones much too big to be moved by hand, adorned the mountain like a crown. I had always seen the photo of Machu Picchu from this spot, the classic tourist shot of the group smiling, posing above the town. Now, as I stood in line to get that very same picture, I noticed that there were lots of people down there, walking in the town itself.

"Wait, are we allowed to go down in there?" I asked Valentin.

"Of course! You can go everywhere," Valentin said.

Our whole group whooped and hollered with excitement. We quickly got our group shot, and then ran down the hill into Machu Picchu. We wandered from room to room, imagining the grass roofs and the people living here hundreds of years ago.

"No one knows why this town disappeared," Valentin explained. "It is believed that this was the king's retreat. And it was a holy place. And when the Spanish came, the people decided to forget it. They didn't tell their children. They told no one, so that the Spanish would never know it was here. That is why it remained hidden for four centuries, until it was found in 1914."

I was so full of wonder that I had a lump in my throat. The beautiful ruins brought to mind our conversations that had seemed to culminate in Annabelle's comment to me over dinner the night before.

"I was a Christian a year ago, walked into our conversation today an agnostic, and walked out of it a mystic, possibly a pagan," she had said, laughing.

Some kind of understanding had died. And something new was taking its place.

Years later, as Pizarro's wealth and power had reached its peak, his home in the newly formed Lima, Peru, was invaded by a mob of political rivals. Apparently, conquest and riches had earned him many enemies.

Twenty heavily armed men stormed his palace. As he tried for his sword, Pizarro was stabbed in the throat. He then fell to the ground, blood pouring from his neck, and they stabbed him many more times. In his final moments, writhing on the floor he painted a cross in his own blood and cried out for Jesus Christ.

One empire falls. Another rises.

Chapter 17

NEW BLOOD INTO BOLIVIA

(Bolivia and Argentina)

4,411 miles to go

After Machu Picchu it was time for all but two of my friends to head home. Over a last dinner we shared how special we had become to one another. My heart was very full, and I felt reignited to continue on toward Patagonia. Plus, Cyrus and Jordan had brought bikes and planned to travel with me for a month.

The original plan was to go straight south, along the Pacific Coast, into Chile. But people warned us about the Atacama Desert. It starts in southern Peru and takes up the entire northern half of Chile. It is known as the driest place on earth. It gets about .6 of an inch of rain a year. A thousand miles of lifeless desert.

Hell no.

So we hatched a new plan. We would travel up over the Andes, bike around Lake Titicaca, drop into Bolivia, then to La Paz, and across to the colonial town of Sucré. From there down to the farmland of Argentina. The new route was more exciting to all three of us. Cyrus and Jordan wanted a taste of the freedom of the road, but that didn't require endless desert. For them, my trip had become emblematic back home for "getting away" and "really living." Just as my dad had predicted, instead of forgetting about me, my friends talked about me as a man "living his dream."

I hadn't heard from Weston the whole week of my friends' visit. On our last day in Cusco, I texted him, "Think you'll make it back on the road?"

He answered a day later. "Still in Hawaii. Maybe I can meet you in Patagonia?"

Wow. He isn't hurrying back, is he? I felt a mix of sadness and relief.

"What do you want me to do with your bike?" I asked.

"Oh, man. Maybe give it to someone who needs it?"

Okay. He's not coming back.

Is he?

No.

I thought back to biking that first day in Oregon. Weston and I weaving back and forth, taking up the whole street, loving the August air and ocean breeze. I remember him calling me his "neighbor" every night as we'd lie in our hammocks. "Oh, how's the family, neighbor?" he'd ask.

"Oh, great."

We'd started with such fire and magic. With a shared destiny and destination. The beginning of a grand adventure is pregnant with a thousand futures. Every possible best thing. But the end is often a fizzle. For us, Weston left for a wedding. And didn't come back. And just like that, a chapter was done.

As we set off from the hostel in Cusco, regrets and self-blame could have buried me if not for Cyrus and Jordan. They were ecstatic. They were biking and singing and laughing and everything was new and exotic. They were discovering bike-touring like toddlers taking their first steps. Tying up their backpacks and sleeping bags between their panniers every morning. Mastering clip-in pedals. Thrilled at the downhills and cursing the uphills. Shouting "Car back!" with the confidence of a seasoned cyclist.

Cyrus would power ahead and bike a quarter mile in front of us. "Sorry, guys, whenever I listen to Kygo my legs start pumping and I become a machine. Electronic music is my pump-up music." He was a lovable jock who was always competing, even if only against himself.

"I'm catching up on podcasts," Jordan would say. "Maybe that's why I'm always in the back. My head is lost in some weird southern town in a *This American Life* episode."

The 400 miles of road from Cusco to La Paz scrapes along the bottom of the sky—breathtaking altitudes, treeless vistas, wind-blown, rock-strewn valleys. Along the side of the road, far from any houses, it seemed, a little gang of high school kids biked up to us from behind and, unsolicited, told us where the best local hot springs were. We found the pools just up ahead behind an abandoned military post. We soaked in boiling baths of water, and steam filled the air around us. We camped nearby in an abandoned schoolhouse and froze all night. The next night we camped on a riverbank. By the time we crossed a mountain pass at 15,000 feet, our highest point, we could hardly breathe.

"How is this safe?" Jordan said. "My head is pounding and I can't catch my breath!"

I was struggling, too, but hid it to show how seasoned I was.

We waited for huge herds of goats to clear out of the road.

There were very few restaurants, and the markets sold only prepackaged junk food. We ate bad soup when we could find it, and Jordan struggled to find anything other than cookies that was vegetarian. We ate lots of cookies. And French fries. We survived on that as best we could.

The boys changed their popped tires like pros.

On the fourth day we were to make it to Puno, a bustling town on Lake Titicaca. That morning, still thirty-five miles from town, we met a farmer who told us to "avoid the next town, very dangerous. Many people get robbed."

That frightened us. So far on the trip, I hadn't heard local people warning me of their own neighbors. I was used to people saying "Americans fear us. But there is nothing to fear."

We biked on, anxious about what lay ahead. Jordan's tire popped and then so did mine. This slowed us down, and we ended up entering the dangerous town at sunset. We found a hostel and dropped our things. The streets were swarming. Tangled power lines clotted in the narrow strips of sky between half-finished brick buildings. Mopeds, cars, and trucks pumped exhaust into the air and made the streets a pulsing mess. We put our bicycles in the hostel and our bags in our room and went to dinner. Jordan brought his backpack because his nice camera and laptop were in it. He didn't want to leave it anywhere. We ate a good dinner and stopped at another place for a drink and walked home. This town didn't seem so bad. As we took our shoes off and prepared to relax for the night, Jordan sprung up like a prairie dog. "My backpack! I left it at dinner."

Oh God.

Jordan was out the door and out of the hostel before we could offer to go with him. I'm certain he ran all the way to the restaurant, which was about four blocks away.

When he got back, he walked through the door holding his bag like a trophy. "The people at the place saw me walk in and laughed and reached behind the counter and lifted it up. Cracking up. They spotted it after we left and held it for me. I love Puno."

The next day, we cycled out of town and along the shore of Lake Titicaca. The lake is so large it looks like the sea. That night we slept on the edge of the lake in the roofless ruin of a barn. We tried to make a small fire out of dried cow patties. We failed. We drank boxed wine. We watched *No Country for Old Men* in my tent. Piling three of us in a two-person tent for movie night was really tight. We talked for a long time about how brilliant the Coen brothers are.

The freshness of Jordan and Cyrus's experience was rejuvenating. They were great companions, helping me navigate, prepping food, and down to explore any- and everything. The trip felt new again.

The next day, while stopping for a snack break, Cyrus said, "I really crave a PB and J right now."

"Holy shit," I said. "That sounds so good. I haven't had one in . . . years, maybe."

"This is our new mission," Jordan said. "We're making PB and Js, eating six each."

We fantasized about the flavors as we rode, and resolved to find the closest grocery store. We found a market in the next town. We looked on every shelf, and ultimately Jordan had to ask, which he didn't mind, because "peanut butter" is his favorite term in Spanish. "*Mantequilla de cacahuete.*" He returned to tell us that peanut butter isn't a thing in Peru. They didn't have any. We asked all over town, and were directed to the only large grocery store in the city, inside the only mall. We parked our bikes at a hostel and took a taxi. We scoured the aisles and found one jar. It was expensive. Like ten bucks. We bought it and jelly and a loaf of bread. We raced back to the hostel discussing how many we would eat. "I'm gonna eat half this loaf of bread," Cyrus said.

We made one each, cheersed them like champagne, and took big satisfying bites. But finishing one, the fever for PB&J wore off real quick. Our dreams of eating six each weren't gonna happen. We made two each and ate them and were done. We watched a World Cup game on the TV at the hostel. We relaxed and felt accomplished.

We biked out of town in the morning and were back in the land of golden grass and bald hills. We laughed every mile. With Cyrus and Jordan, it felt like the beginning of the trip again. Oregon was a million years ago. But I had been on the trip for nine months, approaching ten. The beginning was already nostalgia, a different me. And I had changed. Did I believe Jesus was my savior? I didn't know. I had when I started this trip. And I think I still did. But not in the same way. In some larger way. The salvation of Christ was wider, more mysterious, kinder. I kept thinking about what Annabelle and Jordan and Cyrus had said on the zigzag trail down from Salkantay. About mysticism. About faith. I felt strong, questioning alongside them. The majesty of the Inca, the devotion to their king and their gods, the dissection of my faith, the evil mechanisms of its expansion. In ways I couldn't yet explain, the Machu Picchu experience had been a wrecking ball.

FROM LAKE TITICACA, the three of us crossed the border into Bolivia, paying an unexpected visa fee. From there we had about forty miles to La Paz, along what's called the Altiplano. This is a stretch of high prairie floating in the sky, stretching across much of Bolivia and northern Argentina. The puddles made from the muddy footprints of cattle were thick sheets of ice in the cold morning. By noon, we'd be shirtless in 90-degree heat. We biked at a steady 11,000 feet.

At golden hour, we dropped into the massive city of La Paz. It is another sea of short red-brick buildings, with tall white ones in the center, and snowcapped mountains flanking its edges. It is the highest major city in the world at 11,975 ft. We spent a few days there.

We went to the movie theater. We went dirt-biking. We lubed and cleaned our bikes. We headed out of there and biked for several more days to Potosí, a town that sits even higher at 13,000 feet. It was colder than ever and some days we couldn't even have our hands exposed. We were smack dab in the middle of the South American winter. Nights and mornings were miserable. In Potosí, Cyrus got too sick and cold to bike. He said he'd have to bus to Sucré.

Jordan and I checked the elevation of Sucré. We all decided to bus.

We watched the final World Cup game in Sucré at a German hostel. It was Germany v. Argentina. The excitement was electric. Many of the Bolivians were rooting for Germany, because they didn't like their arrogant Argentinian neighbors. The German hostel became the epicenter of Sucré that day.

Germany won. And we partied hard. I got so drunk that I had the spins and had to sit up in bed almost all night. I had to sit there and play solitaire on my phone. For hours. Because closing my eyes made me spin and lying down made me spin.

After the World Cup, it was time for the boys to leave me.

"You gonna be all right biking alone?" Jordan asked.

"Yeah, will you be scared?" Cyrus said.

"I haven't done it yet, but I'm ready. Not that I'm glad y'all are leaving. Just, at this point, I'm ready to try out the solo thing."

They found large bike boxes at a cycling shop in Sucré and boxed their rides up for the flight. I hugged Cyrus and Jordan goodbye and thanked them for giving me new life. They bused to the airport and left me all by myself.

Jordan and Cyrus had done good things to my spirit. A remembering of my first excitements of biking. A chance for me to show my cycling expertise. A respite from Weston. Well, more like a transition out of Weston.

For the first time in my whole trip, I was truly alone. I had three or four thousand more miles to Patagonia, to the end of my trip. The only person I knew in every direction was myself.

Chapter 18

ALL BY MY ARGENTINA
(Solo Down Argentina)

3,580 miles to go

I sat alone at a café in Sucré to map out the final stages of my journey. I decided I would cycle south along the eastern edge of the Andes, into Argentina's wine country. Mendoza was about 900 miles from the north of Argentina. From Mendoza, I would bike south, another 900 miles to the border of Chile, cross back to the western side of the Andes and into the wind-blown wilds of Patagonia. That's the famous Carretera Austral, a gravel road more than 700 miles long that winds through the fjords and fishing villages of the Patagonian wilderness. I would cycle to the end of the Carretera: Mount Fitz Roy. That would be the end of my cycling. I wanted to do the famous route and then be done, at this famous mountain I'd always wanted to see. To make Punta Arenas, at the tip of the continent, my goal would require six hundred more miles of biking, but bike blogs had described the region as a windy, treeless, and flat expanse. I wanted to end with a beautiful bang, not drudgery for the sake of making a point. So I would finish at iconic Mount Fitz Roy (the mountain range on the Patagonia clothing company's logo), then bus farther down to Torres del Paine National Park to meet my mom for the final hike. Then it would be Christmas and it would all be over. I would head home.

The moment my plan fell into place for the rest of my trip, I felt it as finite. It wasn't my whole life anymore, stretching on forever. For so many months I had seen no shape or end to it.

I was alone now and happy to be alone. Which, for Mr. Social Jedidiah, sounds odd. But it exposes a different side of me. Traveling alone, you get to be whoever you want. I don't mean lie. I mean you get to be a blank slate. You can't leave behind your skin color, or your height, or the handsomeness or homeliness of your face. But you can leave your story behind. If you've broken hearts, the new place doesn't know. If you've lost trust in people and yourself, the new place doesn't know. If everyone thinks you love Jesus, but you never really have figured out what you believe, the new place doesn't care. It may assume you have it all tied nicely in a bow. All your thoughts and histories. Just feeling like your past isn't a vice to hold you in place can be very freeing. Feeling like your family and the expectations and the traditions and the judgments are absent ... it can fill your veins with possibility and fire.

Something about being alone makes me sexual. The moment I'm alone in my house, I walk around naked, I look at porn, I do things just because I can. I'm unwatched. So the things that build up in me, that fear of being watched or found out, show up right when they know they can. But isn't God watching? I don't know. Do I fear that God is watching, or fear that some human will find out what I've done? Maybe I could attribute that to God, the finding out. But still, why don't God's eyes burn me like human eyes do?

I think it's because I've always felt that He understood me. He made me. What could surprise Him?

By myself on the edge of Argentina, these familiar feelings sat up straight. "Jed, you're alone. You can kiss anyone. Be anyone."

I had had a small dream of kissing boys on this trip. Even early on. The thought of anonymity felt scandalous and thrilling. Setting myself free, when and if I found myself alone. I was in a foreign place, far from any watchful eyes, from anyone who knew me. The invisibility. It made me realize how much of decency is built through community, through other eyes. I'd forgive myself just about anything if I felt anonymous.

But for some reason, as I was setting off by myself for the first time, I didn't feel like sex or boys. Maybe it was my spiritual stupor. My foggy thoughts about God and faith and family. Maybe it was the fact that I'd been in mostly rural places that were religious, or indigenous, distant-feeling. I hadn't met a local person that gave me a vibe. Not once. Maybe I smelled bad from this bike. Maybe my busted Spanish was a turn-off. Or maybe it was my lack of confidence, my stumbling ignorance. What is less attractive than a guilt-laden weirdo testing himself against your freedom?

I had heard that Argentina was one of the most developed countries in South America. Meaning I wouldn't have to suffer chicken-foot soup anymore. I heard I'd get good coffee and steak and croissants. That was exciting. So exciting, in fact, that I decided to hitchhike right to the Argentinian border. I stood at a gas station on the edge of Sucré holding a sign that read "Potosí or Argentina?" A truck took me a few hours to Potosí, and then I was stuck, so I got a late-night bus from Potosí to the border. I reached the border at 6:30 a.m. and exited the bus into a little town that seemed to exist solely to serve the border. The morning air was perhaps 15–20 degrees. I wasn't properly dressed, and unloading my bicycle from under the bus and putting the front tire back on caused my fingers to stiffen and sting in the cold. I started shaking. I rolled my bike to the line to cross the border, about twenty people long, waiting to get their passports stamped. I soon became the coldest I had ever been in my life. So cold that I was worried for my fingers. Seriously concerned about nerve damage, or something. My feet felt like blocks of petrified flesh. I had no feeling in my toes. Not even the phantom memory of them. I just had ice hooves. My finger bones ached in their blue-white stiffness.

Damn. I'm all alone out here.

As I walked my bike across the border, I did the now-familiar thing of filling in the visitor form in the margins where there was no bubble to color in. "Mode of transport: train? plane? bus? boat?" and I'd write in "no, bicicleta." The border guard would always see that, look up at me, my bike, all the bags, and smile. They always smiled. It made me happy to give their monotonous day a bit of a perk.

In my frozen-finger misery, I found the only open café on the Argentinian side of the tiny border town and waited until 11 a.m., when it was finally warm enough to cycle.

I set out from town and rode into a new world: Argentina. I had been eager to see it for months. The Argentinian chefs had told me how wonderful their country was back when I tried mushrooms in Colombia. They said it was more developed than most of Latin America. More European. Wealthier. As much as I had loved the back roads, the small towns across Colombia, Ecuador, Peru, and Bolivia, I had grown tired of eating prepackaged food and sketchy roadside fare. I had hoped I would become the most nonmaterialistic human of all time, so at home on the earth that Andean poverty would no more affect me than New York City wealth. I wanted to be zen above it. Floating above the trappings and hardships of human life. Well, that didn't happen. I was sick and tired of all the poverty. I felt bad for the thousands of souls that lived in mud. But the charm wore off, and I knew I could bike away and enjoy my good fortune of being born white in the world's richest country. I still don't know what to do with all that. The hardened soul of reality, dividing rich from poor like it does.

All I can do is be honest. I was ready to see nice buildings well built, to rest in some of the creature comforts of an advanced economy.

Setting out at 11 a.m., I followed a road that was flat to the southern horizon. Mountains to my right, hills to my left. A huge golden valley between, and a road right down the middle. The fields were mostly empty of human interference, apart from the occasional run-down mud-brick hut. I saw lots of llamas. Lots of cows. At one point, a hundred cows meandered across the road. Not being herded. No fences. Just walking across. No more developed and glorious Argentina yet, but I was happy in the sunshine and happy to be on the bike and the long straight road.

AFTER MY FIRST cycling day in Argentina, my first solo day, my new country, my new life, I stopped after fifty miles at the only hotel in a tiny train-stop town and spent the night. I was still at 11,000 feet elevation and it was August, a.k.a. Argentina's winter. I wanted to get inside before the temperature dropped again. My room had a small black-and-white TV playing the movie *G.I. Joe*. An Argentinian guy named Juan that I'd met once in LA had e-mailed me, "Hey, my friend from architecture school lives in the town of Salta, which isn't too far from the northern border of Argentina. You can stay with her. She is great and she will like to practice her English. She is very smart and a good architect. Can I make the intro?"

I wrote back, "Yes of course!" An architect? That sounds good. Maybe Salta was a pretty big city. I was just excited to get out of the hardscrabble countryside. The map said that Salta was a two-day ride. On day one I'd reach Jujuy, which seemed like a pretty big town, then make it to Salta by nightfall the next day.

He introduced me to his friend via e-mail and she said she was happy to host me for a night. She wondered how many people I was traveling with. I replied saying it was just me, that I was very excited to get to know Argentina, and that I'd be a very good guest.

She again replied, "Hi Jed! I'm excited too! As you may know Juan is a very special friend of mine so that you are very welcome here. I hope you have a great time in Salta eating empanadas and meeting new people ;) I'll do my best, See you soon Jed! —Lau"

The next day, the giant golden valley I was riding through began to change. I was rolling more and more downhill. It dawned on me: I was coming out the other side of the Andes. I had risen up them from the Pacific in Colombia, traveled down their spine all the way to Bolivia, and was now on the decline into the lower elevations of Argentina.

I rode downhill for an entire day. A perfect slope. In the lower elevations, trees appeared again. I began riding through thicker air and heat.

At the base of the Andes, the first sizable town in Argentina is Jujuy. As I rode in, I saw something new: big, well-constructed suburban houses. Stucco. Clean handsome construction, and a few that were even fancy, with Spanish tile roofs and swirling iron over the windows and on the gates, and clean cars in the driveways. The houses were still walled off. I realized that almost every sizable home I'd seen in Latin America was behind a wall. I wondered if I'd ever see a house with no walls or fences in Latin America. Like the ones I grew up with in Nashville, where the yard just blended invisibly with the neighbors'. I hadn't seen a yard like that in a town since California, 6,500 miles ago.

As I rode into Jujuy's downtown, I saw tall office buildings. And cafés, with expensive lighting that wasn't simply a dangling LED bulb on a wire. Such expensive building materials struck me as alien. I was encouraged.

I booked myself a bunk bed at a hostel and had dinner at a proper restaurant. I had a glass of wine. I was alone and happy. I got an e-mail from the architect lady. "We are excited to have you, Jedidiah. You can perhaps stay two nights? We can make a bed for you. You can meet my husband and children. We have two dogs."

She recommended a more scenic route between Jujuy and Salta than the busy highway. This one was a winding road through forests and farms that many people enjoyed driving just for fun on the weekends. It was 35 miles. A perfect day's ride.

The next morning I took her advice and the scenic road was extraordinary. Old trees loomed over the road and cows ate in golden fields and people on motorcycles passed me on joyrides. It reminded me of Northern California, of wine country. It felt wealthy. I listened to Anne Lamott's book *Bird by Bird* in my headphones and I rode, and felt very good. I imagined being a writer someday. I was alone and happy and could tell that this architect I was approaching would become my friend.

After a full day of perfect riding, Salta came into view. The houses I was seeing were even nicer than Jujuy's. When I pulled up to the address she gave me, I was met by a large gate and a guard. Not a gated house with barbed wire like Mexico City; a gated community like the kind you would see in Orange County, California, or Dallas, Texas. I told the guard I was here to see Laura, pronouncing it like an American would. "Lore-uh." He looked at me strangely. I tried again. No luck. Then it struck him.

"Ahh, L-ow-ra! Siiii." And he let me in. On a printed map of the community, he circled her house, then handed the map to me. He stared at my dirty bike and smiled with curiosity.

I rode through a maze of mansions. I had, for some reason, assumed she lived in an apartment. Maybe I pictured the apartment of my friend Beatriz in Mexico City. I simply didn't know a fancy gated neighborhood was an option down here. I arrived at her beautiful house—tan stucco, modern and huge. As her dogs ran to meet me, she stepped on the porch, smiling. This was going to be great.

I tried to keep my promise and stay only two nights. But after the first night of testing me out, after wine and stories and plenty of laughter, she announced, "You cannot leave yet. Next weekend is the arts and crafts fair in town. You cannot miss the authentic arts."

"Next weekend? That's in eight days!"

"Is it too long? You truly cannot miss it. And then perhaps we go to our country house. You will love it. With horses."

"Laura, I cannot stay so long! It is an imposition!"

"We insist. And it is good for our children to practice English."

I thought about it. No, I didn't really have the time to spend several weeks in Salta, but this was nice. I liked being alone. And if I'm being honest, I really liked assimilating into a wealthy Argentinian family. I decided to stay.

Over the next days, I created new routines. Every morning I would wake up and come down to the kitchen. The maids had made the coffee. Laura's husband, Mauricio, would be reading the paper. His English was much simpler than his wife's, so we would fumble over our words, and laugh together. I would say something pathetically primitive in Spanish, and he would reply in equally primitive English. But so much can be communicated this way. We had great conversations. We talked about politics and journalism and history. All with baby words and pointing and laughter.

The days turned simple and beautiful. I would ride my bike the short distance into downtown Salta and explore. I would sit and read and write. I would go for walks around the neighborhood and sneak a cigarette.

Every night, after a dinner at 10 p.m., Laura would send the kids to bed and come down for one last glass of wine in the kitchen. Then she would say "goodbye." I knew she meant "good night." But I loved that she ended the day with such unintentional intensity.

I learned of two deaths while at their house.

One, the suicide of Robin Williams. I was reading on Laura's couch when I got a push notification to my phone. I looked at it, stunned. Just then, she came running into the living room. "Did you hear?!" she said. I remember being surprised that she got the push notification, too. A person in Argentina, eleven countries away from the United States, found out the same second that I did.

She had misty eyes. "He is a treasure. I have water in my eyes. I am so sad. Why are so many comedians to die from suicide?"

"I don't know," I said.

"*Mrs. Doubtfire. Patch Adams.* He was one of my favorites. The kids love him."

"I wanted to be him when I was a kid."

She said, "I wish President Cristina, that crook, would commit suicide. Not someone like Robin Williams."

The next day, my Google alerts went off. Harry Devert's body had been found in Mexico after a six-month disappearance. Harry Devert, the motorcyclist who vanished in Michoacán. The one I'd heard about back in January.

Just the week before, an anonymous caller had directed authorities to a body found on a dirt path south of Michoacán—a path that led to a beach outside Zihuatanejo. A week later, DNA tests confirmed that the human remains belonged to Harry. His body had been dismembered, the pieces placed in several plastic bags. The VIN number on the green Kawasaki motorcycle found near his remains matched that of his bike. Alongside the motorcycle and body, small bags of marijuana and cocaine had been discarded.

In my mind, I compared our stories. I had made it to Argentina, safe and sound. Harry had been on his way to Brazil for the World Cup. He didn't make it past Mexico. I had made it without a scratch. Why him? Why not me? Was my bicycle safer than his motorcycle? Was I more cautious? Was it luck? Did God want me to make it, and not want Harry to? Here I was in a mansion in Argentina, enjoying wine and hospitality, while Harry's dismembered body had been decomposing in a bag in the weeds for months. I thought about his mother, praying and worrying and searching for her son. I thought about my mom. I wanted to hug her. I wanted to hear her say "There's my baby, safe and sound."

Laura and Mauricio took me to museums and their country house

and a craft fair. I had felt welcomed and included. I had played video
games with their kids. Then it was time to go. I needed to get to
Mendoza. The land of Malbec. Wine country. It was quite far away,
700 miles. Looking at the months of cycling I had left, and the map, I
realized how large Argentina is. It's almost as big as the entire United
States east of the Mississippi River. I had to get down to Mendoza by
mid-September because my dad had booked a ticket, with his new
girlfriend, to come visit me. They'd rented a couple rooms in a tiny
boutique hotel.

Harry Devert haunted my thoughts on the journey to Mendoza.
He wasn't just dead, he had been murdered. Did he do something
wrong? Or was it chance? What should his experience tell me about
mine? I wanted to understand who lives and who dies, but I didn't. I
just believed that I would always be okay. It was unshakable. Maybe
some people just have that. Harry Devert certainly did, and he died.
But I did, too, and I was still here.

ARGENTINA IS SHAPED like a slice of pizza—the top wide and the
bottom narrow and pointy. The Andes run down the western side,
separating Argentina from Chile. At the top of the pizza slice, the
northern border, the foothills of the Andes flatten into Amazon jungle and swamps. Then as you move south, the plains, or pampas, fill
up with cattle and farms. To drive from the mountainous west to the
coastal east can take eighteen hours. The geography of Argentina reminded me of the United States. It had all the same things we have.
Deserts. Snowcapped mountains. Cattle ranches. Wine country. Big-
city living. Thick forest. Ski towns.

As I followed the Andes south from the border, the land got drier
and drier. The moisture seemed to come from the west, and I knew
that over the mountains lay Chile, wet and lush. But here, on the east
side, Argentina was dry as a bone, with snow visible from the hot
floor of the plains. This dry rocky land was perfect for grapevines,
though. I was excited to go wine tasting and spend time with my
dad. I was looking forward to getting to know his girlfriend better.

I was happy they were coming. I was happy he wanted me to approve of Kelley. I was worried after he quit talking to my sisters that in his newfound unapologetic life he would cut us all off.

I cycled and camped and popped tires and broke my chain and made my way down to Mendoza in a week. At one point as I cycled, I reached the anniversary of starting my trip. August 28. I'd been out here a year. I looked back at photos of Weston and I missed him terribly. I would've given anything to have him railing in my ear against the prison-industrial complex or the benefits of mescaline. Wow. Absence really does its clichéd trick. It turns nagging into charming idiosyncrasy. It turns frustration into character.

I arrived in town a day earlier than my dad and Kelley and stayed at a hostel near the hotel my dad had booked. I had tried to prepare my dad with driving directions from the airport. He had insisted on renting a car. I told him the map on his phone would work if he would just preload it with Wi-Fi. He said he didn't know what I was talking about or what that meant. He said he had walked across America and he would be fine.

The next day, I biked to Chacras de Coria, the quaint historic town where the hotel was located. Fat hundred-year-old sycamore trees lined the narrow streets. Some of the villas, behind beautiful walls and driveways lit by gas lamps, looked like they'd been built in the twenties. I checked into the tiny hotel, just eight rooms, and the concierge said that my parents hadn't arrived yet. That meant they were late. I sat in the lobby, getting worried. I waited for four hours before they pulled up, honking the horn.

Kelley was the first one out of the car, already recounting their trials. "Your damn father will talk to anybody, Spanish or English!" she howled. "We stopped about fifty times trying to find this place. Peter just had the name of the place on a piece of paper—like everyone in this town knows the name of this tiny hotel? We must've asked fifty people. At one gas station, a whole biker gang came up to us, and I thought we were gonna die, but Peter was best friends with them in five minutes. I don't think they spoke a word of English and Lord knows your father can't speak a lick of Spanish, but they were pointing and going on and laughing and then we got here. Can you believe it!? Hi, sweetie!"

All of that seemed to arrive in one breath, then she wrapped me in a tight hug.

It was so great to see my dad. Suddenly, Mendoza felt like Spring Hill, Tennessee. "Hey, Shluh!" He always calls me Shluh, which is a nickname derived from years of revision. Jedidiah first became Jedishliah for reasons unknown, then became Shluhshluhshliah, which found its final form in Shluh. It felt good to hear it.

Kelley loved her wine, so we booked tours at several wineries. These were huge buildings, with high ceilings and art on the walls. Wandering around, our shoes clicked on the polished cement and marble floors. Tasting rooms were packed with tourists and the walls were adorned with plaques detailing this billionaire or that who owned the winery as a hobby. We learned about soil quality, and that grapevines like dry rocky soil. We learned that twist caps are just as good as traditional corks. We learned that Argentina's socialist president had so heavily taxed imports that the wine casks, which were only made in France, now cost double what they used to. It was almost cost-prohibitive. Almost.

We drank wine every day. My dad would have two glasses and slur his speech. It was cute. And listening to them was fun.

"You're such a lightweight, Peter," she told him. "I guess it's better that way. I can't be with a drunk. Absolutely not."

"Kelley makes me a better person," my dad interjected, out of context.

"Oh, Peter. So sentimental. But really, I do. I am amazing," she said and let out a cackle.

"You're the best thing that's ever happened to me," my dad said. Which stung until Kelley chimed in, "Besides your kids, of course!"

"Oh yes, of course," he said, backtracking. "They are truly the best thing in my life. That goes without saying." She rolled her eyes at me.

I enjoyed her. She was age-appropriate for my dad, but she had the wit of a twenty-something. He watched her. She seemed to love him without needing him. She wasn't performing for me, either, which other women had done in the past to win the kids. It wasn't theatrics. She was just a cool woman.

We decided to drive the rental car over the Andes to Santiago, Chile. "I've never been higher than a molehill," said Kelly.

She was so charmed by it all. We drove up over the Andes, at the foot of the tallest mountain in all the Americas, Mount Aconcagua. It's also the tallest mountain outside of Asia, at 22,838 feet. We drove right by it. Kelley was gasping. It was completely white with snow, and unlike Everest or other famous high mountains, Aconcagua stood alone. It was more like a volcano than one peak in a chain of mountains.

"I have never seen mountains like this in all my life. And there are almost no trees. I'm telling you, this is weirder than anything I've ever seen. Makes me thirsty."

At one point we drove through a tunnel that was many miles long—definitely the longest tunnel I've ever been in. Kelley, again, was gasping. When we finally popped out the other side, in Chile, we were quickly surrounded by more vineyards, but this time sprawling, green estates with lush trees everywhere, nothing like Mendoza's brown-and-gold desert.

We had three nights in Chile. We'd go to dinner, then return to our little hotel, where Kelley and my dad would say good night and retire to their room, excited to watch *Downton Abbey*. It was unbearably cute.

As the ten days went on, I watched their kind and encouraging relationship. My dad, in his early sixties. Kelley, fifty. They had been dating over a year, and it was so clear that they fit together. Easily. Without fireworks. Just a key in the door and it opened without even a creak.

Watching them, I found myself rethinking the messiness of my family story, what was right and what was wrong. It still felt wrong for my dad to leave my mom. But because he did, my beloved little sister was born with my stepmom.

Because he did, he eventually met Kelley. I watched him and Kelley and thought, "They are soul mates. It took him a long time, but he found his soul mate."

If our shittiest actions can lead to beauty, what does it mean to do right and wrong? Is it about avoiding hurting others? What about the scripture, "All things work for the good of those who love God." That sounds about right. But some things never get good. They're just terrible and then you die.

Spending time with my dad, who I had always loved and always made me feel loved, got me thinking about the causes of homosexuality, if there are such things. I remember my college pastor taking me to lunch one day and just flat-out asking me.

"Why do you think you're gay? Was your mother overly involved in your early years?" he asked.

"No. I don't think so," I said.

"Did you have an absent father? That's a big cause in homosexuality with boys," he said.

"No, he was a great dad. I mean, he did travel a lot. And they did get a divorce when I was four. I saw him every other weekend and on Tuesdays."

"Well, there you have it."

That conversation planted a suspicion that my father's absence had made me gay. At least it gave me some framework, and I was desperate to understand why I was different.

"Another reason is sexual abuse," he said. He had this thing all figured out.

"I was never molested," I said.

"Well, maybe, but also a lot of people block that stuff out. You may have been, and just can't remember it."

What a cancer in the mind. To be told you could have been molested, but that it's buried in your subconscious. How do you fight that kind of thought? My warm and nurturing childhood was just a delusion, a defense from trauma?

Back in Mendoza, we spent one more night together at the same hotel. By then, my understanding about what made me different was no clearer, but my confidence in my dad's love was strong. Life was complicated. My dad had always loved me. He always made me feel safe and okay in a world where boys need to be good at sports and date pretty girls.

IT WAS ALMOST October when Dad and Kelley flew out. Springtime down here in the upside-down world. Two friends, Parker and Ronnie, were coming down from the U.S. to ride with me for a few weeks. Parker was from Santa Barbara and Ronnie from Saint Louis. I didn't know either of them very well, but south of Mendoza was a long stretch of desert and I didn't want to do that alone. Besides, they'd both reached out, asking if they could join me. I told them to meet me in Mendoza.

I was entering the home stretch. It would be three weeks biking with them. Then three weeks alone again. Then it would be December and my mom would fly down to meet me in Punta Arenas, the southernmost town I'd see on this adventure. The ramp up to the end felt oddly abrupt, the way Halloween begins that sudden slide into the holidays and the new year.

Parker and Ronnie showed up to the little hotel with mouths dropped open. "What the hell have we done?" Parker said, laughing and pulling his bike out of the trunk of the taxi. Right away, their eagerness gave me energy. Parker was a surfer kid. Ronnie was a wide-eyed kid from the Midwest who had never left the country. They were both in their early twenties. We soon packed up our bikes, made a quick stop at the grocery store, and we were out.

South of Mendoza we headed into the desert. Patagonia was straight ahead.

SAN MARTÍN DE LOS ANDES

SAN CARLOS DE BARILOCHE

ESQUEL

FUTALEUFÚ

VILLA O'Higgins

EL CHALTÉN

Fitz Roy

TORRES DEL PAINE ...AKA THE END.

PUNTA ARENAS

Chapter 19

ENTERING THE HOLY LAND
(Mendoza to Bariloche)

2,225 miles to go

Even telling this part of the story is tiring. The light in my eyes, or should I say in my writing, has dulled a bit. I'd been living on a bicycle at this point for more than a year. I don't mean to diminish anything that has come before, but I want to make sure you're with me: I was tired. I had been torn up by Weston's sharp ideas, and softened and changed by whatever happened on Machu Picchu. I had asked this trip to teach me things, turn me upside down, and it was doing that.

But, man, I guess I thought it would've been a bit tidier.

For all the beauty of Argentina, which was quickly becoming my favorite country of all of them, I was ready to see Patagonia and get this whole thing over with.

Argentina's gateway to Patagonia is nothing like the famous and apparently photogenic south. Mostly, it is bleak expanses of sandy, rocky earth. No naturally occurring trees. Very few people. The occasional farm, enclosed by tall poplar trees for a windbreak. As you head down the loneliest road in the world, you see the snowcapped Andes far away on your right, like a wall built to keep the Chileans away, and on your left, flat desert, empty as Mars, extending beyond the horizon to the Atlantic. I knew I would enter Patagonia soon after leaving Mendoza. We biked for three days and then we saw it: not some massive gate or canyon or mountain pass but a tall cement monolith with blue panels on either side reading, "Welcome to Patagonia." Below the words, a photo of a dinosaur skeleton. Parker and Ronnie were biking behind me. I stopped to take a picture.

"Whoa! That's it? This is Patagonia? Just a sign on the side of the road?" Parker asked.

"I guess so," I said.

"Well, dude, you could stop now. You did it. Oregon to Patagonia. Technically you're done," he said.

"Should we turn back and go get a beer?" I joked. But I knew that Patagonia is massive, larger than Texas and California and Oregon and Washington combined. I had so much farther to go.

Still, the desert south of Mendoza looked familiar to me, like a geographical cousin to the American West. Expanses of cacti, and between the cacti, dirt untouched by walking life. The dirt is soft, like brown flour. But the wind is hard, like the blast of a jet engine. There were times on my bike when the wind held me almost at a stop, no matter how hard I pedaled. When the wind was at my back, I could swear I was on a motorcycle. It pushed me up hills, without any help from my legs at all. It felt like a metaphor for life, of fighting against or riding with the current of God. Life can feel effortless, like you're carried along by an unseen force. Or it can feel like you're in a losing fistfight with a brick wall. It all depends on which way you're headed.

After a couple great days cold camping and battling the wind, we pulled into the little town of Tunuyán and booked a room in the only hotel. Splitting it among the three of us, it was six bucks each. They had Wi-Fi. I checked the news and everything was about Ebola in West Africa and the protests in Ferguson, Missouri.

The disease was spreading out of control. In Liberia, people were dying, literally by the truckload. Flights were being screened and canceled. Someone in Texas had contracted Ebola after coming back from Africa. Our interconnected world. Humans carrying diseases, coughing and perhaps carrying death with them, unaware, to every corner of the globe. Except my corner. I felt distant enough from the world I was reading about that it could all implode, and I'd be untouched.

Parker and Ronnie said their moms had e-mailed them about Ebola and told them to be very careful. We laughed at how remote we were and how silly their fears were. But we also wondered if

Ebola would spread over the whole world and kill us all. After that sobering thought, we got some beers next door and decided to double down on our fear by watching the movie *Contagion*, with Kate Winslet and Matt Damon. We watched the world fall apart from a virus no one could stop. I sat on the edge of my hotel bed, wondering if the world would be in ruin by the time I finished the trip.

I couldn't stop reading about Ferguson. Why were there such intense protests in the streets? First Trayvon Martin, and now Michael Brown. I found myself reading a lot of black writers on Twitter and Tumblr. Not mainstream journalists, but activists. I read about white privilege. Maybe I had heard that term before, but it had never hit me. It made me uncomfortable. I am in trouble for existing? I don't think I'm racist. And yet, just by being white, am I oppressing others? That doesn't seem fair.

Ferguson made me uncomfortable with my country and my understanding of it. Uncomfortable with a part of myself I took as nothing: my whiteness. I took it as a floor, unseen and stood on. Now I was becoming aware of how the floor was built, and of the systems in place that kept it there. Seeing police brutality and protests in Missouri reported in the Argentinian press embarrassed me. The way that indigenous South Americans were treated, from Colombia to Argentina, felt different to me. They were second-class citizens, certainly, but at least the ruling elites didn't pretend that everyone had equal footing. In the United States, white kids grow up on a mythology that everyone has the same chances, and hard work and responsibility will lead to success. The American dream was a meritocracy. But all that looked different from down here.

WE CAMPED WHERE we needed to, and stayed in little hotels where we could. The far-flung little towns, no matter how depressing or humble, arrived like welcome resting spots. These towns that crouched in the fields were wind-beaten and crumbling—and very far apart. Every ten or twenty miles, a tree would stand sentry by the road, and we'd stop in its shade to drink water, eat an orange, complain to one another about the goddamn wind. The goal was again sixty miles a day. This was doable on flat roads when there wasn't that god-forsaken headwind, but it was hard in the hills and impossible in the mountains. We bought boxed wine and drank like idiots around fires we made from dried brush. The stars were as bright as anywhere in the world.

Seven days of windy biking later and desert camping under bridges and in dried-out creekbeds, we slept in a field in the town of Malargüe. Poplar trees, which had become ubiquitous since Mendoza, walled in the town. They looked like feathers stuck in the ground. Our little campground—actually just a field not far from the river that ran through town—provided a public restroom but no real campsites. We enjoyed craft beer and pizza at a restaurant that seemed much too metropolitan for this little spot on Mars. I still don't know why it was there, but the pizza was damn good. We slept in our field that night and woke up to intense squawking. Hundreds of parrots had decided to ring in the day from the trees directly above us. We got up early thanks to the birds, found coffee at a gas station, and headed out.

The map showed that the next town was too far to reach in a day's ride. We loaded up on water, cookies, fruit, and salami and crackers. Plus two boxes of the cheap wine.

Outside Malargüe, we reentered the treeless plains, and soon began a descent that lasted thirty miles. This was the longest continuous downhill of my entire trip—and it was a delight. The slope was just right to allow for the perfect speed, one that lets you ride comfortably while sitting straight up, no hands, threading your fingers through the air like claws in water. In moments like these, I couldn't help but sing.

Unfortunately, after fifteen or twenty miles when the hill ended, so did the pavement. As far as we could see down the valley, we saw only dirt. Apparently, the government was repaving the only road through the area.

"Well, fuck," Parker said.

Of course, we had no way of knowing how long the roadwork went on. A mile? Twenty miles?

As soon as we started off, we discovered that the surface wasn't so much gravel as freshly turned-over soil, soft as sand. Ronnie had a road bike with thin tires. He'd make it ten feet then grind to a halt as his tires sliced deep into the soil. We soldiered on for an hour, miserably, making perhaps two or three miles, until the sun started pulling the Andes up over itself, and the sky turned purple. This meant we had about an hour to find a spot to camp and set up our tent.

My camping-spot expertise knew what to look for: thickets of trees. Bridges. Abandoned barns or foundations. Places to hide. Over these thousands of miles, I had developed an instinct for surveying the scene.

But today, no bridge, structure, or tree came in sight. The entire valley was covered in leafless, shoulder-high bushes with thorns as long as my pinky. Even if we avoided the bushes, any thorn on the ground would puncture a tire, a lesson I'd learned in the deserts of Mexico and Bolivia.

With the light fading, we labored around one last bend in the road, hoping for something, only to be met with a vista of inhospitable terrain all the way to the southern horizon. Toward the mountains to our right, the thornbushes looked thick enough to prevent us from even getting our bikes off the road. To our left we could see a river valley, perhaps two miles across. Halfway to the river, the thornbushes seemed their highest, but a cross-stitch of cow paths in that direction offered up a trail. In the center of the valley, another two miles down, we spotted a row of poplar trees—in all likelihood, signs of a farmhouse. The only house in fifty miles.

Not wanting to be seen, we dipped off the road toward the valley and into the soft dirt of the desert. Pushing our loaded bikes through the labyrinth of thorns was stressful and difficult. The bushes were so tall that only the tops of our heads would have been visible. Halfway to the river we came upon a clearing that was big enough to accommodate one tent. Gingerly we laid our bicycles down, careful to avoid any thorns. Ronnie yelped as a thorn ripped at his bike shorts. I quickly set up the tent and we put our sleeping bags inside.

Despite our exhaustion and the oncoming darkness, we decided to walk down to the river. I wanted to walk, loosen my legs up, and lift our frustrated spirits with the beauty of the pink sky over such a barren, hostile waste. About thirty yards from the water, the thorn-bushes cleared and short grass and snow-white tiny thorn shrubs lined the marshy ground. From here I could see the house clearly in the distance. I saw cows but no other sign of movement. The river flowed cold and clear in the sharp air. We remarked on the different types of thorns and the beautiful pink sky. I splashed my face, stood up, and we headed back in the direction of our tent.

But just as we approached the edge of the thicket, we noticed a rising plume of dust coming from the house. I squinted toward it—and made out six men on horseback racing toward us. The horses were galloping so fast that the dust was funneling out behind them like a tornado. I said, "Holy shit," and ducked into the thorns.

"What??" Parker asked. But as soon as he and Ronnie saw the plume, they dropped to the ground.

"Maybe they didn't see us," I said optimistically. "Maybe it's their routine for herding the cattle at sunset." I was making up stuff to appease my fear. We raced through the maze of thorns back to my tent, hunched over like thieves, but somehow the spot where we had set our things now felt much more exposed than before.

We crawled into the tent and sat completely quiet. We heard the drum of hooves approaching, then barking—a lot of barking. Shit. They must have twenty dogs running with the horses to smell us out, to track us down. Soon I could hear men shouting commands to one another.

"We should never have gone for a walk!" I groaned. We'd been seen. I broke the first rule.

As we sat, hunched over and waiting, my mind ran through the scenarios. At best, we'd be booted from our campsite and left with nowhere to sleep. At worst . . . I thought about Harry Devert. The world had been kind to him. Then, in the random Godless world, someone murdered him. Was it my turn? Was my naïveté going to cost me my life? No one knows where we are. Who would find us? I had sent an e-mail two days before to my mom, so at least they'd know the general area. Maybe. And I had lured two young friends out here. What if they were murdered and I survived? What would their parents think of me? What is wrong with me that I am thinking of my guilt more than their lives? Feverish thoughts swarmed to the soundtrack of dogs barking. Getting closer. Closer.

The dogs found us first. They rounded the last few bushes and surrounded the tent.

The sound of hooves came next; the horses slowing to a trot. I peered out and saw a brown stallion with a blond mane and tail, sweat matting dust to its hide. My eyes must've been as wide as an owl's. Parker and Ronnie were as quiet as mice.

On the horse's back was a sun-darkened man—deep wrinkles, a cowboy hat. He towered above me. In his arms was something bright and pink.

This was my Harry Devert moment. I sat there frozen. That absurd moment in *Jurassic Park* came to mind. *If I don't move, he can't see me.* The cowboy sat on his horse and didn't speak. He just looked. The dogs were barking, pleased with their find.

Then I saw what the bright pink thing in his arms was. A little girl. She was small, probably three or four years old, and was wearing a jumpsuit as bright as an Easter Peep. She looked so out of place that I couldn't comprehend the sight of her.

The father said something and the dogs quieted. I kept staring out from the mesh of the tent, Parker and Ronnie holding their breaths behind me. Suddenly, the daughter said something in a high sweet voice. The father said something in reply, then he turned to me and said, in Spanish, "It is very cold here at night. I think you should come sleep in our house. Or camp in our barn. You will be more comfortable."

I looked at him in silence for what felt like a very long time. My heart was pumping so hard that I could hear the blood in my ears.

"Thank you, señor, we are okay," I said in broken Spanish. "Are we on your land? I am sorry. We are on bicycle to Patagonia. I like to camp. I am okay here. Is that okay? I am sorry."

He didn't smile or show any emotion, then he said, "Okay. If you get cold, come to the house at any time. It is okay. You are welcome."

He turned his horse and called the dogs. The little girl in pink held up her hand and kept it there, a wave goodbye.

I slept well and hard. In the morning, we woke to the sound of hooves again. The rising sun hadn't yet made it over the ridge. I could see my breath in the frigid air. The man had returned, holding his child in his lap, and a greasy paper sack. I sprang from my sleeping bag, glad that I'd slept in my jeans for the cold. He handed me the bag, and this time, he smiled.

I peered inside: freshly made doughnuts. He said something in Spanish I didn't understand, but his face was open and smiling and his eyes sparkling. He could tell I didn't understand, so he said simply, "My wife," and gestured to the doughnuts. The little girl watched me, with her hand in her mouth.

WE ATE EVERY last doughnut and packed up and headed back to the soft dirt road, and thanks be to God, within a couple miles the pavement returned. We cycled for three more days through the thorny wastes that now—thanks to the cowboy and the pink girl and the doughnuts—seemed more beautiful and simple than hostile. We slept in the thorns and drank boxed wine and enjoyed the smooth flat road. But I could see on the map that the long straight roads began to squiggle up ahead, and I knew that soon we would enter the mountains. First we saw giant snowy peaks standing alone, with green rolling mountains flanking them. No longer the impenetrable wall of the Andes, this was Patagonia opening up to roads and exploration. Then the desert ended, like a cliff, and we rode a long downhill into a green valley. When a sign welcomed us to "The Lake District," I knew I had entered the Patagonia of my imagination.

Laura, my Argentinian mom from Salta, had described the Lake District as one of Argentina's crown jewels. She said that I would see other cyclists and tourists there, and find wonderful camping. The district contains natural glacial lakes, clear water, snowcapped mountains, and resort towns famous for beer, German-style log cabins, and excellent skiing. This was the Patagonia I knew from *National Geographic*, from photos and dreaming. The desert of thorns was behind us. Now we found ourselves surrounded by grassy meadows and aquamarine lakes fed by mountain streams. It was the Southern Hemisphere's Alaska, Norway, and Nova Scotia combined.

The Lake District alone would make Patagonia famous, but that is only the beginning. From there, you have thousands more miles of mountains, growing ever steeper, the wind growing stronger, the peaks sharper, the glaciers larger, appropriate gatekeepers for the end of the world. It all feels very cinematic, the last place for humans on earth.

We arrived into the squiggly roads with shocking beauty. The mountains popped up like a surprise out of the desert. We jumped in a cold river and hopped from rock to rock. We camped next to the first lake we saw, carrying our bikes on our shoulders along a narrow hiking path to find a private spot. Families were on vacation, taking photos at the various overlooks and waterfalls. The first town in the Lake District we reached was San Martín de los Andes. It is a ski town with pubs and European-inspired hotels and ski shops. I made friends with a young girl from Buenos Aires who had taken a gap year to work at a bar in this little town. She was beautiful, with thick black hair and olive skin. Her English was excellent. We had a few beers and she asked me about America.

"What do you think of America?"

"I'm confused about it all right now. Have you heard about Ferguson, and all the racial tension and stuff?"

"Oh, yes. That stuff doesn't surprise me. America is good with race. Argentina used to have black people. Do you see any?"

"No, actually. I haven't seen almost any. Did they all move to Brazil?"

"No. We killed them all. Black slaves made up almost half our country at one point. But then we only promised them freedom if they'd fight in war. And we sent all the men to the front lines of our war with Spain, and then our war with Paraguay. We killed them all. And then we only allowed Europeans to immigrate here. So, Argentina is worse with race. America will be fine."

"Whoa. I didn't know any of that. Do people talk about that?"

"People don't know. They trust the newspapers, which are all lies. What do you think about Syria and the U.S.?" she said, leaning in like she was asking about secrets.

"What Assad is doing is terrible. It's so terrible. I don't know if the U.S. is going to intervene. It makes me really sad."

"You believe that Assad is bad?"

"Yes, doesn't everyone?"

"I don't believe it. I believe it's the U.S. coming in and lying, the newspapers are lying. The U.S. wants the oil in Syria, to control. I think Assad is maybe a good guy, and the rebels are U.S.-planted terrorists to disrupt. Like what the U.S. did in Nicaragua."

Whoa. There are so many ways to see the world. I tried to counter. "I don't know. I've got friends in journalism," I said. "I've got friends who work at NPR and cover the Middle East. They're there. They see what they see and report it. And our news media is pretty antagonistic with our government."

"Well, that's what they want you to think." She leaned back and raised her eyebrows, looking down at her beer. Her body language pulled away as she realized I was another sheep in the system. I tried to bring her back.

"What makes you think these things?" I asked.

"It's just the truth. The U.S. runs the world through coercion, through fake news stories, through control. Everyone knows this that's outside of the U.S. They keep Americans arguing over guns and black people so they won't look outside the country and see that the U.S. is an empire."

"Wow. That may be some level of true. Thank God I made it out, right?" I held my beer up, and she leaned back in to cheers me.

"I mean, I've always wanted to visit the U.S.," she said, somewhat reassuringly. "I want to do a road trip across it. It's so famous, to do the U.S. road trip. One day I will. I want to see the empire before it falls."

"It is a beautiful empire," I said.

WE CYCLED SOUTH from lake to lake, town to town. Highway 40 is famous for its winding vistas, evergreen trees, spring-blooming trees, wildflowers, and log-cabin lodges. We rode by other cyclists and families camping on the edges of the lakes. We stopped for beer and conversations with tourists from Germany, from Chile, from Australia. We biked into an overlook that offered a crazy view of Lago

Nahuel Huapi, a massive glacial lake surrounded by mountains. A man holding a sign, "Photos with Bruno," sat beside a Saint Bernard puppy. Bruno was a blob of white and brown fur in his youth, and families had lined up, waiting with their happily anxious kids for a chance to pose hugging this absurd dog.

We spent a week in this Patagonian paradise. It would rain for an hour, then stop. Then a rainbow would signal blue skies like a biblical promise. Sometimes we would ride through the rain. It was chilly but fresh. I could feel the end of my trip approaching. I wasn't ready to reflect on it. I was in my animal skin, thinking very little, feeling a lot. I would ride for miles, looking down at my front tire, checking to see if it was getting low.

I watched Parker and Ronnie as they rode. They were nearing the end of their stay with me. I noticed the freedom they felt on the road, free from the world at home and the routines they knew. This bike trip had become my routine now, had been for a while. I didn't feel free. I felt normal. The United States now seemed different and strange to me. The thought of driving a car felt exotic. The thought of speaking English to anyone I met felt like a rare privilege. The idea that in the U.S., I could walk up to any stranger and speak freely, about anything, with thousands of words to choose from, and that they would understand—wow, that felt wild to me.

We arrived in San Carlos de Bariloche, about fifty miles later, at the end of the Lake District's famous route. It is the largest town in the lakes, with a popular ski resort and restaurants and hotels. At more than 100,000 inhabitants, it felt like New York City.

We found a cheap hostel and set up shop. My mom had e-mailed her plans to come finish the trip with me at Torres del Paine. I was very happy to hear this. As much as our relationship confounded me, I always wanted to celebrate with her. I couldn't put a finger on it, but I knew that my deepest wounds were the place of my deepest meanings. And she was ground zero. My salvation was somewhere inside her.

She would fly into Punta Arenas, the biggest town in Chile's deep south. She would rent an Airbnb and a car, and we'd hike and explore and take photos and celebrate. I had another month to make it to Punta Arenas. But soon after Bariloche, I would be leaving pavement again for 700 miles of gravel. Lots of cycling blogs talked about this stretch. It featured the most spectacular scenery, but the government had never bothered to pave it because too few people traveled there.

In Bariloche it was Halloween, the night before Parker and Ronnie left. We had beers and a good dinner and recounted stories of doughnuts and downhill days. The next day they boxed up their bicycles and headed to the airport. In between our goodbye hugs, I could already feel the aloneness approaching. The final stretch. Just me and the road and my bicycle and Patagonia.

FIRST THING, I went to a bike shop in town and bought fatter tires, twice as wide as any I had ridden on. They looked absurd and sluggish. They would slow me down for the next hundred miles of pavement, but I'd be thanking the Lord for them the minute I hit the gravel of the Carretera Austral. Instead of slipping and sinking in and ruining the tires, I'd be able to ride normally-ish.

When I went to pay the bill, the woman behind the hostel counter hardly looked up from her computer. "Gracias," she said, already worrying about something else. I had a coffee. I packed my bike. And I climbed on and began cycling. I was entering the final month of my journey, and no one was watching. Which, though lonely, felt poetically personal and perfect.

The road south from Bariloche took me into ever more dramatic terrain. The mountains higher. The snow whiter. The trees taller and thicker. Rivers of sparkling clarity tumbled over boulders. Sheep became common on the hillsides, with just the occasional horse for aesthetic appeal. I camped some, but mostly I stayed in small hostels. There I'd meet backpackers, day hikers, weirdos, and escape artists. Being alone again gave me a sweet social freedom. I didn't have a travel partner, much less a clique. When you're sitting alone on the porch with a beer, a book, and a friendly face, almost anyone will talk to you.

This has been a common experience for my whole life. Something about the way I hold my face, or my mediocre good looks, my unintimidating stature, my curious and friendly eyes, always leads strangers to talk to me. In any city, people ask me for directions. People ask me what book I'm reading. People talk to me, and I'm sure they don't know why. They might say, "You seemed nice," or "You look like you are from here," but I bet they didn't have the thought first. They just felt familiar with me. It has been a constant reminder of the hidden motivations of all our actions. The signals we send. The language we all speak and cannot hear.

Five days out from Bariloche, I had wound my way around what must have been a dozen more lakes, mountains leaning right over the well-paved road, horses watching me roll by, and the occasional house or gas station. There were little towns with a few cafés and hostels in them. I was nearing the border with Chile, where the road would leave Argentina and dip into the famous Carretera Austral for a long while. From pavement to gravel for more than 700 miles.

The last day to the border was spectacular. A meandering road took me through beautiful farmland and fields of lupines. These flowers were tall spears of purple, made up of hundreds of small purple flowers each, stacked on top of one another. The blue sky, the snow-topped mountains, the sky reflected in the cascading streams, and the purple flowers filling up the green fields made for a world so idyllic that I sometimes felt overwhelmed, even defeated by it. I couldn't take it all in. The photos I took turned out dumb and dull. Nothing captured the colors or scale.

While I biked, I was listening to a podcast episode of *Fresh Air* with Terry Gross. She was interviewing Jill Soloway, the creator of the show *Transparent*, an Amazon series about a seventy-year-old father coming out to his kids as transgender. The show documents his transition into life as a woman. I listened to this podcast enraptured by the evolution of gender, of pronouns, of culture. Terry Gross, a world-famous and seasoned interviewer, stumbled over the proper pronouns with Soloway, who lovingly corrected her several times. "He, I'm sorry, she," Gross would say. "Or do they prefer 'they'?" I remember Soloway explaining that some nonbinary people (between genders) preferred the pronoun *they*, to which Terry Gross seemed to be surprised. "It isn't as difficult as people think," Soloway said. "When your roommate is headed to the airport to pick up a friend that you don't know, whose gender you don't know, it isn't strange to say 'what time do they land?' See how easy that is?" Soloway went on to say that the show was inspired by her life, by her dad transitioning in his seventies, becoming her "moppa," a combination of momma and papa.

As I cycled past the tall purple flowers and over bridges, my mind sorted through the ideas of gender fluidity and identity. I remember thinking that the sight of a cross-dressing man, a man in women's clothes, was funny to me. Strange and silly. I remember thinking, "Does he really think we can't tell he's a man?" I would snicker and think, "What a weirdo." But then I realized, if I held hands with a boy fifty years ago, or even this year in certain places, wouldn't people snicker and point and whisper or worse? What is the difference?

An awareness of my own hypocrisy stung me. I hadn't noticed this in myself. And from this thought, it spread in me an empathy for my mom, for the people in my church. If I, being in a category of oppression, could still mock another who is laterally the same as me, then how common must that hypocrisy be? And in being that way, they are not intentionally evil or bigoted, but groupish human beings wired to question difference.

I thought of the power of storytelling, how exposure to this story of a trans woman was rewiring my brain. How *Will & Grace* had changed my young life. How encountering firsthand my sexuality had rewired the brains of some of my straight friends. Exposure to human stories reminds us that we're all human. I mean real exposure. Listening, hearing. Not pointing from across the room. Engaging. And most of us are just trying to make it day by day without hurting anyone else.

I still look at photos from that stretch of road and remember the sound of Terry Gross's voice, of Jill Soloway's calm surgery on my mind.

Eight days after Bariloche, as I neared the border crossing, I spotted an Andean condor on the ground just off the road. A giant of a bird, the condor can stand four feet tall with a wingspan of eleven feet—perhaps the largest flying animal on earth. This one was metallic black with a white collar of feathers and a bald gray head. It just sat there in the field, not twenty feet away, looking back at me.

Ferguson and Black Lives Matter and *Transparent* and transgendered people and the Bible and my mom and my sexuality and Terry Gross and Ebola. And this bird, unaware of it all. Looking for some roadkill, probably. It was not thinking about identity or gender or going extinct. It hungered for dinner and hungered for a mate. That's it.

I wish, I thought.

Then the condor opened its wings, and with considerable effort lifted into the air, and flew in widening circles over the Chilean border station, and we entered the new country together.

Chapter 20

ALONE IN GOD'S MOST OBVIOUS WORK
(The Carretera Austral)

1,222 miles to go

The road was paved for a few miles, then, as I entered the Chilean town of Futaleufú, the surface turned to gravel. I had arrived at the start of the 700-mile stretch of gravel I had been told about. This was the Carretera Austral, a legendary road through Patagonia for motorcyclists and bikers that winds south through fjords and inlets too numerous to count. The coast is shredded into thousands of islands, with the Pacific Ocean weaving through. What isn't ocean is lake. Lakes everywhere. Evergreen trees and sheep farms and so many waterfalls that most are not named on any map I could find. I would cycle down this for the entire month of November. I would have Thanksgiving alone somewhere. Then, at the town of O'Higgins, where most people end their Carretera adventure, I would ferry across a glacier-fed lake back to Argentina one more time. Then walk or carry my bike twelve miles through a dense forest. Then another ferry. Then I would be in El Chaltén, the home of Mount Fitz Roy.

By now, I was so accustomed to my new routine, to biking and living out of panniers, of eating salami and crackers and sleeping outside, that the approaching end of the trip felt obvious. I was just stepping into completion. It was all surprisingly transactional.

I spent the night in Futaleufú and woke up to tackle the endless gravel. I set off and the gravel was there to meet me. I rattled for the whole day. Several times, my backpack and sleeping bag shook off the back of the bike and fell in the road. I had to tie and retie my things. I was frustrated. My God, 700 miles of this?

The rivers turned an even more absurd color of aquamarine, flowing from glaciers around me. Bits of snow hid in the shadowed places. Everything was beautiful but the shaking really took a toll. Would I enjoy this? After thirty miles of vibrating down the road, I checked into a hostel in a little town. The hostel was actually the upstairs room in a family's home. I slept blessedly rattle free, and in the morning the daughter made me coffee.

The next day, I was prepared to rattle for six hours. I gave myself a pep talk over coffee, and headed out. But right out of town the gravel smoothed and became packed and hard. The riding was actually nice. Now I could enjoy the cliffs and the giant ferns and cascades, one after the other, spilling from mountaintops. The occasional truck roared past, kicking up a funnel cloud of dust. I put a bandana over my mouth to save my lips and throat.

The next night I slept by a river. In a thicket of trees near a pebble beach, the canopy had created a soft brown pad of moss and leaves. My tent fit perfectly.

And the site was perfect for bathing. I saw no sign of humanity anywhere, not a sheep or a fence, just river, mountains, tall trees with gray bark and dark green evergreen leaves, waterfalls, and the river valley extending forever south. I got naked and took a dip in the turquoise river. It was freezing—so cold, I lost my breath and could only submerge for two seconds. Maybe less. I got wet, clambered out to apply soap and scrub down a bit, then took another dip. Then screamed. The whole time, I was talking myself through this out loud. "Okay, now you dip again—AHHGG!!—I know, Jed, you hate it, but it's a necessity—FUCK!—Your bike shorts are disgusting— SHIT!—and you can't have your grundle being a filthy crevice— GRRRR!—You owe it to your bike seat."

I crawled in my tent feeling fresh and clean. I snuggled up and put my winter jacket behind my head on top of my backpack for a pillow. I opened my laptop and checked what movies I had downloaded. It would be nice to have some wine and watch a movie. All alone out here. Outside, the river's white noise filled the air.

I had downloaded season one of *The Walking Dead*.

Zombies walked through the streets and yards, busting down the door of a suburban house and killing and eating the guts of humans. The music was scary. The lighting dark. This kind of thing wouldn't bother me in the least at home. But suddenly my hearing was super-human. As I watched the show, I heard bugs walking outside, or was it a person? Am I being hunted? Will I die out here?

I closed my laptop and chugged my wine, angry that I'd watched even part of the show.

The following day I camped in someone's yard. I rolled up to the little town and asked if there was a hotel. They said no, but pointed to a house. I knocked and asked about camping. The lady said sure, and pointed to the grass next to the toolshed. I paid the family a little bit to let me use their bathroom. After I set up my tent, a group of backpackers appeared in the yard, apparently sent here by the same person. They were gregarious and confident, speaking Hebrew and laughing as they set up their tents. I deduced that they were from Israel. When I greeted them in English, they responded warmly. Soon I had shared my box wine and they gave me a cigarette. But I was tired and not much fun and went to bed early while they cracked one another up all night. I wondered if the lady in the house regretted her generosity.

Ten days down the Carretera, the road had become lonely routine, cycling on gravel, staying at a little house or camping. Everywhere, the wonders of Patagonia rose up around me, but by then, and with no one to exclaim to, I stopped exclaiming. I looked, and my eyes were happy. But I had no one to sing the praises of Creation to. Only the Creation itself. Maybe God was there, proud of His work. But He isn't surprised by things, and He doesn't respond with laughter when I jump for joy. Not that I could tell anyway. So I stopped jumping. I just tried to make the miles. I stopped taking photos of waterfalls.

The days dripped by and I spent a lot of time in silence. I didn't have to camp as much as I'd thought. Even the smallest towns had a room for rent. The Carretera was used to hosting cyclists.

I spent Thanksgiving at a simple hostel on a lake. Chile doesn't celebrate American Thanksgiving, of course, so it wasn't much of a celebration. I sat with my coffee in the morning and wrote in my journal.

Thanksgiving, 2014. Lao General Carretera, Chile.

I am alone. Near no one I know. This is one of America's biggest holidays, at least in respect to family. And they are very far from me. So, as an exercise in mindfulness, and because I believe gratitude is the door to joy, I am going to list some of the things I'm thankful for: Parents I respect. A mother of strong and tender character, endless talent, humor, wisdom, playfulness, taste. A father of kindred heart, with a hunger for adventure, laughter, experience, love. They are both so full of love. My sister Rebekah, her heart and mind of fire, her caretaking powers, her love! My brother, his angelic spirit and perfectly matched wife, I love them so! My little sister. She is a soft voiced, strong-hearted force. I love being near her. What a modern family made whole with grace and kindness!

My health, my strong bicycle, this natural beauty, fjords, so many waterfalls, rivers, God's ridiculous paintings, and all those hearts I carry in my heart, those boards and nails that build my house. . . .

And then I went on for two pages listing every friend that has touched my life. Pushing out words of thanks felt important in my fogginess. Fake it till you make it. It isn't that I wasn't thankful. It's that I felt so bound up in my unknowing that I couldn't figure out who to thank or who to curse. Should I be angry with my past? My faith? My parents? Or should I be thankful?

When I had finished, I closed my journal and went for a walk. I felt fully loved by the people I'd listed. I felt that I had seen them by writing their names, that I'd called them forth. But then, a rush of feeling alone. I knew no one in the nation of Chile. And yet names and faces swirled around me like fireflies. I held my life, so graced with kindness and friendship, in my mind's eye as I walked around the tiny town on the edge of a lake in Patagonia. A stray dog came up and trotted next to me, as if drawn by my thinking. As if responding to some deep calling in every dog to comfort a lost boy.

———

LITTLE HOUSES ALONG the Carretera Austral post signs to attract cyclists. Hotels offer musty lounges, old sofas, and instant coffee. But mostly, I camped. I met only one other cyclist in two weeks on the road. He was a handsome tan Italian with expensive gear and a shiny new bike. We got a beer together at the only restaurant for miles. I drank my beer and he looked at me longer than usual. I didn't give him any cues. But when we parted, I felt handsome for a moment.

I was in the zone, each day biking farther than the last, and becoming ever more accustomed to my solitude. An entire day passed without me speaking to a single human. I did speak though, just to the world. I love talking to the road and to trees and birds. My voice keeps me company.

Cycling alone had me back in my head. Here I was, near the end of the journey, and wondering what I'd learned. Had I found freedom? Did I know what I thought about God? No, I just had more fucking questions. Did I feel more awake and young and alive? Yes, I guess I did, but had I experienced page-turning revelations? Some flag to plant in a new continent of understanding? No.

One day, exhausted from a frustrating uphill stretch where my tires kept spinning out, I decided to take a nap in the midday sun. I pulled off the road and found a grassy meadow next to a creek. I lay down and closed my eyes.

I was roused by buzzing. Not the thin whine of mosquitoes but the sound of something heavier. Bigger. When I opened my eyes, I saw bees. Dozens of bees hovering and circling around me.

Then I noticed that I had lain down next to a hole in the ground. The bees were pouring out of it. They were crawling on me and crawling all over my bike. The bees were much larger than I was used to, more like bumblebees, and solid orange. Like flaming hot Cheetos. But weren't bees from South America supposed to be super poisonous? Or was that Africa?

I got up in a hurry and, using a twig with some leaves, gingerly brushed the curious Cheetos off my shirt and bike. Then I got back on the road.

Strangely, I hadn't seen a bee in months. I'd actually forgotten about the bees from the beginning of my trip. How they seemed to give me encouragement, signaling to me that I was on the right track. They'd left me for so long. But here they were near the end of my trip—different, bigger, friendlier, impossible to overlook.

That night I stayed in an old lady's house. It was full to the ceiling with knickknacks and every manner of thing. She was a little gnome of a woman and a hoarder. I loved her right away. She rented an upstairs room and promised breakfast for cheap. I told her about the strange bees, resorting to drawing one on a Post-it note and saying "naranja" and how I was scared they would attack me. She laughed. "Oh no! Bees here do not sting you. You are safe."

New bees. Bigger bees. That don't sting. I liked that, whatever it meant.

Three days later I took a hard fall. At the edge of a forest, my bike skidded on the gravel, I lost control, and fell into the ditch amid a gnarl of logs and stones. For a minute, I lay on the ground, tangled in my bike and bags, wondering what kind of damage I'd discover when I stood up. A gash, a twisted ankle, a broken bone? I moaned and rolled over and pushed myself up. But underneath the scratches and dirt, I was okay. Banged up but fine. And my bike was fine.

As I got back on my bike and tied my things back on, Machu Picchu and Weston and Jesus came to mind. All those dangerous conversations. Those bike crashes in my head. I had been told that to walk away from Jesus was to walk away from eternal life, from truth, from community and everything. I would be leaving a weeping mother and a broken life. I would be labeled deceived and lost and a backslider. But as the scenario had been playing out on the trip south, it wasn't so black and white as that. Along the way I'd asked hard questions, entertained "wrong" answers, held new ideas with an open hand, and waited to be scalded by fire. Waited for the twisted ankle or broken bone. But it hadn't happened. But then, I wasn't rejecting Jesus, was I? I wasn't walking away. I was just wondering if God was bigger than what I had been told in church. If perhaps He wasn't so jealous, so frightened by the rest of His creation.

Backsliding felt a lot like walking forward. Like expanding into love and wonder. I had dared to crash with my old beliefs into the ditch, and I stood up fine.

A week later on a Tuesday, I reached Villa O'Higgins, the terminus of the Carretera Austral. The hamlet, named for the hero of Chilean independence, is laid out on a grid in a valley near the lake of the same name. I would need to take a ferry across this lake back to Argentina. The houses were constructed of tin siding with tin roofs, and some were falling apart. Grass grew tall in most yards. People sat on their stoops, staring without hurry at the world.

Actually, nothing hurried here, and I was in a bit of a time crunch to get to Punta Arenas and meet my mom. It wasn't dire, but it wasn't like I could sit around either. Just finding the crossing proved a challenge. The woman at my hostel (where I was the only guest) told me that the ferry was operated by a man in the house with the tractors.

"Which house is that?"

"You'll see it."

"Do I just go and knock?"

"Yes."

So I set out on foot to wander the town in search of a house with tractors. On the far corner of the grid, I found it—a lean-to of rusted tin with three or four tractors in various states of disrepair parked around the yard.

When I knocked on the open door and peered inside, a small, elderly woman appeared. She said something in Spanish that I couldn't understand. She didn't seem to have any teeth. I said, "I have a question about the ferry."

"Yes, come," she said, and waved me inside. I walked through a dark room cluttered from floor to ceiling with tractor and boat parts. She led me into the other room of the house. It was so full of oily, dark metal parts that only a hole in the middle of the room had been carved out. In that hole was one recliner holding an old man who was watching a television a few feet from his face.

He glanced up at me then back to the television. "Yes? Hello." He was smoking a cigarette. The entire house smelled like smoke, and the ashtray next to him had at least three packs' worth of butts piled high. The ceiling, what I could see of it above his chair, had turned black.

"Ferry? When is the ferry?" I said, terrified and suddenly forgetting any Spanish I knew.

"No ferry today," he said, looking at the television.

"Oh, yes, ferry tomorrow?"

"No. No ferry."

Oh, God. No ferry. Did he mean ever? Or not tomorrow? He wasn't giving me anything. I was mad at myself for not understanding Spanish better. Not taking lessons. Not trying harder. Letting everyone speak English to me. I couldn't ask the way I needed to. I was so fucked.

"Ferry is possible?" I asked.

"Ferry on Friday. Nine in the morning."

Oh, thank God.

"Okay, come here?" I asked.

"No, take bus to the dock. Bus from the library."

"Okay, thank you thank you thank you," I said. He smiled, but he was smiling at the TV. As I let myself out, I said thank you to the old woman.

I spent three days in Villa O'Higgins. I read my book. I met a few other backpackers and even a bike-touring couple from England. We drank beer. I ate cookies. I hiked to the top of a nearby hill. It was altogether very nice.

On Friday I caught the ferry. We crossed a huge turquoise lake for two hours before we were dropped on the other side. The port here consisted of a cabin painted white with a green roof, and a gravel road leading away from it up the hill and into a canyon between two mountains. That was my route. Twelve miles through the woods, then I'd cross into Argentina again.

I tried to ride but the road was really just a path of baseball-sized rocks. I couldn't ride at all. So I walked my bike. It was already early afternoon and I walked my bike for several miles and then camped in a field with horses.

As I fell asleep, I realized that tomorrow would be my final day on the bicycle. I would reach El Chaltén, and then be done. I would see Fitz Roy, stay the night, and take a bus down to the airport in Punta Arenas, Chile, to meet my mother and friends. Then we'd come back north together to explore the scenic wonders of Torres del Paine. I was almost done. All night, I froze, and only my grin poked out of my sleeping bag.

The next day I walked my bike through dense forest, carrying it over log bridges crossing creek after creek. Before long, my muscles ached. I struggled to stabilize the heavy bike on the skinny path, and actually dropped it all in one of the creeks. But I was so high on finishing that I hardly cared. I sang to myself, mostly "look at this stuff, isn't it neat" from *The Little Mermaid.*

Finally, I saw a sign, "Welcome to Argentina." In the distance, behind the sign, were the peaks of Fitz Roy. I took a photo of my bike in front of it all. My day ended with another ferry ride across a small lake, then, after three miles on a nice gravel road, I was in El Chaltén.

In town, I parked my bike outside a hostel, where I found myself surrounded by tourists and backpackers, some of whom had also cycled the Carretera Austral. After setting my stuff on a bunk bed in a crowded room, I walked back out to the main street.

It was sunset. 11,700-foot Fitz Roy showed itself through shifting clouds. I had cycled to Patagonia. I drank a beer, feeling proud but calm. I was simply done. Like the last grain of sand dropping in an hourglass, my experiment in time ended without a sound.

I never got on the bike again.

Chapter 21

MOM AND THE MOUNTAIN
(Torres del Paine)

592 miles to go

The next day, I hiked alone to the base of Cerro Torre, which is next to Mount Fitz Roy and almost as famous. The peaks here present an incredible skyline of skinny granite spires shaped by the brutal and endless winds and rain. Like knives stuck blade-up in the snow. I asked a tourist to take my photo. I stood in the hateful wind and let my face get chapped. I hiked back to town and had dinner with some hikers I'd met from England. Then I wandered the main street and thought how alone I was in my accomplishment. All these people were on vacation, doing their own thing. They saw me and assumed I'd flown here. Or didn't think about me at all. I was just an extra in the movie of their life. But I knew what I'd done. And so did God.

That evening, I stowed the bike in the baggage compartment under a big bus and boarded it for Punta Arenas, Chile, another thousand miles south, where I'd meet my mother and two of my friends.

On that bus, I had a lot of miles to stare out the window and think about my journey. About expectations. About destinations. I had wanted my spirit quest to answer questions for me. More than that, I needed it to reveal my questions to me, then answer them. What a burden to put on travel, which in itself is ignorant and indifferent. It becomes so hard to just enjoy the thing as it happens. We make the journey about arrival, not travel. We are so goal focused. We are the dog that won't stop paddling as long as he sees the shore. But, man, my shore had been hidden by the fog for so long.

Of course, goals help us get a lot done. But they often remove our attention from the experience to the achievement. When we arrive at the goal, we think, *then* we will be happy. When we finally get there, we can celebrate and have fun. When I get that job, I'll be fulfilled then. When I get married, I will be happy. The Eden we pine for is not under our own feet or bike tires, but over the next mountain.

I had crossed the mountain. I was in the Eden of my dreams. I had a couple weeks left in the adventure of a lifetime, but I was here. I had arrived. Now what? I suppose I'd worked through some things on the road. My faith had gotten rearranged, the puzzle pieces disassembled and spread across the table. Not put back together, but not a total mess either. I guess I did feel a warm direction, a positive pulling toward something else. I had always worried that if I took my inherited beliefs off the throne, if I took the Bible out of God's hands and put it in mine, that my life would spin into relativistic nonsense. That's what I'd always been told. Yet I didn't see that happening. I had asked and been asked heretical questions. I had looked straight at the sun and demanded answers, and I was still standing. And I was not blind.

Thousands of miles from Peru, from saying goodbye to Weston, he was with me in my heart. His critical mind, fearless to excavate all possibilities, had been hard for my fragile ego. He wasn't afraid to let things change. He'd done that his whole life. He'd fought for heaven then discarded it like a rumor. He'd tried all the fruits of pleasure and remained unsatisfied. He'd sought the world for truth and freedom, and perhaps he was closer than I was. But his liberty had done something to me. I missed him terribly. I wished he'd been with me. I wished he had been there for Fitz Roy, blowing smoke in my face and hugging me.

Thanks to him, I had come to realize that there were doors and rooms in the house of my mind that had always been there, but had been boarded up. He'd kicked some of those doors open. I had peeked through, broken rules, walked down dark hallways. And the house, even in its mystery and darkness, was still my home, and surprisingly still felt like it.

On the Carretera, some of my spiritual discomfort had settled. In my aloneness, I had forgiven people. Now they couldn't hurt me.

Only nature was real. Christianity couldn't tell me what to do. My mother couldn't tell me what to do. My need to belong and fit in had fallen away into meaninglessness. Mile by mile, only discovery mattered.

Yet now, at the end of the trip, I felt a dull melancholy. The way DayQuil can mask a cold, but leave you with a muffled head. I was excited, sure, but I was tired. I wondered if old age felt like this. If the end is not a triumph and fireworks, but a simple, quiet arrival. A beer in a pub and wondering what it was you had wanted so desperately. Looking back at a complex grab bag of lessons, but seeing no through line. Feeling pride of accomplishment, as I did now, but struck by your own cheating and laziness. And finally you take a cosmic bus to see your mother.

Punta arenas, a port on the Strait of Magellan, lies halfway between the Atlantic and the Pacific. It is the bottom of the world. The shore faces Antarctica. It is the southernmost significant habitation on the continent of South America, with only the islands of Tierra del Fuego and the stormy Drake Passage separating the mainland from the Antarctic. This was as far south as I would get.

I arrived and slept in a dingy hostel, my last night alone. I should say I hardly slept. I was so excited to see my mom and my friends. I woke up, had my coffee, and felt both sad to say goodbye to this weird season of my life and thrilled to be done with it.

Mom had been texting photos of things she was buying for the trip. Hiking boots on sale at TJ Maxx. A men's rain jacket from Goodwill. Protein powder that can be mixed with creek water in case of emergency. Ebola-protection materials from a website dedicated to preparing for the end-times. A Spanish phrase book, though when she realized it only had slang and curse words, she sent me a picture of the book in the trash.

The airport in Punta Arenas had no Wi-Fi and I knew my mom's phone wouldn't work. It felt like trips to the airport in the early nineties, when no one had cell phones and you had to hope that the time they said they would arrive turned out to be the right time.

But standing in the terminal waiting for my mom, I felt proud and strong. I felt like a man. I still couldn't throw a football. But lots of dudes can throw a football, and none of them have lived on a bicycle for sixteen months. I wasn't looking forward to my mother's direct questions, her probing, even though I felt okay in my sexuality and my ambiguous faith in a way that I had never been. I just didn't want my mother to be sad with who I'd become. I didn't want her to be mourning her son's dead soul as we explored the mountains together.

Then I spotted her curly brown hair and unnecessarily bejeweled sunglasses rounding the corner. She was already yelling for me, laughing through her words. "Jed, I did it! I'm a world traveler. Ecuador and now Patagonia! And at my age!" Her brightness and presence made me instantly happy.

She pushed past the other passengers and dropped her purse and roller bag for a long hug. When we pulled away, she said, "You look so skinny! Handsome, but skinny. Momma's here, I'm not about to cook, but we're gonna eat our way through this Patagonia!" She had booked a hotel in an old building that looked like an English castle. We would be staying a night before renting a car for the week and heading north up to Puerto Natales, the closest town to Torres del Paine National Park.

Later that evening, my friends Mila and Willow flew in. They had decided to join me for the final exploration of Torres del Paine. I was very happy about that. And honored. Plus, it was easier to be around my mother with the buffer of a third and fourth party.

My mother showed us all the ridiculous things she had packed. She had a folded, tightly packed yellow hazmat suit. She said, "You know, with all the Ebola going around the world, on planes, I didn't want to take any chances." She knew she was funny. But she was also serious. From under her T-shirts she pulled out a gallon bag of almonds. Willow and Mila laughed at every new revelation.

"Mom, why so many almonds?!" I said.

"Did you know you can live off of just almonds for months? Maybe forever? They're just a backup plan." She had nonperishable food in sandwich bags tucked in every corner of her bag. She pulled out a big plastic bag of pills.

"What are those?" I asked, incredulous.

"Water purification tablets. Just in case."

"In case of what, Mom?"

"I didn't know how the water would be down here. Or if we'd be lost in the wilderness and need to survive."

I laughed. "Mom, we're staying at an Airbnb."

"You never know."

The next morning we picked up the rental car and began the three-hour drive north to Puerto Natales. The trees ended at the outskirts of town, the terrain becoming rolling hills of grass with clumps of trees around the few farmhouses. In the distance, we could see snow-covered mountains. We saw rheas running along the fences by the side of the road. Rheas look almost exactly like ostriches. We were simply driving across prairie land when a huge bird began racing next to us on the other side of a fence. No one had told me that South America had its own version of native flightless birds.

"Look at that ostrich!" my mom screamed. My eyes took a minute to register what we were seeing. It was smaller than an ostrich, but tall as a man, and keeping pace with our car for no apparent reason. I didn't have cell service or Wi-Fi so we just had to speculate how there could be ostriches down here. It wasn't until that night that I remembered to google it and learned of the existence of these feathery indigenous giants.

We arrived at the cottage my mom had rented just outside Puerto Natales by midafternoon. It was attached to a boutique hotel sitting on a broad grassy field that rolled down to the bay, which is connected by a series of channels to the Pacific. The distant mountains were white with snow, but in town, the grass was neon green and lush. Horses waded through it.

Puerto Natales swarmed with serious hikers from all over— Europeans, Australians, Israelis, and Americans. They come here to do the circuit hikes around the peaks of Torres del Paine and Cuernos del Paine. The full circuit takes about a week. You camp along the way, stop at ranger cabins to replenish or have a beer, and meet hikers from all over the planet. For two days, we played tourists along with the crowds—shopping, horseback riding, and eating well. Then we drove the final two hours to the park itself.

The landscape in this part of Patagonia is unbelievably expansive. With very few trees, the bare skin of Patagonia shows through. The naked beauty of a raw planet. In the fields stretching away on either side we saw cows and rheas and vicuñas (which are in the llama family, though with shorter hair, golden brown with white bellies). Clouds would pile up thick and tall over the mountains one moment, then swirl into mist the next, strands of sunlight streaming through over the course of the day in a cycle from hopeful to ominous and back.

In the distance, we could see the granite towers of the Torres del Paine massif approaching. The spires sit on top of a wide-set mountain like a crown. I knew from obsessing over the map that Cuernos del Paine, one of the world's most daunting ascents, was situated on the opposite side of Torres del Paine from us. Instead of a lineup of peaks, Cuernos del Paine looks like a jumbled collection of shardlike spikes rising in a triangle, almost like God had taken a machete to a mountain in a drunken rage. Hiking trails completely encircle both of these wonders.

We stopped at a lodge at the foot of Torres del Paine for lunch. While eating, Mom asked, "How many miles is that Torres del Paine hike?" I told her it was about six miles, all uphill, then six miles back.

She swirled her wineglass. "We should do it," she said.

"Mom, it's a strenuous hike. I don't think . . ."

"I want to do it. I'm in good shape. I'll go at my own pace."

"Are you sure? What if you get hurt?"

"I'll go at my own pace and I won't get hurt. I can't come this far and not try. I feel great. I walk a lot."

"I don't know, Mom."

"Okay, don't start this. I've always known that one day my kids would start to baby me as I got older. I know it's coming. But not yet. I am an adult and I have my wits about me and I am healthy and I want to do it."

"Whoa, Momma! Okay! Sorry to trigger all that!" I said, laughing.

"OK, let's do it tomorrow. On your thirty-second birthday. You know they say Jesus walked on water when He was thirty-two. He lived to be thirty-three. You're in your years of ministry."

"I know, Mom."

We drove back to our cottage in the long twilight of the Patagonian summer. In the morning, I woke to her calling me from the kitchen.

"Jaayyyuuuddd," she crooned, "Happy Birthday, my favorite oldest son." She came into my room and hugged me in my covers. "It's time to go climb a mountain. I've packed us sandwiches and little individual bags of almonds and dried fruit I found at the market the other day. All this fresh organic South American fruit."

"Mom, that fruit is probably from a factory just like at home."

"Well, I don't know. It seems fresher. I have us big water bottles, metal ones, lightweight, so we don't get that BPA poison in our systems. Oh, and here." She handed me a crystal. "I got these at a gift shop, they are crystals from the top of the Andes and the lady said they are charged with good energy. I think we should have them in our pockets! For good luck."

I laughed. "Mom, when I was a kid, you forbade me from having those little troll dolls with the poofy pink hair because you thought it was witchcraft and un-Christian. And here you are giving me a crystal?"

"God made crystals. The Chinese made those troll dolls. Trolls are demonic. Crystals are okay. And so are pennies."

"Oh my gosh. You always pick up pennies from the ground and say, 'Oooh, good luck!' I'm just realizing how superstitious you are! You hypocrite!" We were both laughing.

"Stop micromanaging me," she said. "I see those coins as little blessings from God. You're supposed to give them away so both of you will be doubly blessed. Don't be a hater!"

"Mom, never say 'hater' again."

We had some coffee and pastries in the lobby of the boutique hotel, and in a moment while Mom was sitting across the lobby looking at her phone, I asked the owner, who was also the concierge, about the hike.

"Is the Torres del Paine hike difficult?"

"It is long. Very long. But you don't need any mountaineering equipment or anything," he said.

"Well," I asked more quietly, "do you think my mother could do it?" He said the only person he'd seen who had done the hike at her age had been a climbing instructor from Switzerland. "Is she healthy? It isn't impossible. It is just long."

"She is very healthy," I said, considering her across the lobby. She was now eating granola and texting. She was sixty-seven years old, but her dyed-brown hair, straight posture, and fast talk had made her seem ageless to me. Was she capable of climbing this mountain? Was it a mistake to let her try?

Willow and Mila joined us, and we put on our hiking boots. I carried the backpack full of snacks, water, and sandwiches. My mom hung her point-and-shoot camera around her neck with a bright multicolored neck strap. And the four of us headed back to the park.

On the drive, a memory came back to me.

I must've been eleven or twelve. My parents were already divorced and I was sitting in the backseat of my dad's truck. We were driving to Sonic, to get me a Dr Pepper as a reward for helping my dad feed hay to the cows. Maybe my dad said something to trigger it, I don't know, but for the first time, it dawned on me that my mom would one day die. The thought bulldozed my mind and knocked everything over. I can remember exactly the bend in the road where I thought it. Mom would die. I would be without her. It felt like a terrible injustice. I remember turning my face to the window so as not to be noticed, pretending my sniffles were allergies.

IT WAS 12:30 by the time we parked at the base of the trail. Lots of cars were parked there when we arrived. The hike seemed like the most popular thing to do in the park. That gave me confidence in bringing Mom. There had to be other moms and dads on this hike.

As we gathered our stuff and put on our rain jackets, I said, "It definitely looks like it's going to rain. You sure about this, Mom?"

"Honey, I walked across America, I slid down a glacier, and got hit by a car going sixty miles an hour. I can handle a little rain."

The trail started flat, along the base of the great mountains, through low grass and over bits of broken rock. We walked for perhaps a mile, crossing streams of meltwater from the snow high above.

Mom just crept along, but we all hiked together at first. The trail quickly gained elevation, curled into a canyon at the base of two mountains, and headed up the side of one of them, hugging the canyon. Soon we moved along a steep ridge with a long black-rock slide down to the right, to white water below. At that point, Mom told us not to wait for her. "Just go at your own pace," she said. "It's not a race and I'd rather be careful than injure myself and ruin our day."

"Mom, we don't want to leave you. It's fine," I said.

"No, I insist. I won't have fun or enjoy any of this nature if I feel like you're waiting on me. Go on. I'll enjoy God's creation at my own pace."

With that, the girls and I went on ahead. Still, for a while, I dallied, checking on Mom from a hundred yards up the trail. She would walk a little. Stop. Take out a snack. Walk some more. Stop. Look at a flower. Take twenty pictures of it. Twenty identical photos. She didn't seem to think about the hours of sunlight we had left, or how much progress she was making.

Finally, I turned around and pressed on to catch up with the girls. We had decided to regroup at the halfway point, where a *refugio* served food and hot chocolate. For the next two hours, we hiked mostly straight up. The trail wound along bluffs and then entered an old-growth forest. Under the towering trees, everything gleamed wet and fresh. Ferns grew from black soil, and fallen logs sprouted mushrooms and lichen. A rain shower came and went, but the canopy of the forest kept us dry.

Willow, Mila, and I made it to the *refugio*, a dark green cabin on the river with a large deck and lots of picnic tables. At this point it was late afternoon. Hikers there were stopping on their way back down. A young Australian working behind a counter told me we were halfway, and that we should hurry. "You don't want to be hiking after dark."

After forty-five minutes, Mom strolled up brandishing a new walking stick, and pulling little rocks from her fanny pack to show around. Each had a story. I told her we shouldn't rest long.

From there we crossed a log bridge over rushing snowmelt. The ground was black and moist. Moss and green ferns grew everywhere. It had begun to drizzle or mist or that strange in-between place where water seems to float in the air and collect on your face and sleeves. Mom was getting tired, but she kept up a pleasant conversation anyway. She pointed out delicate ferns and flowers. One little collection of flowers looked like chubby maids in white and yellow bonnets, and my mom squealed in delight and knelt down to take a photo. Twenty photos. I told her we needed to keep moving.

"If I can't enjoy the trail, what's the point in the hike?" she said.

I started walking on ahead again, letting my thoughts drift back over my trip, thinking how far I'd come, wondering whether or not I had changed at all.

I had. I knew I had. But how? These walkabouts, these rites of passage, these spirit quests are meant to transform. We want to meet Jesus on the road, to be stopped in our tracks by a white light or a burning bush. I didn't get any of that. I got the erosion of the shoreline of a river, one pebble at a time. I wanted to change. I wanted to be born different. To be replaced and born again. New. Forgotten and remade. I don't know how that happens. I guess you have to completely erase your past, which I wasn't ready to do. So I carried it with me, no matter how hard I ran from it.

Clunking up the trail in my boots, I was making great headway. By now, the girls were somewhere up ahead, out of my view, and my mom was somewhere behind. These stunning monoliths of Torres del Paine would mark the true end of my journey. The trip felt like forever, but also here I was, in the present, with the moment rushing past me as though I were a stone in a creek. Time didn't quite move like I'd thought. I had wanted to slow it down. I wanted to be aware of every moment passing, in reflection and contemplation. I wanted to leave my office life in order to feel time passing in some more holy way, holding it in my fingers and studying each minute like a prayer bead.

But that isn't how we experience life. The first miles in Oregon, I had been self-conscious in the extreme. I had felt my knees and hands and breath. On our bikes, Weston and I rushed through the pungency of sea foam and evergreen, crazy with euphoria, sure the newness of it all would be eternal. But then we slid into living the trip, and my awareness dulled into routine. I had been reborn into a different life, a different normal. The bicycle, the camping, the two-lane highways, the people and cultures had become patterns I could predict.

I had wanted slowness, but I got life.

An older couple, perhaps in their fifties, came from around a bend ahead of me. They were headed down the mountain. I asked how close I was to the top, and they said "perhaps another hour" with German accents. It was now 6:00 p.m., and it got dark at 10:30. I kept myself calm by thinking that the walk back down would take half the time. I waited for a few minutes for my mom to catch up, then decided to keep going. She was going at her pace, and she asked for that, and I would go at mine.

The trail got steeper. How was my mom doing now? I got it in my head that she had fallen, that those Germans would find her and think me a terrible son. But I kept hiking. "This is your trip, your finish," I told myself. "You go, and she can catch up. If you don't see those towers, those Torres del Paine, you'll never forgive yourself, or her. She asked for this hike. She doesn't want the end of your adventure to be babysitting."

I immediately felt guilty for the thought. That she had taken care of me and raised me and I was inconvenienced by her slow pace.

When the forest ended the trail came to a giant pile of boulders, an uphill cascade of gray stones, each one larger than a car. The trail snaked around and through them, but it was easy to lose. Any young climber would have simply crawled and scampered up and over the giant rocks. I was almost to the top. But the end was the hardest. I sat down on a rock and waited again. I didn't want to see the end without Mom.

I waited there for thirty minutes. She must have stopped. She wasn't coming. Maybe she was too tired. Maybe she went back to the *refugio* for hot chocolate. Maybe all this waiting for her, which she told me not to do, was actually slowing us down. The sky was dimmer and grayer and I was so near the end of the trail. The end of my trip. The girls must already be at the lake, at the granite spires of Torres del Paine. I decided I had to go on. I couldn't wait for my mom, because she wasn't coming.

I climbed full speed up the boulders, crawling over them like a lizard, and entered layers of mist that came and went. It would mask the trail ahead of me in total gray whiteness, and then be gone, like a paintbrush dragging the ground. As I climbed, for a moment, the higher fog parted and there were the towers, each one the size of the *Titanic* turned on its stern. Maybe bigger. Truly giant spears striking at the sky. No wonder this was a destination. It was holy in its grandeur. I kept climbing to reach the end of the trail, which, based on photos, was a lake at the base of the three spires.

The air was cold. But by now I had slipped into my animal brain. I was looking from rock to rock, boulder to trail to hand-hold, focused only on what was before me. *My hands are cold. Put them in your sleeves and don't touch the rocks with your bare skin. Climb over this boulder. Put your right foot here. Breathe through your nose. This boulder is wobbly, step lightly and watch your ankles.* It was meditative.

I rounded a massive boulder, and suddenly there I was, at the top of the boulder pile, staring at a lake. It looked like the top of a volcano, a hole scooped out of the summit. The scoop was filled with perfect blue-green water. Lining the lake were the three granite towers rising up like God's fat fingers above the lake in the palm of His hand. Photos made it seem so approachable. It was not. It was mighty. The sheer scale of it reminded me of the Old Testament God, a God who struck fear in the hearts of men. A humbling, respectful terror. For me, only mountains and canyons have this effect on me. The ocean, much bigger than any mountain, lies flat to the horizon. The flatness doesn't have the same effect on me. But seeing a mountain, I am frightened by the giant standing over me, looking down at me with indifference or maybe love. Or with a canyon, I am frightened by the cliff, the ease with which I could lose my mind and jump. Experiencing those things leaves me properly reduced. I think it is a good feeling. The fear of God.

Willow and Mila were down at the water's edge, taking pictures. When they spotted me, they yelled with excitement, but the wind tore the sound of their words away. We were the only people up there. I walked clumsily to join them. My fingers were freezing. The wind penetrating between my socks and my pants, that one tiny millimeter of skin, chilled me all over. I stared at the giant Torres. I took photos. I posed with the girls and we hugged and they were so excited for me.

"Your trip is done!!! Soak it all in!" Willow shouted. I filled my bottle from the lake so that I could make coffee in the morning with the lakewater. I wished my mom was up here. But I imagined her sipping warm hot chocolate at the *refugio*, deep in conversation with an Australian or an Argentine.

I had reached the Torres del Paine. The peaks that had fired my imagination since high school. The holy calling. I was there. The trip had dismantled me. But I didn't feel lost like I had been. For the first time in my life, I felt that my only allegiance was to the truth. Not to tradition. Not to safety. Not to what I had been taught. But to whatever was true. And that made me feel strong.

I tried to meditate on the beauty of the place. I tried to love it for its worthiness and grandness. I sat there, smiling at the rocks, the water, the spires, and said thank you. Thank you to God, to the whole universe, to the atheists, to the weirdos, to the conspiracy theorists, to the unpaved gravel shit, to all the miles. I let the whole place sit on my heart for a minute. I let the cold get too cold. I wished my mom had been there.

But she was having hot chocolate at the *refugio*, befriending the Germans. Of course. I held it all in my chest. I grinned and took snapshots by blinking slowly. I had done it. Willow, Mila, and I headed down the mountain.

———

As WE CRAWLED down from boulder to boulder, we were all talking about how perfect the place was. Then, at the edge of the woods a few hundred yards down, I saw a bright red raincoat.

Red raincoat? Mom? I thought, "No way." There was no way she was still coming. There was no way that she had made it this far. But as I got closer, I noticed her poof of brown hair coming out of her hood. I noticed her walking stick.

"MOM!"

She stopped and held up two walking sticks in triumph. She had added another, and was using them like ski poles. She had kept on hiking, at her own pace, mostly alone, for all these miles.

I scrambled down as fast as I could. When I reached her, I could see she was struggling to breathe. But she was ecstatic, too. "Oh, honey, it's so beautiful," she said. We hugged and laughed. There was no time now for her to make it all the way to the lake—at her pace, that would've taken another thirty minutes.

But she had made her own summit.

"Mom! Look, you can see the towers! Do you see?"

"I see the towers. I made it," she said between huffs.

I looked back and the towers were covered with fog. Maybe she hadn't really seen them. But she was happy. "I'm just so thankful to God for my walking sticks," she said.

"Okay, Mom, we need to head back now."

"Yes, honey. I'm so glad"—she took a deep breath—"that I made it to the finish with you."

We turned to go down. I was worried. "We may end up walking in the dark if we don't hurry."

"I can't hurry. My knees are really hurting me. Real bad. Have to go at my pace."

"Mom. It's dangerous to be out here if it gets dark, we could get lost," I said. I was overcome with the desire to protect her. To care for her. "We'll go as fast as we can."

"I'll try," she said, tired.

The rain started again. Not the misty mountain rain from before. Real rain. Pouring. Willow and Mila looked at my mom with obvious concern. Seeing their faces made me worry more.

"Y'all go on down, I'll stick with her," I said. "Just go on to the car. I'm sure it'll go by fast since it's all downhill. We won't be far behind you."

As we walked, I asked her about her time on the trail. "How was it, Mom? I'm sorry I didn't wait and walk with you. I should have."

"No, honey, this was your trip." Her words came in quick, breathy spurts. "I'm here to support you. I'm glad you got to go and see it at the top. That's what I wanted. I'm just so thankful to be out here, thankful for my walking sticks."

The light was gone from her voice. She was exhausted and laboring. "Did you enjoy this hike, Mom? You're so strong! I can't believe you've done this. I wonder how many sixty-seven-year-old women have done this?"

"I took breaks. Looked at flowers. Took some great pictures," she said. I could tell that she didn't want to talk. It took too much energy.

So we walked. I stayed right beside her. And I kept talking, trying to take her mind off the walk and how cold it was and the rain. So much rain. Pouring now. Sometimes she would say, quietly, "My knees." She said it to herself, hoping I wouldn't hear. There was fear in her voice.

When we reached the *refugio*, it was nearly dark and we still had three more miles. But now the rain was howling. This time, we didn't stop.

I led the way, worrying that once we left the forest, the trail would be more difficult to see in the darkness. I was shivering, my hands in pain from the cold. My hiking boots were now wet inside, and my feet felt like ice blocks. My poor mother.

I heard her voice soft and weak behind me. "I'm just so thankful to God for giving me this opportunity," she said. "How am I so lucky?" She was praying.

"Mom, we have to speed up."

"Honey, I can't."

I couldn't help it, I got annoyed. This hike was too much. Too dangerous. Why did she want to do this? She was going to get hurt or we were going to get hurt together and we shouldn't have done it. I should've been a man and stood up to her and said no.

We walked. I tried to set the pace but she was moving very slowly. She was in pain. It was pouring rain. It was soon pitch black. I tried to use my phone's flashlight, but couldn't. The rain was dumping so hard that the light only lit the falling water droplets; it looked like a blizzard, and anyway, the water would ruin my phone. I put it away and tried letting my eyes adjust. Time was crawling. I cursed my old wish for it to slow down.

I tried talking loudly about nothing as I walked, to make sure she could hear me. Behind me, she whispered, "Oh, my knees."

Now I couldn't see the trail at all. I had to drag my feet to feel the pebbled path. As I walked, if my feet hit dirt or bushes, I knew I was off trail. The rain stung my face. Was it hail? How far did we still have to go? It felt like we had been hiking for days.

Eventually, we came to a bridge over a noisy creek. I remembered this bridge. It was one of the first things we had crossed. I looked back and didn't see even the silhouette of my mother. Where was she?

Then I heard her.

"Jed?!" she cried out from the dark. The tone of her voice pinged something visceral in me. I had scuffled ahead too fast and left her too far back in the dark. She couldn't hear my feet or steps anymore because of the creek.

I responded with an annoyed and loud "What?"

"Help! I can't see!"

I had never, in my thirty-one years, heard her voice sound like that. Frightened. Calling out for help. A scared girl. Something jumped in my heart. My stomach. My being. My mom was scared. She didn't know where we were, that we'd reached the bridge. She was in pain. My mother, the direct spokeswoman for the God I feared, was frightened and needed my help.

I held up my phone and turned the light on to show her how close I was.

"I'm right here, Mom!"

When she caught up to me, she said, "I got frightened. I lost you."

"I got you, Mom. We're almost there. We're close."

I felt an incredible strength of purpose rising in me. I had to get us home. The rest of the way, she walked right behind me and I used my phone light. I didn't care if it broke.

We came around the final bend and we saw the lights of the lodge where we had parked the car. I've never been so relieved to see anything in my whole life. I was shaking from the cold but tried to hide it from my mom. As soon as she saw the hotel, she burst out with praise. "Oh, thank You, God, thank You for not abandoning us, thank You, Jesus."

We were as wet as rats in a flood and we sat down in the lobby. It was after midnight. Willow and Mila were there waiting. They hugged us with their dry and warm bodies. They laughed and didn't seem to know how scared we'd been. The restaurant in the hotel was closed, but upon seeing us, and feeling deep pity, they brought us both hot toddies.

My mom sat down and closed her eyes. She wasn't laughing. She wasn't making light of it all. She had always laughed through the hardest things. She had never complained about anything in her life. Never shown weakness.

She was too weak to put on a face. She closed her eyes and sat in the deep relief of being alive and inside and warm and out of the rain. She had both of her walking sticks, leaned against the table.

"I love you, Mom. I'm so proud of you."

She smiled, half opening her eyes at me, blinking slowly. "I'm so proud of you," she whispered.

I sat there, exhausted and watching her, and I didn't think about my trip. I didn't think about thousands of miles. About Oregon, Baja, or Argentina. I didn't think about my identity or my faith or my loss of it all. I didn't think about Jesus or sex. I didn't think about Weston or my father.

It was over. My trip was done. On my thirty-second birthday. And I was wet and frightened and shaking. But the claustrophobic kid who needed escape, needed approval, needed hatred or fire, was not there.

Afterword to the Paperback Edition

In the six years since this trip, I have uncoiled and exhaled. I have wondered why my twenties had to feel so stunted, and then thanked them for protecting my heart. I have since fallen in love and had my heart broken. Even in the hurt, I have loved the freedom to hurt. The liberty of being off the bench and in the game. (A sports reference is still wild for me, but here we are.)

Weston now lives in the mountains of North Carolina, making things with his hands and running through the forest barefoot with his dog. We chat pretty often and laugh, and he feels far more like family than a friend.

Mom can't drink wine anymore. It gives her headaches, so we drink margaritas instead. She keeps forbidding me from posting videos of her online. "I don't have my makeup on, and I sound ridiculous." Then she sits, hunched over her phone, reading all the comments about her. "People really think I'm funny, don't they?" "They really love me." "This person says I'm iconic." She often brings up our hike in Patagonia. She loves being the only person among her peers to have done such a thing. A couple years ago, she broke her back after falling from a bunk bed, but it hardly slowed her down. She may be Wolverine. She sends me encouraging Bible verses. She prays for me, I'm not always sure about what. But I know she wants me to thrive and to love God.

I do love God—and rarely provide definitions.

Next to Mom's bed is an easel with a large painting of Torres del Paine. She's been painting it all these years. Little by little. She promises to give it to me when she's finished. I don't know that she will ever finish. That's kind of how this work goes.

JEDIDIAH JENKINS
Los Angeles, California, December 2019

Acknowledgments

Special thanks to Lincoln City Fellowship from the Speranza Foundation and Kathy Treat for believing in artists and believing in me.

Thank you to David Kopp, Derek Reed, and Ashley Hong for reading my every word, teaching me what I'm really saying, and being my therapists.

Thank you to Tina Constable for threatening me with greatness, for telling me my potential before I would even daydream it.

Thank you to Bryan Norman for seeing a diamond in the Dumpster. You honestly changed my life.

And thank you to these friends, family, and heroes for giving me the wings to write. You didn't even know what the book would be, and you said, "Write it." That is brave and beautiful. Thank you,

Tom Shadyac
Aaron and Lauren Paul
Mila Elizabeth Fischer
Gregg Foxworthy
Jonathan Chu
Barbara Jo
Alice Lutz
Shervin Pishevar
Pablo del Olmo
Ryan Smith
Alex Rice
Jay Faires
Toby Salz
Robert Hemple
Clint Russell
Kelly Craven

Lydia and Michael Slaby
Jordan Foxworthy
Erica Shay
Daniel
Shawn Parr
Bobby Chang
Jeffrey Boal
Michael Gonzales
Jason and Danica Russell
Travis Tidmore
Marloes van Bedaf
Taylor Bruce
Krista Moore
Steve Witmer
Kristina Stover
Tiffany Newcomb

Spencer R. Scott
Rachel Ashley
Caleb Noordmans
Cara Bubes
Julia Plomer
Philippe Lanier
Andrea
Niki Mangan
Amy D. Jones
Becca May
Stephanie Mack
Diana Evans
Molly Franken
Paula Fuga
Mallory Ross
Stephanie Harmon
Harry Chemko
Greg Spencer
Dag Gano
Timothy
Mitchell Moses
Brian Cheng
Jack Shanks
Melis Kuris
Madison Clark
Taylor Dybdahl
Mary Gomes
Tyler & Jenn Jones
Elizabeth
Winky Jenkins-Rice
Brenda Frye
Whitney Black
Susan Ennor
Liz Anderson
Kerryn Devenny
Matt Obermeier

Olympia Rizzo
Krista Tchir
Christina Sambor
Grant Hughes
Samantha Hansen
Allison Findlay
Amanda Hobert
Samantha Marq
Debra Bowne
Melanie Smith
Tyler Karr
Brady Peters
Chrysi Philalithes
Alison Hansen
Taylor Smith
Preston Caffrey
Katie Stjernholm
Scott Lamming
Molly Thompson
Nathan Ah Quin
Larry Pahl
Courtney Poole
Blake Bartlett
Ahna
Beks Opperman
Holly Gonzalez
Randy Scott Carroll
Still Fighting
Nicki MacGregor
Claire
Roko
Lindsay Brandt
Doris Zampella
Lisa Coleman
Lauren Thomson
Jessie Bailin

Tiffany Keesey

Katherine and Jay Wolf

Hiyasmin Samala

Amy Louise Collins

Stephanie Sambor

Kevin Stock

Kyle Wood

Bobby Bailey

Esther Maria Swaty

Chad Bowker

DC

Kimberly Vandivort

Michael George

Steve Rogers

Matt and Jen Wood

Robyn Corcoran

Steven Mole

Maddie Devonshire

Pam Faulkner Tomalin

Jim Ganus

Maleeha Ahmad

Brent Mayberry

Samantha Lacy

Chaz Vetter

The Lammings

Karen Mulvaney

Noemi Mueller

Meredith Ann Harris

Albert Nguyen

Jaclyn Visbeen

Paul Gillcrist

Matt Hughes

Angélica Suárez Poveda

Ballard C. Boyd

Lalo Perez-Varona

Tim Wyand

Amy Barth

Miki Agrawal

Meg "Yates" Hill

Danny Dubin

Mandi Ashley

Amanda Leigh Brown

Ana Jaya

Eva Frazier

Nicola Odemann

Collin Roberts

Helena

Chad Clendinen

Ryan Nibouar

Ben McKenzie

Olivia Meinhardt

Westley Austin

Christopher Louie Szabo

Emalee Eichorn

Lindsay Ratowsky

Heather Brown

Alissa Pure

Stephanie Flores-Gomez

Hayley Cox

Robb Erwin

Chris Paul

Lauren Andrews

Tawny Burgess

Ice Cream Expedition

Henry Muehlhausen

The Bundys

Liza Martin

Kevo Rivera

Alicia Reese

Alexis Trimble

Brendon Reed

Katey Bundy

Michael Reddish

Mark Griffith

Erik Einwalter

Angela Diange

Yuki Roig

Carrie Platts

Lauri Olmsted Makuck

Kaylinn Douthett

Lorie and Bevans Branham

Nancy and Dan Pryor

Bryan Funk

Kristine Wong

Pat Loughery

Janes Timmons

Callie Moser

Erica Schwalm

Katharine Dowd

Sheila McMahan

Azita Ardakani

Andrew Abitbol

Jessi Fikan

Craig Hampton

Tessa Joe Caprella

Justina Buzza

Zach Prosser

Seri Wheeler

Lauren Painter

Karen Weiss

Rebecca Bechtel

Sarah Barritt

Sharon Maori

Nicole Eanes

Veena Rangaswami

Anna Thomas

Levent Yungul

Ruth Ann Harnisch

Rebekah Jenkins

Hannah Elizabeth

Karla Wehling

Cristina Thompson

Bridget Connelly

Cameron Woodward

Joyce Smith

Josiah Lamerson

Anna Nicles

Parker Shinn

Ellen Bockius

Robin Townley

Niamh Byrne

Ryan Flynn

Jennifer Simmons

Vanessa Spenuzza

Marina Barcaglioni Hanahan

Eric Martinez

Molly Biter

Jordan Brown

Nathalie Isabella

Brice Crozier

David Dry

Cameron Heavican

Jessica Malaty Rivera

Coy Whittier

Lindsay Branham

Andrew Herbert

Justin Boreta

Mary Burford Bailey

Kristin Finch

Hayley Biraghi

Margaret Hollins

Dan Hagerty

Nathan Phillips

Patty Steinman

Lisa Tucker

Olivia Kaplan

Scott Ellis

Darling Magazine

Brittany Beltran

Claire Biggs

David Zaborowski

Emily Ellina

Ben Weiland

Christian Miller

Grace Christian

Shoshauna Schmidt

Dave Pahl

Kim Sturgeon

Renee D. Santos

John Kobs

Susan Avery

Amanda

David & Diane Fatke

Juliette Arcodia

Julia Scullion

Rachel Jonas

Alex

Kysaundra Phillips

Scott Frentrop

Tristan Kirwan

Corey

Asquith

Maren Brown

Brennon Bloemendaal

Krissy Estrada

Gabriel Kreuzer

Monica Silvestre

Abby

Ryan Youngblood

Tony Boenzi

Lauren

Gabriella Giron

Jordan Bellamy

Dale McCarthy

Becca Bower

Ashley Gutierrez

Austin Flack

Jutta Stieglmeier

Gustav Persson

Sarah Milstein

Ellen Gustafson

Lindsey

Sarah Harmeyer

Sara Jawhari

Devra Lane

Paul Gi

Linnessa Kellogg Scott

Carly Parmer

Sara Hutton

Catie Serex

Ben Price

Kevin Vandivort

Katherine Eifert

Lissa Eng

Malia Mia

Aaron Henderson

Matthew Woods

Valerie Hulme

Jessica R. Pearce

Christopher Collins

Kristin Weaver

Vicki Ross Bechet

Missy Swanson

Bonnie Thomas

Mandana Ighani

Julia Funicella Gullotti

Erin Quinn Mundy

Eyasu "Josh" Felleke

Tyler Bartlett

cmd112

Nicole Elizabeth Shehab

Kevin Trout

Doug

Melanie Holland Tracey

James Ramos

Tara Peters Barrows

Jessica Wood

alexandra003

Clinton Stapleton

Katy Irving

Jessica Xiao

Camela Giraud

Jeremy Danenhauer

Cody West

Melissa Martinez Leo

Emily Wilkinson

Jameson Detweiler

Keith Comer

Josephine Jenkins Gibbs

Julia Denni

Joshua Ballantine

Brian Mircheff

Andy Blair

Cameron Connerty

Danielle Deabler

Lucy Patterson

Ezekiel Duran

Michelle Hart

Amy Boyd

Megan Sutherland

Adam Finck

Ryan Sisson

Guy Raz

Michelle Costales

Jordan Bentley

Lisa Calzailla

Cindy Ortiz

Xochitl Hernández Ivanov

Alyssa Medrano

Patrick Dodd

Bettina

Erin Nicole

Vita Angiulo

Rachel Tobac

Geoffrey Wickersham

Zena Ah Chin

David Young

Jess McAlister

Caleb & Janelle Warren

Megan Marshall

Maya

Brenna Murphey

Kelli

Fallon Buckelew

Hayden Wyatt

Jill Smayo

Jennifer Bolay

Tiffany

Madelyn Webb

Christina VH

Shane Chard

Ashley Stephenson

Amy Lubbering

Ben Seliner

Joseph Hargan Calvopina

Alexis Levine

Katie

Stephen Claybrook

Jamison Monroe

Alan Zelez

Sarah Reynolds

Simon Moons

Jeanne Le Guyader

Barbara Benedini Walbridge

Isaac Widdicombe

Liz and Steven Coufal

Lauren and Bret Harrison

Jaclyn

Hunter Lyall

Venum Skillmethodz

Adam Blumenthal

Maraldy

Andrew Witmer

Katherine Collins

Sarah Kelly

Kenworth Reeves

Rebecca

Lynn Wilkerson

Amber Sundell

Judy Johnson

Erika M. Dobkins

Charles Izard

Katie Swenson

Chandra Joy Shoalmire

Carolyn Berg

Jackie Connery

Jeff Shimabuku

Matthew Doak

Rebecca Adler

Ragni Lunkan

Jacob May

Danielle Mignogna

Monica Del Vecchio

Lonnie L. Liston

Andrea Kollmorgen

Leigh R. Hendry

Marissa Holloway

Christine Bergman

Erin Ensor

Aaron Echols

Krystal Rodgers

Lee and Ashley Gagne

Emily Ip

Taylor Engen and Ted Olson

Brent

Odette Annable

Chris Lowell

Mariana Blanco

Steph

Saren Oliver

Amy Kitchel

Mary Ellen Feinberg

Michele Haicl

Jacob Bixenman

To SHAKE
the SLEEPING SELF

by Jedidiah Jenkins

A READER'S GUIDE

Questions and Topics for Discussion

1. Early in the book, Jed chronicles the grind of becoming an adult and trying to find a meaningful career in his twenties. At the same time, he makes clear that his "itch" to leave his job was rooted in deeper doubts and questions. "An important part of me was covered and squirming," he writes. Have you ever felt a similar itch in your own life?

2. In the opening chapter, Jed writes, "I was holding tight to the narratives of my youth like treasure. But with hands full, I couldn't receive anything new." What are some things you were told to be true in your upbringing? As you developed into the person you are today, what do you still affirm and consider true, and what are some things you've decided are not so fundamental? What are some "truths" you are reckoning with today?

3. In Chapter 3, when Jed wonders if it's safe to hitchhike, Weston says, "It's probably safer than it was in the fifties. The only difference is public perception and the news media." Jed makes a similar point when his mother expresses fear for his safety while biking through Mexico. In what ways is our perception of safety shaped by secondhand accounts? Have you ever held expectations about a place or experience, only to be surprised by the real thing once you encountered it?

4. While we aren't all given the chance to bike from Oregon to Patagonia, have there been moments in your life when you needed to escape the routines you had laid down for yourself? What are ways—however big or small—you might spark a similar shake-up in your life?

5. In Chapter 4, Jed writes, "Each of us has a mash-up of talents and experiences and potential that plants something in us, and becomes a dream. . . . Dreams are like a compass that points us in a general direction, and goals are the islands in the ocean along the way." What dreams and goals do you carry? What might be keeping you from pursuing them?

6. In Chapter 6, Jed writes about the difficulty of growing up gay in a conservative Christian family. In your own upbringing, were parts of your identity repressed or punished? How can the communities we're a part of—be it a religious community or a friend group—celebrate these parts of our identities?

7. In the same chapter, Jed describes having an existential crisis while riding through the desert: "I was excavating my past, thinking over the years and my pain and my fragile masculinity." In contrast to the iron-clad confidence Jed once carried, much of the book shows him earnestly seeking to understand his own heart. Did you relate to this part of Jed's journey—his struggle to acknowledge and tell the truth of his insecurities and fragilities, and ultimately be kind to himself?

8. In Chapter 7, Jed writes, "Fear is like a thorn in your foot. It may be proportionally small in relation to the body, but it hurts and demands attention and everything halts until the thorn gets pulled." What fears do you carry that, as Jed writes, might be demanding your attention? What are ways you can turn your focus toward them?

9. In Chapter 8, while reflecting on America's colonial history, Jed writes, "Mexicans tell their story in a different way than we do in the United States. They show patriotism, but less confidence." Is there a difference between patriotism and nationalism? What questions do you think those in power—whether in government, religious communities, or other realms of leadership—

need to ask about their histories and the persistent gap between the powerful and the marginalized?

10. By the time Jed reaches Central America, he writes that the trip itself had turned into a routine of its own. In what ways do our problems follow us, no matter how we try to escape? Is it truly possible to escape routine and pay attention to every moment of our lives?

11. It's hard to forget the visceral, brutal discomfort of some conversations between Jed and his mother. Still, Jed's love for his mother remains constant and undeniable throughout the book. What did you make of his devotion to someone so close, yet so capable of saying hurtful things to him? What does it take for you to choose to love or to cut ties?

12. What do you think Jed learned by the end of his journey? In what ways did the trip change him? Do you think it met his expectations?

13. Jed grapples with his faith through the book. In what religious or philosophical tradition were you raised, and how have you shaped that tradition to fit your life now? Do you believe what your parents raised you to believe? How did you make it your own?

Read on for an excerpt from *Like Streams to the Ocean*

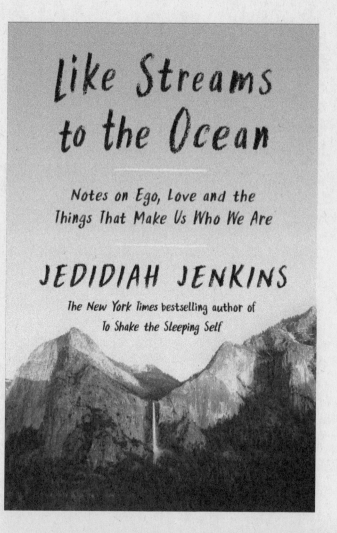

Like Streams to the Ocean

Notes on Ego, Love and the Things That Make Us Who We Are

JEDIDIAH JENKINS

The *New York Times* bestselling author of
To Shake the Sleeping Self

Introduction

S ometimes I wish I could stop thinking and exist in the full contentment of an animal. I envy the staring of a lizard, how it sits in the sun and looks out onto the world. It is not worried about things it can imagine. It is not smiling. It is not happy at its contentment. How could it be? It doesn't know discontent. If it is scared, it is scared for a reason, for a danger it can sense and see. It is not imagining what could happen ten years from now. Its mind is perfectly present. Free.

But we are not like that. We are conscious. We are self-aware. We have a triad of worlds inside us: our mind in the present, our mind holding the past, and our mind guessing at the future. Our consciousness unites these things in a mysterious and muddled way. It feels things it cannot explain—urges and sadness and lusts without names. We have to sort out these many longings and instincts, or live in anxious confusion.

For a sentient unicorn such as you or me, the unexamined life is a curse. It leaves the mind at the mercy of the gut, cluttered with confusing information coming from below. Who we are cannot be fully realized until we tidy up the room and see what's under all those piles of clothes.

The summer before my first book came out, I got very sick. I had a 105 degree fever. At night, I soaked the bed with so much sweat that I started sleeping on six towels, peeling them away when they became unbearably soggy. Over two months of this, I lost twenty-five pounds. I went to the hospital ten times and had enough blood drawn to deflate a whale. They couldn't figure out what was wrong with me.

The illness came at the worst possible time, in the ramp-up to the release of my memoir. In the book, I had written about my struggle to be a good church kid from Tennessee in a family who loved me but thought being gay was a death sentence. For weeks, I had been going back and forth with my mother about things she didn't like in the book. Things she thought were unfair representations and caricatures. When she confronted me, it led to an exchange of no-holds-barred emails, in which I spelled out my homosexuality, the dismantling of my faith, and the new boundaries I needed to set with her. Much of it for the first time. She was willing to listen, but wounded, and she wrote with a firmness in what her faith said about me. By the end, I basically told her I was prepared to walk away from the family.

I remember shaking as I typed those emails. I love no one more than I love my mother, which is why she can rock me and warp my spine. I knew I had a story to tell, one that I'd desperately needed to read when I was younger. But the book was about to blow up my relationship with my family, and now my body was falling apart.

My mystery illness reminded me of a universal truth: It is good to have a doctor for a friend. Toby is that doctor for me. I met him in San Francisco through my old roommate and reveled in his stories from the hospital. He's worked in the emergency room for years, and my god, the things he has seen. The things people stuff into their bodies' orifices are impressively varied (ex: a dead crow, because it was "cold"). Toby's experiences in the ER have made him calm and rational at all times.

After my fever had kept me up for two full weeks, I texted Toby. He told me to get my blood tested. Maybe it was Lyme disease. After the third week, he said, "This is odd, most fevers are gone after two weeks." I kept getting more blood tests, stool tests, urine tests. Negative. Nothing. I was as healthy as an athlete, except for the fact that I was too weak to walk to the bathroom. At six weeks, Toby no longer sounded calm and collected. He was worried, tired of my local doctors not taking this seriously. He told me to go to the ER. If I told them I'd been having chest pain—which was true by then—they would fast track me to see the doctor.

I poured myself into an Uber and hobbled into the ER. The doctor looked at my most recent test results with a furrowed brow. "You could have testicular cancer," he said, looking up from the sheet. "Drop your pants please so I can check."

"Cancer?"

"Yes. The fever could be your body's way of trying to cook it and kill it."

Wow. I had thought I had a flu, maybe, or Lyme disease. Cancer never crossed my mind. I stood up and pulled down my pants and underwear. The doctor felt around while I braced to hear words that would change my life.

"I feel nothing; that's good. But you could still have cancer. Let me order you a CT scan."

I went home buzzing with mortality. I called Toby. He told me that I'd entered into a category called FUO, Fever of Unknown Origin. This is like unlocking a secret level in a videogame. Suddenly, all kinds of bad things are on offer to explain what's wrong with you: extrapulmonary tuberculosis, typhoid fever, malaria, chronic active hepatitis, HIV/AIDS, leukemia, lymphoma, colon cancer, testicular carcinoma, and more.

After a horrible week of waiting and wondering, the scan came back negative. My body was frying itself, and no one could figure it out. Toby called and checked on me multiple times a day.

Then, eleven weeks into my illness—the week my book came out—the sickness vanished. Poof. Lifted like a fog.

I went back to the doctor to make sure it could really disappear like that. He wasn't fazed. "Believe it or not, this happens all the time," he said. "People get better, and we never find out what happened." I was baffled, annoyed that modern medicine couldn't tell me what was wrong. "We have a robot driving around on the surface of Mars right now, and you can't tell me why I was sick?" I said.

"We know a lot," he said, "and if you remained sick, we would keep testing. But when people get better, they stop getting tested. And it stays a mystery."

Toby agreed with that doctor. In his controlled and toneless way, I could hear how relieved he was.

Later that week, I talked with my friend Connie, who, like most of my friends, had been really worried about me. She brought up a possibility I hadn't considered. "I bet it was psychological," she said.

"No way," I said. My sickness had been real. Toby wouldn't have checked on me every day if it was some made-up thing. This wasn't mental.

"Think about it," Connie said. "You're about to release a very personal memoir, one that you're afraid might hurt your relationship with your mom and family. You're always saying that you don't feel emotions, but the body knows. They get stored up."

I didn't believe her then, but here I am a year later, and I am convinced she was right. The book was published. My mother didn't disown me. Somehow, it brought our family closer. At the time, however, I didn't know that would happen. So my body took the reins from my mind. It shut me down.

Psychologists believe that between the ages of eight and ten, we wake up into a sense of self. These are the years when our brains develop a distinct identity. We realize that we aren't our mothers. That we are individuals with one life that ends in death. This is a frightening experience. As individuals, it is our job to stay alive. Mom won't be there forever. So, we observe the world around us for danger. It is that world, the one we map in those opening years, that we spend the rest of our lives trying to fix. I didn't know this when I got sick, but when I heard it later, it clicked.

When I was eight, I lived in a home where my mom was overwhelmed by the demands of raising three children. So I learned to be independent and never bother her. At the same time, my body was betraying me, giving me strange thoughts and "bad" desires. I adapted by disassociating from my body, floating at a thousand feet and watching life unfold. I believe this defense of becoming a mind at a distance, rather than a soul in a body, turned me into a writer. I am grateful for that. But it also severed me from my emotions. From knowing my body. From the right to have needs.

This I have come to believe: If we don't examine ourselves—our walls and defenses and blind spots—in the daylight and out in the open, we run the risk of a shutdown. What is buried will rise up and take over.

We must dig around under our houses and shore up the ground floor of our thinking, making it as sturdy as it can be. Not with answers, but with a way of looking actively at our world. We must invite our consciousness into full awareness of itself. To be astonished that we are alive, and aware of it, and wonder what it all means.

We can do this by thinking about the most important things in life.

In these pages, I have compiled eight elements that I believe form the foundation of who we are. The way we think about ourselves, the people in our lives, our relationships, and our homes affects everything else. Until we know ourselves, the language of our gut and spirit, we will continue to expect wrong things and misunderstand our motives. Misery is in direct proportion to expectation. And getting comfortable with this mystery of self, with the great unfolding of our lives, is the biggest step we can take toward existential joy. The death of anxiety. The embrace of the "why" behind all of our doing.

Some of what you'll read are essays I've written specifically for the book. Others are thoughts I've collected over the past five years and published in spurts elsewhere, online and in magazines. (Indeed, the idea of this book came when readers asked me to put my online writing in one physical place.) Some are snippets and thought-sparkers, meant to be read on a fifteen-minute subway ride. Others are longer and meant to be read under the covers on a slow Saturday morning. You'll find an evolution, a bit of "working it out" over several years in these pages. I am trying to be that friend who sits with you until three A.M., talking in swirls like milk poured in coffee.

We are not thoughtless lizards. As much as a blank mind would calm our twisted senses, it is not on offer. What we have are complex thoughts, spiritual meditations, and brains that want to hold the universe in our consciousness. This is the miracle of being human. If there is no God, and we are just atoms bouncing through a giant something, then the mystery of consciousness is all the more amazing. We are pieces of matter, perfectly organized in such a way that we are able to see ourselves. What an honor. What a commission. And if the saints and mystics are right, and we really are children of God, then wow. We are creations of the Most High, main characters in the cosmic drama of meaning. Maybe those two options aren't as different as we think.

This is my attempt to lean into the duty of consciousness. To think wide and deep.

JEDIDIAH JENKINS is a travel writer, entrepreneur, and Instagram personality. A graduate of USC and Pepperdine University School of Law, Jenkins began his professional career with the nonprofit Invisible Children, where he helped orchestrate multinational campaigns to end the use of child soldiers in central Africa. His parents, Peter and Barbara Jenkins, are the authors of the bestselling *A Walk Across America* series. He is the executive editor of *Wilderness* magazine, his work has appeared in the *The Paris Review, Playboy,* and *Good* magazine, and his journey was covered by *National Geographic.*